Also forthcoming from Routledge, a companion reader to
Global Business: Positioning Ventures Ahead

The Future of Global Business: A Reader
Edited by Michael R. Czinkota and Ilkka A. Ronkainen

In the fast-paced world of global business, success is marked by the ability to stay on top of current events, to recognize new trends, and to react quickly to change. This book offers contributions by global marketing authorities to help you understand this rapidly changing international environment and respond to opportunities and perils.?

Editors Michael R. Czinkota and Ilkka A. Ronkainen use their years of experience in policy, business, and academia to provide these readings noted for their currency, relevancy, and scholarly depth.

978–0–415–80093–8
Available 2010

To order or for other information, please visit www.routledge.com.

Table of Contents:

1.4 Czinkota, Michael R., "Academic freedom for all in higher education; the role of the general agreement on trade in services," *Journal of World Business*, 41, 2, 2006, 149–160.

1.5 Czinkota, Michael R."International Information Cross-Fertilization in Marketing: An Empirical Assessment," *European Journal of Marketing*, 34,15, 2000; 1305–1314. Winner, Article of the Year Award.

1.6 Czinkota, Michael R. and Ilkka A. Ronkainen, Trends and Indications in International Business: Topics for future research; Management International Review, April 2009

1.7 Kotabe, Masaaki and Crystal Jiang, "Contemporary Research Trends in International Marketing: The 2000s," in Alan Rugman, ed., *Oxford Handbook of International Business*, 2nd ed., Oxford: Oxford University Press, 2008, 447–501.

2. Competition from Emerging Markets
2.1 Malik, Omar R. and Masaaki Kotabe, "Dynamic Capabilities, Government Policies, and Performance in Firms from Emerging Economies: Evidence from India and Pakistan," *Journal of Management Studies*, 2009. forthcoming.

2.2 Gao, Gerald Y., Janet Y. Murray, Masaaki Kotabe, and Jiangyong Lu, "A 'Strategy Tripod' Perspective on Export Behaviors: Evidence from Domestic and Foreign Firms Based in an Emerging Economy," *Journal of International Business Studies*, 39, 2009.

2.3 Aulakh, Preet S., Masaaki Kotabe, and Hildy Teegen, "Export Strategies and Performance of Firms from Emerging Economies: Evidence from Brazil, Chile, and Mexico," *Academy of Management Journal*, 43 (3), 2000, 342–361.

2.4 Aulakh, Preet S. and Masaaki Kotabe, "Institutional Changes and Organizational Transformation in Developing Economies," *Journal of International Management*, 14 (September), 2008, 209–216.

3. Marketing Mix
3.1 Dimofte, Claudiu V., Johny K. Johansson and Ilkka A. Ronkainen, "Cognitive and Affective Reactions of U.S. Consumers to Global Brands," *Journal of International Marketing*, Volume 16, Number 4, December 2008

3.2 Czinkota, Michael R. and Masaaki Kotabe, "Entering the Japanese Market: A Reassessment of Foreign Firms' Entry and Distribution Strategies," *Industrial Marketing Management*, 29, November 2000, 483–491.

3.3 Swan, K. Scott, Masaaki Kotabe, and Brent Allred, "Exploring Robust Design Capabilities, Their Role in Creating Global Products, and Their Relationship to Firm Performance," *Journal of Product Innovation Management*, 22 (2), March 2005, 144–164.

3.4 Clark, Terry, Masaaki Kotabe, and Dan Rajaratnam, "Exchange Rate Pass-Through and International Pricing Strategy: A Conceptual Framework and

Research Propositions," *Journal of International Business Studies*, 30, Second Quarter, 1999, 249–268.

3.5 Gencturk, Esra F. and Masaaki Kotabe, "The Effect of Export Assistance Program Usage on Export Performance: A Contingency Explanation," *Journal of International Marketing*, 9 (2), 2001, 51–72.

4. Global Sourcing and Supply Chain Management

4.1 Czinkota, Michael R. "An Analysis of the Global Position of US Manufacturing," *Thunderbird International Business Review*, October 2003: 505–519.

4.2 Kotabe, Masaaki, Michael J. Mol, and Sonia Ketkar, "An Evolutionary Stage Model of outsourcing and Competence Destruction: A Triad Comparison of the Consumer Electronics Industry," *Management International Review*, 48 (1). 2008, 65–93.

4.3 Kotabe, Masaaki, Michael J. Mol, and Janet Y. Murray, "Outsourcing, Performance, and the Role of E-Commerce: A Dynamic Perspective," *Industrial Marketing Management*, 37 (1), 2008, 37–45.

4.4 Murray, Janet Y., Masaaki Kotabe, Joe Nan Zhou, "Strategic Alliance-Based Sourcing and Market Performance: Evidence from Foreign Firms Operating in China," *Journal of International Business Studies*, 36 (2), March 2005, 187–208.

5. Emerging Issues

5.1 Czinkota, Michael R., Gary A. Knight, Peter W. Liesch and John Steen, "Positioning Terrorism in Management and Marketing: Research Propositions" *Journal of International Management*, 11, 2005, 581–604.

5.2 Czinkota, Michael R., David A. Grossman, Rajshekhar (Raj) G. Javalgi, Nicholas Nugent, " Foreign Market Entry Mode of Service Firms: The Case of U.S. MBA Programs ", *Journal of World Business*, forthcoming

5.3 Czinkota, Michael R., "How Government Can Help Increase US Export Performance." Testimony before the House Committee on Small Business"

5.4 Kotabe, Masaaki and Crystal Jiang, "Three Dimensional: The Markets of Japan, Korea, and China are Far from Homogeneous," *Marketing Management*, 15 (2), 2006, 39–43.

5.5 Kotabe, Masaaki, Srini S. Srinivasan, and Preet S. Aulakh, "Multinationality and Firm Performance: The Moderating Role of R&D and Marketing Capabilities," *Journal of International Business Studies*, 33 (1), 2002, 79–97.

See page xii in this book for information on how these readings compliment each chapter in *Global Business*.

Global Business

Global Business: Positioning Ventures Ahead alerts every business to the new windows of opportunity open to those willing to explore global markets. Authors Czinkota and Ronkainen bring readers quickly up to speed on the essentials of international marketing, explaining all the strategic alternatives for going global—from exporting and licensing to distributorships and joint ventures. They illustrate how to present, promote, and price products and services to appeal to multiple world markets and how to strike back when world competitors move into one's territory. *Global Business: Positioning Ventures Ahead* equips readers with the skills to ride out the risks and reap the rewards of world-class engagement.

Michael R. Czinkota is faculty member at the McDonough School of Business, Georgetown University and the University of Birmingham, U.K., where he holds the chair in International Marketing.

Ilkka A. Ronkainen is a Professor at the McDonough School of Business, Georgetown University.

Global Business

Positioning Ventures Ahead

Michael R. Czinkota

McDonough School of Business, Georgetown University and the University of
Birmingham, U.K.

Ilkka A. Ronkainen

McDonough School of Business, Georgetown University

Routledge
Taylor & Francis Group

NEW YORK AND LONDON

First published 2011
by Routledge
270 Madison Avenue, New York, NY 10016

Simultaneously published in the UK
by Routledge
2 Park Square, Milton Park, Abingdon, Oxon OX14 4RN

Routledge is an imprint of the Taylor & Francis Group, an informa business

© 2011 Taylor & Francis

The right of Michael R. Czinkota and Ilkka A. Ronkainen to be identified
as authors of this work has been asserted by them in accordance with sections
77 and 78 of the Copyright, Designs and Patents Act 1988.

Typeset in Berling
by Keystroke, Tettenhall, Wolverhampton
Printed and bound in the United States of America on acid-free paper
by Edwards Brothers, Inc.

Library of Congress Cataloging in Publication Data
Czinkota, Michael R.
    Global business : positioning ventures ahead / Michael R. Czinkota,
Ilkka A. Ronkainen.
        p. cm.
    Includes index.
    1. Export marketing. 2. International trade. I. Ronkainen, Ilkka A.
    II. Title.
    HF1416.C947 2010
    658.8′4—dc22   2009052412

ISBN13: 978-0-415-80194-2 (hbk)
ISBN13: 978-0-203-87510-0 (ebk)

To Ilona and Margaret, my sources of strength
Michael

To Susan, Sanna, and Alex,
who encouraged me in every way
Ilkka

Contents

Global Business: Positioning Ventures Ahead
Michael R. Czinkota and Ilkka A. Ronkainen

together with

The Future of Global Business: A Reader
Edited by Michael R. Czinkota and Ilkka A. Ronkainen

Build on the insights of *Global Business*.
This list matches the chapters in this book with complimentary readings found in
The Future of Global Business: A Reader.

Chapter 1: The Global Imperative

1.1 Czinkota, Michael R. and Ilkka K. Ronkainen, "An International Marketing Manifesto"

1.2 Czinkota, Michael R. and J. Samli "The Remarkable Performance of International Marketing in the Second Half of the 20th Century"

Chapter 2: Establishing The Context

2.1 Malik, Omar R. and Masaaki Kotabe, "Dynamic Capabilities, Government Policies, and Performance in Firms from Emerging Economies: Evidence from India and Pakistan"

2.3 Aulakh, Preet S., Masaaki Kotabe, and Hildy Teegen, "Export Strategies and Performance of Firms from Emerging Economies: Evidence from Brazil, Chile, and Mexico"

2.4 Aulakh, Preet S. and Masaaki Kotabe, "Institutional Changes and Organizational Transformation in Developing Economies"

3.5 Gencturk, Esra F. and Masaaki Kotabe, "The Effect of Export Assistance Program Usage on Export Performance: A Contingency Explanation"

Chapter 3: Doing your Homework on Global Markets

1.5 Czinkota, Michael R. "International Information Cross-Fertilization in Marketing: An Empirical Assessment"

1.7 Kotabe, Masaaki and Crystal Jiang, "Contemporary Research Trends in International Marketing: The 2000s"

5.3 Czinkota "How Government Can Help Increase US Export Performance"

Chapter 4: Getting there with customers and suppliers

3.2 Czinkota, Michael R. and Masaaki Kotabe, "Entering the Japanese Market: A Reassessment of Foreign Firms' Entry and Distribution Strategies"

3.3 Swan, K. Scott, Masaaki Kotabe, and Brent Allred, "Exploring Robust Design Capabilities, Their Role in Creating Global Products, and Their Relationship to Firm Performance"

4.3 Kotabe, Masaaki, Michael J. Mol, and Janet Y. Murray, "Outsourcing, Performance, and the Role of E-Commerce: A Dynamic Perspective"

Chapter 5: Creating a Global Footprint

2.2 Gao, Gerald Y., Janet Y. Murray, Masaaki Kotabe, and Jiangyong Lu, "A 'Strategy Tripod' Perspective on Export Behaviors: Evidence from Domestic and Foreign Firms Based in an Emerging Economy"

4.1 Czinkota, Michael R. "An Analysis of the Global Position of US Manufacturing"

4.4 Murray, Janet Y., Masaaki Kotabe, Joe Nan Zhou, "Strategic Alliance-Based Sourcing and Market Performance: Evidence from Foreign Firms Operating in China"

5.2 Czinkota, Michael R., David A. Grossman, Rajshekhar (Raj) G. Javalgi, Nicholas Nugent, "Foreign Market Entry Mode of Service Firms: The Case of U.S. MBA Programs"

Preface

There has been unprecedented change on the global business front. We know that when domestic economic activities are down, international ones are down as well, only much more so. Austerity brings changes in production and consumption patterns and introduces new dimensions into the decision-making process. The role of governments is growing by leaps and bounds, dictating the direction and strength of international business activities. There is rising potential to restrict imports, and encourage exports, in order to keep home industries safe and to gradually reduce global imbalances. However, though periods of economic crisis may lead to short-term interruptions in globalization, the important changes in production, consumption, and lifestyle brought about by international business will be inexorable.

In dire economic times, international business actors are a key agent of social change, who provide their insights and their knowledge to help society to understand the trade-offs and consequences of actions and to make good decisions while considering a broad variety of stakeholders. They are crucial for implementation as well. For example, how does one reshape the U.S. economy into a more export-oriented one? How can Chinese savers be convinced to consume more, spend more, and save less?

"Think globally, act locally, and change personally" has become the business battle cry around the world. But being involved in global sales and having global brands or operations in different countries is not enough to maintain a sustainable long-term competitive advantage. Managers need to exert leverage of corporate capabilities around the world so that the company as a whole is greater than the sum of its parts. The origin of these capabilities matters little. What counts is to find, develop, and use them in operations worldwide.

Globalization has been associated typically with large-scale multinational companies in globally contested industrialized markets. However, sheer size is no longer a buffer against competition in markets where customers are demanding specialized and customized products that draw from worldwide best practice. The advent of electronic processes and the opportunities associated with e-business, has given rise to mini-nationals which are able to compete on price and quality – often with great flexibility. By taking advantage of today's open trading regions, they can serve the world from a handful of manufacturing bases, sparing them from the necessity of building a plant in every country. Information technology allows for access to data throughout the world, which enables service firms to run inexpensive and responsive operations across language and time zones. In addition, companies from emerging markets are establishing their own operations in developed markets independently or as part of strategic alliances.

More than 1 billion people use computers and cell phones, the vast majority in the developed markets of Europe, North America, and Australasia. Those markets alone may not be the source of global growth needed. The next billion consumers to be reached internationally will come from the emerging markets of the twenty-first century: China, India, Russia, South Africa, and Brazil. These countries are experiencing burgeoning ranks of millions of middle-class consumers. These newly wealthy consumers are showing preferences for fashionable brands as well as for features every bit as sophisticated as their developed-country counterparts. As a consequence, companies such as Cisco, Del, and Microsoft dominate global markets. However, many new challengers are using their low costs and intimate knowledge of emerging markets to expand their businesses. Chinese network systems company Huawei can charge 50 percent less and succeed in the markets of Africa and Europe.

Developing new technologies or products is a resource-intensive task. Without the efforts of international managers, nongovernmental organizations, local governments, and communities would flounder in their attempts to bring development to the poorest nations in the world. The emergence of these markets presents a great growth opportunity for companies. It also creates a chance for business, government, and civil society to join together in a common cause to help the aspiring poor to join the world market economy. Lifting billions of people from poverty may help avert social decay, political chaos, terrorism, and environmental deterioration that is certain to intensify if the gap between the rich and poor countries continues to widen.

Many managers have to face the increasing globalization of markets and competition. In many industries, the major players have decided to compete in all of the major markets of the world. The challenges in this process are considerable. Managers will have to assess their core businesses, formulate global strategy in terms of target market choice and competitive strategy, develop appropriate business approaches to match the need of the markets, and make sure their organizations are ready for these new programs.

International managers develop the knowledge and talents that disentangle the competing priorities confronting individuals, companies, and governments. They explain the tenet that nations must be able and willing to buy each other's goods if world economies are to blossom. They can show how competition and consumer choice are crucial to the achievement of a higher level of well-being. By having field-specific knowledge, by understanding the effect of culture and emotions, and by sitting at the table, and making their contribution, international managers help to ensure a better life and a better world.

We thank all the participants in our labors – particularly Sandra Beckwith of Beckwith Communications, who made key contributions to this work and always communicated her good mood. Jane Autler suggested some new directions in our thinking and we are grateful for that. Dafina Nikolova and Rebecca White helped with research – thank you both. Charles Skuba was always there to help out, and brought enthusiasm and capabilities to all his involvement. Thomas Czinkota continuously provided support in terms of thoughts and ideas. Vielen Dank and Kiitos!

This book will help you understand the complexities of international markets, to interpret change and find new directions for your activities, and develop ways to make use of new opportunities. We wish you well. Please contact us to add examples, new views, or to just have a chat about international business. We will be pleased to hear from you. You can also track our latest thoughts, analyses and interpretations in international business and let us know your perspectives by coming to our blog: www.michaelczinkota.com.

Michael R. Czinkota
(czinkotm@georgetown.edu)

Ilkka A. Ronkainen
(ronkaii@georgetown.edu)

Chapter 1

The Global Imperative

International marketing is a necessity, not an option.

A nation that does not participate in the global marketplace will see its economic capability and overall standard of living decline. A company that overlooks the potential of global marketing might not even survive – let alone thrive. Successful international marketing benefits both nations and employers, promising an improved quality of life, a better society, more efficient business transactions, and a more peaceful world as trading partners "make love, not war."

THE GLOBAL ECONOMY DEPENDS ON TRADE

The reality is that the world depends on continuity in trade. Trade flows and currency values shape the global economic outlook, competition, and consumer choices. In the U.S., for example, trade-related activities comprise more than 25 percent of the country's GDP – which is more than the housing and banking sectors combined. Trade also accounted for the entire U.S. economic growth in 2008.

Patterns identified during the global recession of late 2008 highlight the remarkable impact of any ripple in trade worldwide. According to U.S. Commerce Department data, combined U.S. exports and imports dropped 18 percent from July to November 2008, with a decline in imports accounting for two-thirds of the drop. With the U.S. importing less, nations that export to America suffered as a result. For example, during this period, Japan experienced its biggest drop in exports ever, while China and Germany experienced their biggest drops in a decade. This, in turn, means that other countries that are exporting less will also import less from the U.S. and other nations. As a result, the World Bank predicted that global trade would decline 2.1 percent during 2009, just two-tenths of a percent more than the last big decline in 1975.

Of course, when demand is down among the world's global trading partners, little or no trade growth is likely to occur until a recovery begins. This lull in trade creates an opportunity for companies that are new to global trading to study, learn, and become knowledgeable. This is the time to prepare for the inevitable point when global buyers regain confidence – and they will regain confidence. Research shows that it typically takes new exporters about two years to get their international legs before they begin to realize good sales results. The best time to get that experience is when there's less pressure to learn it quickly to keep up with a booming industry or with the competition.

University MBA program applications reflect this – increasing numbers of students, knowing that job prospects are not as robust as in the past, are staying in school to accumulate knowledge and capabilities that will prepare them for the economic turnaround to come.

Companies can do the same. Now is the time to use slack resources to explore new market opportunities, new cultures, and new customers. Company leaders and managers can take international business courses at local universities, attend regional trade seminars and industry conference workshops on global business, and read books and newsletters. They can network with managers of local companies already marketing their products and services in other countries. U.S. businesses can contact the local office of the U.S. Commercial Service to learn more about how this arm of the International Trade Administration can assist. Then, when economic conditions get better, companies can pounce on the markets they have researched and prepared for.

This applies to all nations. Many countries have export promotion capabilities and the expertise needed to help more of their firms market overseas. There has never been a better time to take advantage of the knowledgeable support that they offer.

U.S. Leadership is Essential

As we write this, governments worldwide are working to counteract the 2009 economic crisis by developing stimulus plans. The efforts of any one nation will have an impact globally because national economies are intertwined, but economic activity is highly concentrated among a few players – the U.S., European Union, Japan, China, and Canada – who account for more than 75 percent of the world's economy. That clout makes it critical for U.S. companies to become more involved in international marketing, whether it is export–import trade, licensing, joint ventures, wholly owned subsidiaries, turnkey operations, or management contracts.

There is a tendency today toward domestic protectionism and while it is not surprising, it is also not wise. Using the U.S. as an example, those with global marketing experience know that a "buy American" attitude will cost the U.S. and the world billions of dollars and reduce the number of jobs. The U.S. needs the companies from other nations with facilities in the U.S. to continue to pump money and jobs into the economy. These companies should be welcome to do so, particularly when they create products Americans want at an affordable price.

Conversely, when an American company ventures abroad, it wants its contribution to another country's economy to be welcomed, not feared. The reception it receives in those countries will be driven by the openness the U.S. offers outside companies. Every time a U.S. firm loses business abroad because of retaliation for American restrictions, the economy suffers. Keeping the U.S. open to trade will avoid a new global battle of trade restrictions that will undo decades of effort by corporations and governments to eliminate the trade barriers that keep businesses from thriving.

Recent economic recovery plans in the U.S. and abroad have provided both an opportunity to send a signal to markets about what they can expect in terms of U.S. trade, and a chance to reassert U.S. leadership on the global stage. Discussions of U.S. economic improvements must go beyond domestic issues and include a focus on global recovery. Countries must be willing and able to buy each other's goods – in increasing quantities – if economies are to blossom. Financing is key to their success, so recovery plans that include governmental efforts to help companies finance overseas ventures, including providing buyers with credit, will boost the domestic economy as well.

Global Opportunities Yield Success

The potential is exciting. A new world order and curious and open-minded consumers offer a vast array of new marketing opportunities. At the same time, international specialization and cross-sourcing have made production much more efficient than ever before. New technologies and resources, especially connections made possible through the Internet, have changed the way we do business, allowing us to both supply and receive products from across the world. Even the smallest companies that had never thought in terms of global marketing have been able to actively expand to international markets because of buyers who have discovered their products or services online and purchased them. These buyers, while similar to domestic customers, might never have been targeted by the companies for global outreach.

The number of markets in a position to buy our products and services is increasing, as well. As more traditionally poor regions enjoy access to improved communications technology – television sets, satellite networks, and Internet access, for example – more people become aware of products available elsewhere, creating demand for them in unexpected places. Microfinancing designed to help poor households meet basic needs or assist entrepreneurs starting or expanding a business will have a profound impact. The funding will improve not only the quality of life for borrowers in emerging markets, but will also help build a workforce for manufacturers establishing operations in these regions. Citizens with new employment opportunities offered by international investors will also be better able to afford those enticing products seen in television and movies or the Internet.

World traders have forged networks of global linkages that bind us all – countries, institutions, and individuals – much more closely than ever before. A drought in Brazil and its effect on coffee production and prices is felt around the world. Hurricanes Katrina and Rita on the U.S. Gulf Coast disrupted oil production so severely that there was a spike in gasoline prices worldwide, raising transportation costs for countless industries and businesses. These linkages have also become more intense on the individual level. Communication has built new international bridges, whether it is through music or international programs transmitted by CNN, BBC, Al Arabiya, and other networks. We share similar interests and activities with others worldwide – many of us wear jeans, listen to the same music on iPods, and eat kebabs or curry or sushi. Transportation linkages let individuals from different countries see and meet each other with unprecedented ease. Common cultural pressures result in similar social phenomena and behavior, such as the rise of dual income families searching for ways to save time with shopping and housework.

Trading blocs – the European Union in Europe, NAFTA in North America, Mercosur in Latin America, and ASEAN in Asia – encourage trade relations between member countries while having an impact on the trade and investment flows of nonmember nations. They remind companies that they are competing not only domestically but also globally – whether they have an overt presence overseas or not.

LEVERAGE OPPORTUNITIES, MINIMIZE CHALLENGES

Today's international marketer is subject to a new set of macro-environmental factors; to different constraints than they are accustomed to; and to quite frequent conflicts resulting from different laws, cultures, and societies. The basic principles of marketing still apply, but their application, complexity, and intensity might vary substantially. Interestingly, an international marketer can take on the role of marketing as a key agent of societal change as well as an instrument in the development of socially-responsive business strategies.

Companies expanding into other countries must consider whether their marketing will contribute to economic development and societal improvements. For example, with a banking infrastructure in Russia that is less sophisticated than that of the U.S., an American company that hopes to finance automobile purchases in Russia must be prepared to implement a different business model. And while there might be challenges to doing so, the rewards of the effort include greater stability for the lender and improved quality of life for the new auto owners.

Firms expanding into additional global markets must tackle distribution systems, pricing, and address a wide range of ethical issues such as legal systems related to monitoring pollution, maintaining a safe work environment, copying of technology or trademarks, and dealing with demands for bribes. As the 2008 attacks in Mumbai show, terrorism continues to pose a risk. Terrorism can be a threat to plants and their people or, more likely, have an impact on a manufacturing supply chain. A company's ability to master these challenges will present it with potential for new opportunities with significant rewards.

International marketing is also leading to a shift in corporate processes. It is easier, and more important than ever, to gather, manipulate, analyze, and disseminate information. As a result, products can be produced more quickly, obtained less expensively from sources around the world, distributed at lower costs, and customized for individual customers and clients. Just a decade or so ago, we would have thought it was impossible for a company to produce computer motherboards, monitors, and software in different countries, assemble the computer in yet another nation, and sell it in still other markets. Today, the computer industry depends on this model to survive.

Adaptation is Key

Companies that want to succeed need to actively adapt to the changing world environment. By absorbing and providing knowledge around the globe, a company can build and strengthen its competitive position. A global company with units in multiple nations can create a knowledge intranet populated with best practices and "here's how we solved this problem" information capitalizes on the intellectual capital of its employees worldwide. It can then move ahead quicker and with greater ease than its isolated competitors. Businesses that depend on long production runs can expand their activities and reach far more customers, increasing the payoff. Companies can avoid the stagnation that comes with market saturation by creating new product life cycles in other countries.

Production sites are more flexible today, as plants get shifted from one country to another and suppliers are increasingly available in more nations. Cooperative agreements let all involved parties bring their strengths to the game, emerging with better products, services, and ideas than they could ever create individually. What is more, research shows that multinational corporations face a lower risk of insolvency and pay higher wages than domestic-only companies. Stability like this attracts top talent in a competitive marketplace. Consumers benefit, too, since international marketing gives them a greater variety of lower-priced products that can help improve their lifestyles and comfort.

Companies and industries that do not participate in the global marketplace must recognize that in today's trade environment, they will suffer. Willing or unwilling, we all are drawn into global commerce. Even if it does not happen by choice, companies and individuals are affected directly or indirectly by economic and political developments that occur in the international marketplace. It does matter to Americans when the European Central Bank makes interest rate decisions in Frankfurt, or whether Russia and Ukraine have disagreements over the use of gas pipelines. Companies that ignore such events or decline to participate can only react and are unprepared for harsh competition from abroad that can have a profound impact on business success or failure.

Some industries are more progressive about this than others. Farmers, for example, understand the need for high productivity in light of stiff international competition. Computer makers, software firms, and high-technology-related businesses large and small have learned to embrace global relationships so they can stay in the race. Companies in the steel, textile, and leather sectors have shifted production in response to overwhelming onslaughts from abroad. Other industries in some countries have been caught unaware and have not adjusted, resulting in failed firms or entire industries such as coal mining and steel smelting in certain countries.

PROCEED WITH CAUTION – BUT PROCEED

Thoughtful companies explore the opportunities before making the global leap. They examine global developments, understand their meaning, and develop the ability to adjust to change. This ability to adapt to changing global conditions is, in fact, essential to success. Sometimes companies do not adapt because they do not see a need for it, assuming that international customers are just like those they serve at home. Such assumptions can lead to inefficiency, lack of consumer acceptance, and give the more responsive competition a leg up. It will be clear in subsequent chapters that there are substantial differences – along with similarities – among consumer groups around the globe.

Small Businesses Can Thrive

Do not be fooled into thinking that only huge corporations can succeed in the global marketplace. It is true that some very large players from many countries are active in the world market. But smaller firms have a significant presence, too.

Success in the art of international marketing requires solid answers to these questions:

- Should I obtain my supplies domestically or from abroad?
- What marketing adjustments are or will be necessary?
- What should I expect in terms of threats from global competition?
- How can I work with these threats to turn them into opportunities?
- What are my strategic global alternatives?

These questions need answers. Integrating these issues into all of the global marketing decisions can help overseas efforts become a source of growth, profit, needs, satisfaction, and quality of life that would not exist if the company limited itself to domestic activities.

Small Business Exports Grow

The Commerce Department's Exporter Data Base reveals that companies with fewer than 500 workers accounted for 97 percent of all U.S. exporters. The number of small and medium-sized businesses that exported merchandise more than doubled from 1992 to 2008. Increasingly, smaller firms, particularly in the computer and telecommunications industries, are born global, since they can achieve a worldwide presence within a short period of time.

Businesses differ widely in their international activities and needs, depending on their level of experience, resources, and capabilities. For the company that is just beginning to enter the global market, the level of knowledge about international complexities is low, the demand on time is high, expectations about success are uncertain, and the international environment is often inflexible. But should that stop them? Of course not. Knowing there was a global need for its oral diagnostics products, U.S.-based Zila Inc. was selling its products in just the U.S. and Canada in 2007 but a year later had strategic distribution alliances in a number of European markets. By early 2009, the company with fewer than 300 employees had expanded even further to get its products into distribution in the United Kingdom, Germany, France, Spain, Portugal, and Greece. New distribution agreements in the Pacific Rim will ensure future sales in that region as well. Conversely, the multinational firm with thousands of employees on multiple continents has more leeway in terms of resource availability, experience, and information. The multinational marketer can respond creatively to the environment by shifting resources or even shaping the environment itself – options that are not always available to the smaller company.

But large firms started small. Their managers had to learn the basics before directing far-flung global operations. Those starting out must understand the operational questions that are crucial to success while those that have become multinational corporations must constantly learn and adjust to achieve global synergies. Mastering the global marketing imperative involves learning:

- How international marketing differs from domestic marketing
- Whether or how marketing principles apply when they are transferred to the global marketplace
- Whether there is a market abroad for their product or service without spending a fortune on research
- How a company can promote its products in global markets
- How marketers find and evaluate an international distributor
- How to ensure payment
- How to minimize government red tape while taking advantage of helpful government programs.

Once we understand the opportunities of global trade and how to deal with the challenges, international markets can become a source of growth, profit, and needs satisfaction. Around the world there is hope, expectation, and willingness for U.S. leadership in international marketing. There will be great potential when the U.S. leads its economic partners on the basis of trust and fair play and when governments, companies, and business leaders work together collaboratively.

FOOD FOR THOUGHT

- Is your company already selling products or services outside the country?
- What is the global marketing potential for your company – how much can your business grow by reaching beyond borders?
- What international market most closely resembles your domestic market in terms of customers and use?
- Who do you know at local global companies who will talk to you about how to move forward with the growth that will come from international expansion?

Further Readings

Bhagwati, Jagdish. *In Defense of Globalization*. Oxford, UK: Oxford University Press, 2008.

Gatignon, Hubert and John R. Kimberly. *The INSEAD Wharton Alliance on Globalizing: Strategies for Building Successful Global Businesses*. Cambridge, UK: Cambridge University Press, 2004.

Krugman, Paul. *The Return of Depression Economics and the Crisis of 2008*. New York, NY: W. W. Norton & Company, Ltd, 2009.

Nelson, Carl A. *Import/Export: How to Take Your Business Across Borders*. New York, NY: McGraw-Hill, 2009.

Stiglitz, Joseph E. *Making Globalization Work*. New York, NY: W. W. Norton & Company Ltd, 2008.

Online Resources

BNET Today: Resources for International Marketing
Marketing resources from a website that provides managers with business intelligence
http://resources.bnet.com/topic/international+marketing.html

Global EDGE: International Business Resource Desk
A collection of thousands of business resources selected based on content and usability
http://globaledge.msu.edu/

Regional Trade Blocs: UC Atlas of Global Inequality
A useful website with maps and data for the world's regional trade blocs
http://ucatlas.ucsc.edu/trade/subtheme_trade_blocs.php

Chapter 2

Establishing the Context

Constant and rapid changes in the international marketing environment make it essential for marketers to understand the forces behind the changes and their impact on global trade. Marketers must be acutely aware of the policies, politics, and legal and financial environments of the countries or regions where they plan to do business. Behaviors or practices that are accepted or even encouraged in one region might be banned in another.

UNDERSTANDING TRADE POSITIONS

It helps to put the current trading environment in context. Over time, international trade positions have changed significantly. In the 1950s, 25 percent of the total world exports came from the U.S., in large part because the U.S. economy was not destroyed by the Second World War. It had the manufacturing power and products to sell elsewhere while many European economies did not. Later, as other trade partners worked aggressively to secure a larger world market share for themselves, U.S. export growth did not keep pace with total world export growth. By 2008, that 1950s share of 25 percent had dropped to 8 percent, with both Germany and China having a higher share in world merchandise exports than the U.S.

Ironically, it was the leadership role of the U.S. after the Second World

War that led to the shift in trade positions. American policy-makers have long seen the U.S. as the leading country in world power and trade. This opinion brought with it a sense of obligation to assist other countries with their trade efforts. Americans believed that without their help, other countries would never play a meaningful role in the global economy. While there was continuing aid to other countries and their businesses, U.S. domestic firms received no special support or aid. These policies continued for decades, eventually placing U.S. companies at a distinct disadvantage in the world trading environment.

At the same time, U.S. companies were continually assured that the American domestic market was large enough to support the nation's businesses. That market availability and the relative distance to overseas markets led U.S. manufacturers to remain content to keep their trade within domestic borders. The perception was that exporting and international marketing were not worth the risk and effort.

Meanwhile, as smaller nations were forced to look beyond their borders to grow and thrive, their companies trained executives about markets abroad and cultural sensitivities and differences. U.S. managers did not learn this on the job and students did not learn about it in business schools. They lacked global interest, information, and education. This, combined with an overall ignorance of where and how to market internationally and unfamiliarity with global market conditions and trade regulations, nearly ensured that the U.S. would continue to lose its share of the international market.

Conditions are changing, though, as U.S. businesses realize that their survival depends on a global, rather than domestic, marketplace. E-commerce has made it easier for many to think past their borders and expand outward, serving a wider, more international audience. Universities and their business programs, in particular, are stepping up to educate students not only in theory but also in practice, sending students abroad for internships and other learning experiences. Some universities actually "export" globally by opening up subsidiaries or branch campuses around the world. Even the U.S. Department of State has come on board, offering training in business–government relations to new ambassadors so they can help U.S.-based companies doing business abroad. The collective attention in the U.S. to international markets as a source of new customers and supplies continues to expand. There is increasing demand for knowledge and understanding of global markets and how they differ from those at home.

Market environments have been favorable to globalization in recent years, although the recent recession did cause many countries to reinstate trade barriers that had fallen years before. In early 2009, countries suffering from decreased consumer spending and purchasing power scrambled to protect their economy but, in the process, might have hurt those of others by making it harder for other countries to export to them.

This is not an unprecedented response to an economic crisis. In 1930, the Smoot-Hawley Tariff Act in the U.S. raised the tariffs on more than 20,000 goods, causing other countries to retaliate by increasing the tariffs on imported U.S. goods. In the decades since, however, nations have realized how their societies have benefited by increasing, rather than restricting, trade, so the barriers of 2009 are expected to be temporary.

WHY TRADE IS GOOD FOR YOUR COUNTRY AND COMPANY

It is hard to understate the value of global trade and exports in particular. Exports can determine the level of imports that a country can sustain, affect currency values as well as the fiscal and monetary policies of countries, and shape public perception of a nation's ability to compete. In 2008, the U.S. was importing 1.5 times as much as it was exporting, creating a trade deficit of $680 billion (see Figure 2.1). Large trade deficits are not sustainable in the long run. They are a strong indicator that a country is consuming more than it is producing, which reduces independence by making it increasingly reliant on the products and services of other nations.

Increasing export volume helps reduce the trade deficit. This is a wise course of action for many reasons, but one of the most important is that exporting creates jobs. In fact, the International Trade Administration of the U.S. Department of Commerce reports that, in 2006, exports of manufactured goods supported 6 million U.S. jobs. Just as importantly for companies, however, is how exporting can help them achieve economies of scale. By broadening reach and serving customers abroad, it is possible to produce more and to do so more efficiently in industries

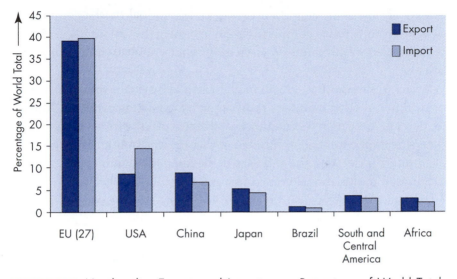

FIGURE 2.1 Merchandise Exports and Imports as a Percentage of World Total, 2008

Source: World Trade Organization

affected by economies of scale. This often leads to lower costs and higher profits both at home and abroad.

Market diversification that results from selling products and services in other countries can bring greater stability to a company. If one region experiences an economic downturn, the company suffers less if it operates in other areas with greater stability. For example, Breeze Industrial Products Corporation, a Michigan-based maker of hose clamps, has diversified both in terms of industries served and in global regions where it markets its products to protect the company from either industry or economic downturns. Establishing a plant in Germany to serve European markets has allowed the company to expand the business by as much as 25 percent in two years and offset problems plaguing the domestic U.S. auto industry. Selling products to companies other than U.S. auto manufacturers both domestically and abroad also provides more stability.

An economy that imports offers benefits as well. Competitors selling in a company's home market can raise the bar by introducing new approaches, better processes, or improved products and services. To maintain market share, home countries are forced to compete more effectively by improving their own systems and products. Consumers benefit from a more competitive environment by gaining access to a wider variety of products or services at what are often more appealing prices.

Many businesses participate in global trade by establishing businesses or facilities in other countries rather than by exporting products. Known as Foreign Direct Investment, this strategy offers strong growth and diversification potential for businesses that understand the need for globalization. For decades, the U.S. was the leading foreign direct investor as U.S.-based multinational companies and subsidiaries popped up nearly everywhere. Increasingly, though, we are seeing the opposite, with businesses from other countries investing in companies or facilities in the U.S. The Organization for International Investment reports that U.S. subsidiaries of foreign-owned companies employ 5.3 million Americans and account for an annual payroll of $364 billion. In addition, global investors in general contribute to the host country's economy not only by providing jobs but also by importing supplies and exporting products.

Not all countries eagerly embrace foreign direct investors. It is an emotionally charged topic for both citizens and policy-makers, some of whom aggressively oppose outside investment even when there is little economic evidence of any negative impact. Many governments review the effect and desirability of foreign investment projects before allowing them to move forward. In the U.S., the Committee for Foreign Investments in the United States scrutinizes such investment activities primarily for their impact on national security. For example, due to pressure, it blocked the acquisition of American oil company UNOCAL by the China National Offshore Oil Corporation in 2005. In France the same year, the government prevented Swiss-owned Novartis from acquiring the pharmaceutical company Aventis.

Government Policies Can Help or Hinder

Governments often impose barriers that interfere with trade. The Office of the U.S. Trade Representative (USTR, www.ustr.gov) defines trade barriers as "government laws, regulations, policies, or practices that either protect domestic products from foreign competition or artificially stimulate exports of particular domestic products." One typical barrier consists of "voluntary" import restraints that are applied selectively against trading partners, an approach used primarily with the textile, steel, and automotive industries. Voluntary restrictions, ensured through severe threats against trading partners, are designed to help domestic industries reorganize, rebuild, and recapture their trade prominence. Countries that do not use voluntary measures often implement tariffs. This approach helped preserve the Harley-Davidson Company in the U.S. during the 1980s when the duty on imported Japanese heavy motorcycles was temporarily bumped from just over 4 percent to almost 50 percent.

Global Trade Barriers

The Office of the U.S. Trade Representative's *National Trade Estimate Report on Foreign Trade Barriers* published annually classifies barriers into ten categories:

- Import policies that include tariffs and other import charges as well as customs barriers
- Standards, testing, labeling and certification, which includes refusal to accept U.S. manufacturers' self-certification that they conform to a country's product standards
- Government procurement, including "buy domestic" and closed bidding processes
- Export subsidies including export financing on preferential terms and agricultural export subsidies that displace U.S. exports in third world markets
- Service barriers such as limits on the range of financial services that can be offered by outside financial institutions
- Lack of intellectual property protection – endangering patents, copyrights or trademarks
- Investment barriers, including limits on global equity participation, access to outside government-funded research and development programs, and restrictions on transferring earnings and capital
- Anticompetitive practices with trade effects tolerated by other governments, including anticompetitive activities of both state-owned and private firms

■ Trade restrictions affecting e-commerce including discriminatory taxation
■ Other barriers, such as those that might encompass more than one category – bribery and corruption – or that affect a single sector.

Each year the report outlines the specific barriers in each of the largest export markets for the U.S., breaking them out according to 57 countries and several regions including the European Union and the Southern Africa Customs Union. It is essential reading for global marketers looking to expand into one of these nations or regions.

Non-tariff barriers are much more subtle and difficult to detect, prove, and quantify than their tariff counterparts. They might be "buy domestic" campaigns or preferential treatment to domestic bidders on government projects. The primary result of trade restrictions is that they take us away from what we know is good for the world and its citizens. While industries are preserved, it is done at the expense of world trade and at a cost to consumers, whose choices are restricted by government intervention.

In the U.S., government policy responses to trade issues have consisted primarily of political reactions to specific situations rather than a coordinated set of continuous activities in the legislative and executive branches of government. Because of persistent trade deficits, increased foreign direct investment, and the tendency of some industries to seek government shelter for their market problems, the U.S. Congress has for the past two decades been willing to give the president increasing powers to restrict trade but has failed to provide the resources to substantially encourage trade. The emphasis has been on threats against importers rather than encouraging conditions for exporters. Trade legislation has become increasingly oriented to specific trading partners and industries, such as bilateral trade agreements between the U.S. and Korea, which are, after passage, renegotiated against strong opposition.

Like many other countries, the U.S. does help its companies promote their exports. The key objective is (or should be) reducing risk or increasing rewards. The U.S. Department of Commerce (www.commerce.gov/) provides a wide range of helpful data on international trade and marketing developments. The trade promotion unit of the International Trade Administration, the U.S. Commercial Service (http://trade.gov/cs/), has trade specialists in more than 100 U.S. cities and 80 countries who provide help with exporting and other forms of global sales. In addition to providing counseling, the local offices offer access to market research, trade events for product or service promotion to buyers, and introductions to appropriate distributors and buyers. Relatively speaking, though, U.S. support lags behind that provided by other major advanced economies, particularly since the largest portion of what is provided goes to the agricultural sector.

Many nations offer financial assistance through subsidized finance rates, too. In the U.S., the Export-Import Bank, the "official export credit agency of the United States," offers mixed aid credit, loans composed of commercial interest rates, and highly subsidized developmental aid interest rates. It works to help level the playing field for U.S. exporters by matching the financing that other governments provide to their exporters.

Governments can also support businesses marketing their products and services abroad by enacting appropriate trade policies that recognize that the country's economic platform determines a nation's global competitiveness. This means that trade policy must become more domestically oriented at the same time that domestic policy adopts a more international vision. In general, policy-makers must be willing to trade off short-term achievements for long-term goals and to appreciate the linkages between domestic policies and international capabilities.

Trade Policy Goals

A trade policy should have these goals:

- Improving the quality and amount of information shared by the government and businesses
- Encouraging collaboration in areas such as goods and process technologies
- Overcoming a reluctance to export and a short-term finance attitude

- Educating and training workers so they are qualified to handle global competitive challenges
- Giving the executive branch the authority to negotiate international agreements without fear that the agreements will be altered by Congress
- Building on a domestic framework that allows firms to fully bring their competitive capabilities to bear internationally.

UNDERSTANDING POLITICAL AND LEGAL ENVIRONMENTS

It is essential to understand the political and legal environments in home and host countries. It also helps to understand the treaties, agreements, and laws governing the relations between home and host nations. For example, minimum wage legislation in any country where a company has employees has a competitive impact, particularly on labor-intensive processes. Country-based legal issues common to many companies involved in global trade include safeguards for intellectual property rights and how gray market activities are policed and prosecuted.

The political environment in most countries tends to support its corporations' international marketing efforts, but not those of foreign direct investors. In addition, there are often specific rules and regulations that restrict international marketing. These rules are usually political in nature and involve other concerns that might include foreign policy and national security.

Be Alert to Risks

Even when doing business in a country with a stable and friendly government, marketers must monitor the government's policies and stability for changes that could cause problems. Be alert, in particular, to the political risk that comes from changes in tax laws, tariffs, expropriation of assets, or restriction in repatriation of profits. The types of risk encountered most frequently include:

- Ownership risk, which exposes property and life
- Operating risk or interference
- Transfer risk involving attempts to shift funds between countries

Political risk can be quite dramatic, as in when a coup d'état results in a new government. Less exciting but still worrisome risk develops when policy changes are caused by pressure from nationalist or religious factions or from widespread anti-Western feelings. Alert marketers work to anticipate these developments and have a plan in place for dealing with them. Common outcomes in these situations include violence against employees or company property, confiscation, and expropriation.

Expropriation, or the compensated seizure of foreign assets by a government, has been appealing to some countries because it demonstrates nationalism while immediately transferring a certain amount of wealth and resources from the outside company to the host government. In Venezuela, for example, the government has specifically targeted the petroleum industry, giving itself 60 percent ownership of oil companies in that country. ConocoPhillips and ExxonMobil have resisted, charging the government with expropriation. While expropriation does compensate the owners, negotiations are drawn out and often shortchange the owners. The result is a short-term gain for the host country – that transfer of wealth – with long-term consequences – companies stop bringing their business to that nation.

Confiscation is similar, but harsher, because there is no compensation for what has been taken from its owners. Some industries, including mining, energy, public utilities, and banking, are more vulnerable to confiscation because of their importance to the host country's economy and because the nature of the industry makes it difficult for the businesses to shift operations elsewhere. An increasingly common and more subtle form of control is domestication. When this happens, the government demands partial transfer of ownership and management responsibility while imposing regulations that ensure that a large share of the product is locally produced. A larger share of the profit is retained in the host country, too. Ramifications for the company range from imposed local managers who lack appropriate skills, experience, or training to increased costs, inefficiency, and lower quality products.

Most businesses operating abroad face a number of other risks that are more common and less dangerous than these, however. Host governments facing a currency shortage sometimes impose controls on the movement of capital in and out of the country. Sometimes they leverage exchange controls to reduce the importation of goods that are considered to be a luxury or unnecessary, no matter that they might be important components.

Governments might also try to control outside companies and their capital by raising the tax rate. These selective tax increases might result in revenue for the government, but they can severely damage the global investor's operation, which, in turn, can lead to decreased income for the host country in the long run. Political pressure can also force governments to control the prices of imported goods or services. This happens most often in sectors considered to be highly sensitive from a political perspective, such as food or health care.

Avoiding Risk

Companies face political and economic risk whenever they conduct business overseas, but there are usually ways to reduce the risk. The most important step is learning about and understanding the host country's history, political background, culture, and current policies and political climate before making a long-term investment decision. It is also necessary to have a high degree of sensitivity to country-specific approaches and concerns so that the company blends into the local landscape and does not call attention to what is different.

If a country's citizens feel exploited by global companies, government officials are more likely to take action against those companies or others like them. Reduce that risk by being a good community citizen. Hire and train local people. Pay well. Be a leader the community. Show that the company is willing to share the fruits of its labors with nationals by forming joint ventures with local partners. In addition, be certain to monitor local political developments through local partners or by contracting with a firm that specializes in this service.

It is also possible to purchase insurance to cover losses that might result from political situations – most developed countries offer insurance programs for their companies doing business abroad. Germany offers its companies an export credit guarantee known as Hermes cover. In the U.S., The Overseas Private Investment Corporation (www.opic. gov) offers insurance.

Risk Insurance in the U.S.

In the U.S., The Overseas Private Investment Corporation (www.opic.gov) offers insurance for three types of risk:

- Currency inconvertibility
- Expropriation
- Political violence.

Rates vary by country and industry, but for $100 of coverage per year for a manufacturing project, the base rate is $0.25–0.45 for protection against inconvertibility, $.50–0.70 to protect against expropriation, and $0.70–1.10 to protect against political violence. Policies do not usually cover commercial risk and cover only the actual loss – not profits – in a claim.

None of this guarantees that a company will eliminate risk, but it will certainly help manage it. Remember, too, that many governments encourage outside investments, particularly when they see a benefit to their country. Some even offer incentives in the form of subsidies. Pay close attention to the extent and forms of incentives available from governments and factor them into global trade decisions.

Laws Vary from Region to Region

Many host countries have laws that have an impact on how companies can execute their marketing and business plans. For starters, some have laws that impose tariffs or quotas. There are antidumping laws, which prohibit companies from selling their goods below their cost, as well as those requiring export and import licensing. Many also have health and safety standards that might, either on purpose or accidentally, restrict the entry of nondomestic goods. For example, after high levels of lead paint in Chinese-made toys prompted U.S. toymaker Mattel to recall more than 21 million products in 2007, India banned imported Chinese toys in early 2009. It eased the ban six weeks later after China said the sanctions would hurt bilateral trade relations.

There is also global controversy about genetically modified products. Australia, for example, requires that food produced using biotechnology be assessed by the Australia New Zealand Food Authority. Other laws might be in place to protect domestic stakeholders but might have the effect of reducing imports. There is often very specific legislation that regulates where a company can advertise and what is considered deceptive advertising, information that is particularly important in the marketing process. Some countries even regulate company names or the foreign language content of a product's label. It is essential that marketers research the laws that will have an impact on their business when making global market decisions. Understand a country's legal and political systems and work with people who understand how to work within the systems.

Marketers committed to a region can also work to influence the legal system to generate more favorable environments. Some develop coalitions or constituencies designed to motivate legislators and politicians to implement change by highlighting the benefits of the changes they are seeking. These coalitions often need to employ lobbyists who bring to play their experience and networks to influence policy-makers and legislators. Successful lobbying also involves local citizens and companies to help demonstrate how a particular issue affects a decision-maker's constituents.

The Impact of International Politics and Law

In addition to considering each country's political and legal climate, marketers expanding overseas, particularly with direct investment, must take the more global scene into account. The global trading environment is influenced both by bilateral political relations between home and host countries and by multilateral agreements governing the relations among groups of countries. The impact of government-to-government relationships can be profound, particularly when the situation becomes hostile or adversarial, which is how some might characterize U.S.–Iranian trade relations.

International political relations can have a positive impact, as the world has seen with the thawing of relationships between countries of the former Soviet Bloc and those in other parts of the world. This political warming has opened up new markets for U.S. companies in Hungary, Poland, and Russia. Improvements in relations now permit many new business ties between Libya and the U.S. It pays to be aware of political currents worldwide, to anticipate changes, and to be prepared for them.

Although there is no international body that creates and enforces international laws, certain treaties and agreements honored and respected by a great number of countries influence international business operations. The World Trade Organization defines internationally accepted economic practices for its 151 member nations, influencing how companies do business by providing a more stable and predictable market environment. Bilateral agreements between nations also have an impact. The U.S. has signed bilateral trade treaties with a wide range of countries. They usually define the rights of U.S. companies doing business in another country – and vice versa – guaranteeing that U.S. firms will receive the same treatment in the host country as a domestic business.

Because there is no international body of law, there are often questions surrounding jurisdiction during legal disputes. Which nation's laws apply – those of the country where the agreement was made or those of the one in which the contract will be fulfilled? Deciding on the laws to be followed and the location to settle the dispute are two different decisions. This is why a dispute between a U.S. exporter and a French importer could be resolved in Paris with the resolution based on New York State law. Smart negotiators add a jurisdictional clause to their contracts so there is no question if a dispute arises. Alternatively, it is possible to make provisions for arbitration to speed up decisions and reduce costs in case of disputes.

Minimizing Terrorism's Impact

International terrorism is the systematic use or threat of violence across borders to attain a political goal while conveying a political message. One of the most recent high-profile examples is the 2008 attack in Mumbai, India, by ten Islamic militants who killed nearly 200 people in more than a dozen locations, including two luxury hotels and a Jewish center. Bombings are most common, followed by armed assaults, kidnapping, vandalism, and hijacking. Global mass media has ensured the visibility of these types of attacks, spreading fear, creating unfounded expectations of other attacks, and harming economies. Unfortunately, according to the U.S. Department of State, businesses are most often the target of terrorists. Figure 2.2 shows the number of terrorism incidents in 2007.

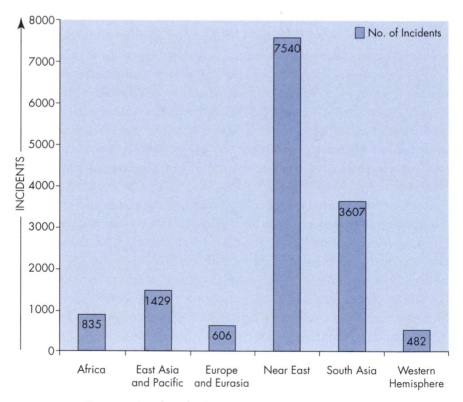

FIGURE 2.2 Terrorism Incidents by Region in 2007

Source: National Counterterrorism Center, 2008 Report on Terrorism

Terrorists often succeed in disrupting economic systems by affecting supply and demand. Companies suffer, enduring reduced revenues or increased costs and, as Americans saw in the attack of the World Trade Center in New York City, a long rebuilding period. Companies doing business in other nations need to be prepared for the range of potential terrorist risks or for the impact on their businesses of attacks taking place elsewhere. In fact, the greatest risk is not a direct attack, but the indirect effect of an attack elsewhere on a company's supply chain, transportation systems, or other factors. Today's global climate requires that companies be prepared for more than survival – the goal is continuity.

Preparing for exposure to terrorism by minimizing risk and maximizing flexibility of response is particularly important for companies doing business in countries or regions where attacks are more frequent, but should happen for all locations. Risk management involves conducting a risk assessment that compares the severity of possible outcomes with the probability of an attack to help determine the likelihood of direct damage to the operation. It includes creating a disaster plan that might be similar to what is used for a natural disaster that disrupts power, causes structural damage to a facility, or even injures workers. Figure 2.3 illustrates our model of corporate preparedness for terrorism.

In some situations, companies might chose to work with customer segments or regions that are less susceptible to terrorism. Many times, companies feel safer working in domestic markets because they are more familiar. However, staying domestic is becoming difficult in our increasingly globalized world. The reduced willingness of firms to sell to or buy from terrorism-exposed countries demonstrates why governments need to work on prevention: terrorism creates poverty.

ETHICAL ISSUES IN GLOBAL TRADING

Whether doing business domestically or internationally, corporate governance, responsibility, intellectual property rights, and corruption all fall under the ethics umbrella. But what is permitted in one country might differ from what is allowed in another. As a result, some wonder whether companies from a developed country with stringent ethical laws should be allowed to use looser local principles in emerging or other economies

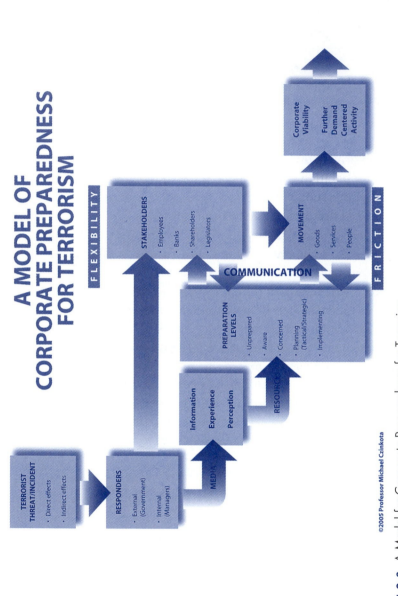

FIGURE 2.3 A Model for Corporate Preparedness for Terrorism

Source: Michael Czinkota, testimony for the U.S. House of Representatives (109th Congress) Committee on Small Business in Washington, DC on November 1, 2005

to their advantage. Marketers must understand the ethical rules of the global marketplace where they are doing business in order to make informed decisions, whether the topic is corporate governance or corruption. In addition, global marketers need to be forward-looking and lead in key areas such as ethics, human rights, and best practices.

Corporate Governance Varies

Various cultural views on stakeholders affect corporate governance and lead to different practices across countries, economies, and cultures. Major factors driving differences include financial market development, the degree of separation between management and ownership, and transparency. In regions such as Hong Kong, Singapore, Malaysia, and France, for example, corporate governance is family-based and management and ownership tend to be combined. Corporate governance in Korea and Germany is more likely to be bank-based, with government influence in bank lending and a lack of transparency in operations. China and Russia, on the other hand, employ government-affiliated governance that reflects state ownership and a lack of transparency. The U.S., United Kingdom, Canada, and Australia have a market-based system leaning toward efficient equity markets and dispersed ownership.

Market-based regions rely on the interplay of supply and demand and let price signals guide their activities rather than relying on government intervention. This results in a market environment that respects profitability and private property and relies on a trust established between investors and managers. That trust disappears when bribery, corruption, or obscurity appear, so it is important that these issues are eliminated in market-based regions. Transparency and trust are important not only within a country, but also across borders with international business partners.

In addition to being responsible to stakeholders, corporations are often expected to exhibit responsible behavior in the markets where they do business. Their obligations often include environmental sustainability, reasonable working conditions and wages, and overall concern about the well-being of their employees and their families. The European Union has surpassed the world in implementing these types of programs. CSR

Europe is a business networking group designed to help companies integrate corporate social responsibility with daily business practices.

Protecting Intellectual Property

While developing a new product or technique can bring lucrative opportunities, it is a vulnerable process. Competitors can make it difficult for an innovator to leverage a new product's potential if they are able to copy the innovation, so it is important for companies to protect their intellectual property. Historically, intellectual property violations or issues had to be pursued for each country. The World Trade Organization changed that in the mid-1990s when it implemented its "Agreement on Trade-Related Aspects of Intellectual Property Rights" (TRIPS) and the corresponding enforcement mechanisms (including trade sanctions). Its requirements apply equally to all member nations but emerging economies are given more time to implement necessary changes.

One particularly ethically-charged issue within intellectual property rights concerns the availability of new medicines. The issue is whether a corporation should retain all rights to manufacture a life-saving drug or vaccine when it cannot manufacture enough to meet global demand. In the case of the AIDS cocktail, the three large multinational companies holding the patents for the drugs involved have filed lawsuits against South African producers of a generic version of the cocktail. Unlawful music downloads are a more common, but less emotionally charged, global intellectual property issue.

Bribery and Corruption

In many countries, bribery and corruption are part of the business lifestyle. "Greasing the wheels" is expected for government services. Decades ago, U.S. companies doing business in other countries played by those rules, paying bribes or doing favors for government officials in exchange for lucrative contracts. A different perspective – one that argued that U.S. companies should provide ethical and moral leadership – emerged in the mid-1970s and forced passage of the Foreign Corrupt

Practices Act (FCPA), making it a crime for U.S. companies to bribe officials in other countries to obtain contracts.

While it is certainly the more ethical way of doing business, there is no question that this puts U.S. firms at a disadvantage when competing for business in markets where bribery and corruption are the norm. In fact, research conducted in the years after the antibribery act was passed revealed that U.S. business in regions where government officials routinely accepted bribes declined significantly. The problem is one of ethics versus practical needs. Some argue that one country should not apply its moral principles to other societies, especially when the gap is wide, but that argument does not do much for U.S. companies – they would be breaking their home country's law if they acted on that viewpoint. In addition, a system that operates on bribery can lead to shoddy performance or materials, which in turn can undermine the reputation of the company responsible for the end result.

Corruption Avoidance Guidelines

To help global companies distinguish between reasonable ways of doing business internationally – including compliance with the expectations of other countries – and outright bribery and corruption, the 1988 Trade Act included revisions to the Foreign Corrupt Practices Act. The revisions clarify when management is expected to know about violations and draws distinctions between the facilitation of routine governmental actions and governmental policy decisions. Routine actions involve tasks such as obtaining licenses or permits, processing governmental papers that might include visas or work orders, providing phone and mail service, and cargo handling. Policy decisions concern situations where a company might receive or retain a contract.

The Organization of American States officially condemned bribery in 1995. In 1999, the Organization for Economic Cooperation and Development agreed to change bribery regulations among its member nations not only to prohibit the tax deductibility of bribes, but also to prohibit them entirely.

There is also a distinction between what is referred to as "functional lubrication" and individual greed. Functional lubrication might include an "express fee" charged in many countries. It is usually relatively small, is standardized, and does not stay with the official making the request – it gets passed through the system or network to others involved in processing the documents. With individual greed, the amounts are higher and the official keeps the money. While facilitating routine actions with an "express fee" is not prohibited, illegally influencing policy decisions can lead to severe fines and penalties.

The 2002 U.S. Sarbanes-Oxley Act designed to protect investors by improving the accuracy and reliability of corporate disclosures has been effective in reducing questionable practices in the developing world. There has been a sharp increase in the number of companies self-reporting illegal payments overseas and cleaning up their overseas procedures.

International marketers need to consider general standards of behavior and ethics. What complicates the effort, though, is different global attitudes or perceptions related to issues that some might think are obvious, including global warming, environmental protection, and moral behavior. For example, cutting down the Brazilian rain forests might be acceptable to that country's government, but scientists and environmentalists elsewhere advise against it. Similarly, it might be legal for U.S. cigarette manufacturers to export their tobacco products, but some view that as exporting death to other countries. And while it is acceptable in China to use prison labor to produce products, U.S. law prohibits importing the resulting products.

In addition, companies are not only subject to governmental rules, but they must also face the values of the public at large. Activists concerned about issues such as child labor, low wages, or sweatshops, campaign to educate consumers, who voice their opinions at the retail level by boycotting brands made in ways that violate their personal ethics. Companies might then suffer from public scorn, consumer boycotts, and investor scrutiny. It is possible they lose more as a result of what might be considered unethical behavior than if they had avoided the practices in the first place.

All of these issues – from the political and legal climate in host countries to the ethical standards of target customers – need to be taken into account when doing business in other nations. To avoid the problems that can result from confusion, misunderstandings, or ignorance, research the markets, anticipate changes, and develop coping strategies. The goal is to avoid being taken by surprise. When necessary, work to change laws in the host country or encourage the company's domestic government to conduct government-to-government negotiations to improve the marketing environment. In the end, a company is subject to the vagaries of political and legal changes. The best one can do is to be aware of political and legal influences and laws, work to conform as much as possible, and to develop a leadership role in blazing new paths for the future.

FOOD FOR THOUGHT

- Does your company have a plan for how to react in a crisis? How can this be modified to address terrorism risks in your global markets?
- What are the trade restrictions to and in markets where you plan to do business? How will you work with or around the restrictions?
- What leadership role does your company assume in its home market? How would you "export" this leadership to other regions where you have a marketing or manufacturing presence?
- Does your company have an ethics policy? How will you apply it in global markets?

Further Readings

Cohen, Ed. *Leadership without Borders: Successful Strategies from World-Class Leaders.* Singapore: John Wiley & Sons Ltd., 2007.

Collins, Denis. *Essentials of Business Ethics: Creating and Organization of High Integrity and Superior Performance.* Hoboken, NJ: John Wiley & Sons Ltd., 2009.

Czinkota, Michael R., Ilkka A. Ronkainen and Masaaki Kotabe, *International Business: The Cutting Edge.* London: Routledge, 2011.

Fisher, Colin and Alan Lovell. *Business Ethics and Values: Individual, Corporate and International Perspectives.* Essex, UK: Pearson Education Ltd., 2009.

Richardson, Harry W., Peter Gordon and James E. Moore II. *Global Business and the Terrorist Threat.* Cheltenham, UK: Edward Elgar Publishing Ltd., 2009.

Online Resources

Annual Report on the OECD Guidelines for Multinational Enterprises 2008
www.oecd.org/document/39/0,3343,en_2649_34889_42416807_1_1_1_1,00.html

International Business Ethics Institute
Content from an organization dedicated to promoting business ethics and corporate responsibility www.business-ethics.org/

Office of the United States Trade Representative: Reports and Publications
www.ustr.gov/about-us/press-office/reports-and-publications

Chapter 3

Doing Your Homework on Global Markets

The most important reasons for international failure are insufficient preparation and lack of information. Most companies understand the need in the domestic marketplace to study what customers want, why they want it, and how they go about filling their needs. Yet, many overlook these components when expanding into global markets. Whether they blame lack of funds or manpower for failing to properly research new markets for the company's goods or services, the end result is, at worst, a failure, and at best, an unnecessary struggle.

Solid international market research is essential to an organization's success when entering the international market. Companies have to understand consumer needs and wants and learn as much as possible about the target region's political, economic, and governmental environment (as discussed in Chapter 2). They must also understand the culture and how it is similar to or different from that of the home market. It is not "business as usual" in a global market. Even regions within nations can be remarkably different not only from the domestic market, but from neighboring regions, as well.

Some companies that have already been filling unsolicited orders from international markets believe that their anecdotal experience is a substitute for formal market research. They are usually wrong. It is simply not enough to know that there is a demand for a product in a particular country. Marketers also need to know whether they can get their product to customers there and whether they can market effectively without breaking any laws.

International marketing research helps management pinpoint and develop strategies for global trade. This task includes identifying, evaluating, and comparing potential outside market opportunities and subsequent market selection. Research is also required for a marketing plan – how else will the company know how to enter and penetrate the market successfully? It provides the facts needed to determine the marketing mix in each region, identifies key cultural factors, and offers the continuous feedback required to fine-tune the marketing plan. Just as importantly, it helps decision-makers anticipate events that will have an impact on the business, take appropriate action, and prepare for global changes.

WHAT IS DIFFERENT WITH GLOBAL MARKET RESEARCH?

Information resources vary from nation to nation. There is more information available about some regions than for others, but failing to gather whatever information is available before moving into new markets might doom an endeavor. The tools and techniques of international marketing research are the same as those used for domestic research, but they are used differently because the environments they are used in can differ significantly. The four primary environmental differences that are important to note and understand are:

- *New parameters*. These might include duties, foreign currencies and changes in their value, different transportation modes, and unfamiliar documentation requirements. There are also new and different parameters linked to doing business in a different country. Exporting, licensing, joint ventures, and foreign direct investment all have their own idiosyncrasies from market to market.
- *New environments*. It is essential to learn about the culture of the host country and its demographics and acknowledge differences in societal structures and language. It is also important to understand the country's unique laws and regulations along with its political system and stability.

- *Number of factors involved.* Companies that expand internationally often enter more than one additional market, making it even more important that they understand not only how the dimensions differ from market to market, but also how they interact. Market research helps manage that process.
- *Broader definition of competition.* Global markets introduce a greater variety of competitors. Determine the breadth of the competition, track competitive activities, and evaluate the actual and potential impact on operations with research.

Start the research process internally by evaluating the company's readiness to go global. Do a general review of the company's personnel and resources. Identify the degree of financial exposure and risk the company is able and willing to assume. This understanding of the company's capabilities can generate confidence or encourage the organization to be better prepared before moving forward.

Next, select the markets. There are two ways to evaluate global markets. One is country ranking and the other is clustering, and both should be used. The first step is indexing or ranking countries by their market appeal to the business or product. Then cluster countries into similar groups for screening and evaluation.

Market Analysis

Analyze general market variables such as total and per capita GDP, GDP growth, mortality rates, and population figures. Population size and concentration offer clues to market size. Age distribution and life expectancy provide insights to market development level. Household size is another important variable, particular when marketing consumer products. Income, however, is the best predictor for most consumer and industrial products and services. In highly developed countries, for example, the richest 10 percent of the population consume 20 percent of all goods and services, while in less developed countries, the respective figure might be as high as 50 percent. In general, the more developed the country, the more income distribution tends to converge toward the middle class.

Country Income Classifications

Marketers use four types of country/income classifications:

1. *Very low family incomes* with subsistence economies characterized by rural populations in which consumption relies on personal output or barter.
2. *Very low and very high family incomes,* with the majority living barely above the subsistence level and others who are truly affluent and spend accordingly.
3. *Low, medium, and high family incomes* with an emerging middle class and the very low and high income classes remaining because of social class barriers.
4. *Mostly medium family incomes* seen in economically advanced countries with institutions and policies that reduce extremes in income distribution.

Understand that per capita income figures might not be an accurate reflection of purchasing power if the currencies involved are distorted by factors such as family self-sufficiency or governmental currency controls. Researchers sometimes use purchasing power parities (PPP) instead of exchange rates to overcome that distortion. PPPs show how many units of currency are needed in one country to buy the amount of goods and services that one unit of currency will buy in another. Often, a monetary measure is not always the best definition of income. For example, in emerging economies where most consumption is self-produced or bartered, financial data alone misrepresent the standard of living. In addition, while lack of income in a market might preclude marketing an existing product, there are still options. The market might respond to an altered product that either has fewer bells and whistles or is made with less expensive parts and materials. The new $2,500 "people's car," Tata Nano, was created to offer Indian families an affordable first vehicle. The low, affordable price is possible only because of the simplicity and small size of the vehicle.

Consumption patterns, when available, are useful as well. The share of income spent on necessities, for example, indicates the market's development level and suggests how much money consumers might have for other purchases. This type of research helps show that expensive, labor-saving devices might not succeed in China because of their high price as a proportion of the target customer's annual salary and the lack of value attributed to "free" time.

Data on product saturation or diffusion – the percentage of households that own a particular product – provide more market potential detail when used with other information, such as household income. For example, in most cases, an expensive product is not going to sell well in extremely low-income markets because consumers will not be able to afford it. There are exceptions, of course, particularly with products that have strong perceived prestige. A China-based manufacturer is testing this theory by marketing a product to rural Chinese residents that can cost them more than half of their annual income. Lenovo Group Ltd. announced in 2009 that it would try to leverage government subsidies for electronic goods by introducing a lower-priced line of computers to Chinese residents in rural locations. With the computers priced at from $365 to $510, subsidies of no more than 13 percent of the purchase price, and an average annual rural income of $700, other computer manufacturers will be watching to see the progress of Lenovo.

The availability and quality of a nation's infrastructure is also critically important when evaluating market potential. International marketers will be relying on the local market for transportation, communication, and energy as well as those systems that facilitate marketing functions. Helpful indicators include steel consumption, cement production, and electricity generation because these correlate with the level of industrial development and the availability of the types of suppliers needed for support. Analyze transportation capabilities by investigating rail traffic by freight tons per kilometer. Use the number of passenger cars, buses, and trucks to assess the state of road transportation and networks. Communication is as important as transportation. Data on the number of telephones, computers, broadcast media, and print media provide solid indications on how well a company can expect to communicate inside and outside the market.

Marketers also study quality of life. This involves reviewing the share of urban population, life expectancy, number of physicians per capita, literacy rate, percentage of income received by the richest 5 percent, and the percentage of the population with access to electricity. They take cultural indicators into account as well, and increasingly focus on emotion research. This tracks how people feel about advertisements and products. Researchers are finding that emotional responses, measurable through magnetic resonance imagery (MRI) or by analyzing breathing, heart rates, perspiration, or body motion, add an important element to understanding high context decisions.

If the company plans to move forward with foreign direct investment, analyze its degree by country and industry in any given market, and study the rules governing this type of investment. There could be restrictions based on industry type or investor origin. Many nations also have screening agencies that assess foreign direct investment proposals.

Evaluating these general market variables will reduce the list of nations from 194 to a more manageable number. Next, assess each of those markets on the list in greater depth. Identify the fastest growing markets, the largest markets for the product, market trends, and market restrictions. While there might not be detailed information for specific products, market researchers can usually find comprehensive information for general product categories. A necessary and cursory review of government restrictions will often help narrow down the list of markets even further.

This is the point where marketers need to learn enough about each market opportunity to make an informed decision about where to consider expanding. Emphasis shifts to market opportunities for a specific product or service, including existing, latent, and incipient markets. Get as specific as possible. Identify demand and supply patterns, evaluate regulations and standards, and assess the competition.

SECONDARY DATA SOURCES

International market research requires using resources and tools that might not be familiar to the researcher who has only gathered and evaluated domestic information. Whether gathering information on the macro level – tariff information or data on government trade policy, for example – or on the micro level – data on local laws and regulations, local standards and specification systems, and distribution systems – there are a number of potential sources of information:

■ *Governments.* These usually have the greatest variety of data available, making them an excellent starting point. Macro information available from governments includes population trends, general trade flows between countries, and world agricultural production. Micro information usually includes details on specific industries in the country, their growth prospects, and their international trade activities. Most countries have a wide array of national and international trade data available online for quick access. Always remember! Government data serve governments.

■ *International organizations.* Many international groups provide useful data online and in directories.

International Information Sources

Here is a sample of the most useful global information sources:

■ The *United Nations Statistical Yearbook* (http://unstats.un.org/unsd/syb/) is an annual compilation of a wide range of international economic, social, and environmental statistics for more than 200 countries and areas of the world, compiled from sources including UN agencies and other international, national, and specialized organizations.

■ The *digital library of the UN Conference on Trade and Development* (www.unctad.org) gives companies access to the knowledge generated by the organization through its intergovernmental and expert meetings, as well as its analyses and research.

■ *Market analysis tools from the International Trade Center* (www.intracen.org/mat/) are available at no charge to users in developing countries.

■ The *United Nations Centre on Transnational Corporations* (http://unctc.unctad.org) publishes the *World Investment Report* covering the latest trends in foreign direct investment around the world and other resources.

■ The *World Trade Organization* (WTO) publishes *International Trade Statistics* (www.wto.org), which offers a comprehensive overview of the latest developments in world trade. The WTO also covers the details of merchandise trade by product and trade in commercial services by category.

■ The *International Monetary Fund* offers financial statistics by country, all of which is available online, as well as several special reports, including the *World Economic Outlook* (www.imf.org/external/pubind.htm). This resource is particularly accurate and useful.

■ *Vendors* – companies that provide services to corporations, including banks, large accounting firms, airlines, trade consultants, and freight shippers, often provide data on business practices, legislative or regulatory requirements, and political stability as well as basic trade data. Shipper DHL, while no longer serving the U.S. market, offers extensive international export and import information for other countries on its website.

■ *Trade associations* – industry associations often collect data from their members and publish them in aggregate form. While often quite general in nature, this information is still useful to marketers for providing initial insights and establishing benchmarks, for example. World trade clubs and domestic and international chambers of commerce, such as the American Chambers of Commerce Abroad, also provide valuable information about local markets in more detail than other less localized sources can offer.

■ *Trade magazines, newsletters, and directories* – many trade magazines publish special issues or resource directories designed to help subscribers who are international marketers. *Appliance Magazine*, for example, publishes an online Global Supplier Directory (www.appliancemagazine.com/ensd/) while *World Trade Magazine* offers a number of white papers on topics ranging from risk mitigation to global sourcing.

■ Banks and accounting firms, among others, publish client newsletters on specific issues such as international trade finance, contracting, bartering, counter-trade, payment flow, and customs news. There are many industry-specific directories, such as the one mentioned from *Appliance Magazine*. These tend to identify companies and contact information and provide general background information about the companies. They are useful for helping to identify sources or partners.

■ *Electronic information services* – entities known as "standards institutes" in most of the G8 nations (Canada, France, Germany, Italy, Japan, Russia, United Kingdom, and the U.S.) provide online access to their databases of technical standards and trade regulations on specific products. In the U.S., the National Center for Standards and Certification Information (http://ts.nist.gov/Standards/Information/index.cfm) provides research services on standards, technical regulations, and conformity assessment procedures for nonagricultural products.

■ The U.S. Department of Commerce offers trade leads and market research through its combined "GLOBUS (Global Business Opportunities) & NTDB (National Trade Data Bank)" resource (www.stat-usa.gov/tradtest.nsf? OpenDatabase). There, users can access the country commercial guides, industry sector analysis reports, and international market insight reports – and that is just a sample.

It is worth noting that data privacy laws might make gathering certain types of information difficult or impossible. In the European Union, it is particularly difficult for direct marketers to get international access to voter rolls, birth records, or mortgage information. In addition, EU law permits companies to gather personal data only if the individuals involved consent to it, know how the data will be used, and have access to the database so they can correct any errors.

Because it is sometimes impossible to get precisely what one needs when working with international secondary data, it is important that they be analyzed in a context going beyond the scope of the data. Analysis requires using creative inferences to reach conclusions that will be useful. Doing so often involves combining and cross-tabulating various sets of data and using proxy information – a comparable stand-in when data on the actual product being studied is not available. For example, a researcher who cannot find information on CD or MP3 players might need to rely on information on television set sales instead. Double-check conclusions by cross-checking the results with other information sources or experts.

GATHERING PRIMARY RESEARCH INFORMATION

Different environments, cultural conditions, attitudes, and market condi-tions can make conducting primary research at the international level challenging. But these differences make the research-gathering process a requirement – how else will a marketer be able to understand and leverage those differences if they are not aware of them?

Many companies are interested in gathering information about market segments, including their size, responsiveness, wealth, and approachability. To obtain such data, companies need to expand their research beyond variables such as income per capita or consumer spending on certain product categories. They have to include lifestyles, attitudes, and personalities. This helps identify similar consumer groups in different countries and aids in marketing that crosses borders.

Executing Primary Research Plans

Once the company has decided what questions the primary research needs to answer, it needs to decide how to manage the process. Most organizations use either a centralized, coordinated, or decentralized approach. The centralized method gives headquarters the greatest amount of control because focus, thrust, and design are directed there and forwarded to the local country operations for execution. This approach helps ensure continuity between regions when the company is conducting research in multiple markets.

Sample Market Research Questions

Marketers give careful thought to the questions they need research to answer. The following are examples of the types of marketing questions that need answers:

- What is the market potential for our furniture in Australia?
- How much does the typical Brazilian consumer spend on soft drinks?
- What will happen to demand in Poland if we raise our product price along monthly inflation levels?
- What effect will a new type of packaging have on our "green" consumers in Germany, Liechtenstein, and England?

A coordinated research approach uses an outside specialist to link the company's headquarters with the country's operations. This offers better support of both strategic and local concerns.

The decentralized method might be guided by the corporate home office, but it puts design and implementation in the hands of the local operation. The downside of this approach is most clear when comparable research is being conducted in multiple markets – local variations might lead to results that are not comparable. In addition, this approach often offers the least amount of knowledge transfer to the home office.

Companies large and small often contract with an outside research firm for international research. Smaller companies usually do not have the talent on staff, and larger companies, even though they might have research departments in-house, appreciate the value that a specialist can bring to the assignment. When hiring a research consultant for international assignments, the most important criterion should be previous research experience in a particular country and industry.

Effective Research Techniques in an International Environment

The culture of the region being researched will have an impact on how marketers conduct the research, what is asked, and the length or form of the information received. The willingness and ability of respondents to spend time on the process and provide a free-form response are influenced by factors that include culture and education, the market conditions, and the segments being studied. Cultural and individual preferences, which vary from country to country, also have an impact on research techniques. While U.S. businesses often like to generate research that gathers numbers they can sort and manipulate, companies in other nations might use other approaches. In Japan, for example, researchers might gather hard data about details such as shipments, inventory levels, and retail sales and combine them with soft data from interviews, conversations, and personal experience that come from site visits.

Traditional qualitative data tools – interviews, focus groups, and observation – are used in international research but researchers might need to use or evaluate the results differently. Interviews work best when the company needs in-depth answers to specific, narrow questions. Focus groups are effective at helping researchers learn more about attitudes, perceptions, and opinions. Technology also makes it possible for focus groups in different regions to interact with each other. When using focus groups internationally, though, it helps to understand that some cultures are uncomfortable with the frank and open discussions that might happen freely elsewhere. In addition, some cultures believe that disagreeing with another – a hallmark of focus group discussions – is rude, while others consider certain topics to be taboo.

Observation is especially useful for those who are completely unfamiliar with a region because this method provides a first-hand opportunity to watch and learn. Trade missions to other nations are excellent opportunities for experiential information through observation in new markets. Observation can also help with the details of product refinements for specific regions. Knowing this, Toyota once dispatched a team of engineers and designers to the U.S., where they discreetly observed as women got into and operated their cars. Key observations – such as how women with long fingernails had trouble opening doors – led to subtle design changes. But, be aware of regional regulations regarding observation. In Europe, for example, researchers and marketers must schedule retail store checks with store managers in advance.

Surveys, which are quantitative tools, are typically conducted with questionnaires that might be administered in person, by mail, or over the telephone. While they can generate useful information, their level of insight depends on a number of factors in a global market – such as availability of telephones or even telephone numbers, cell phones versus landlines, the quality of the postal system, and whether or not the targeted demographic can even be reached (for example, in some regions, women are inaccessible). All of these factors can vary from region to region so understand the options before investing in this method in a given market.

Societal demands and restrictions also influence how or whether people answer questions. In some situations – for example, when asking questions regarding income in countries where taxpayers are not paying what they should – respondents might even willingly provide inaccurate information. In addition, because of government restrictions in Brazil, individuals will rarely admit to owning an imported car – even though they might be everywhere – so there is no point in asking that question in that market.

Cultural Sensitivity in Questions

When generating survey questions, it is important to be sensitive to cultural differences that can have an impact on what is acceptable and what is not. Questions about age or income will be accepted differently in different countries. In regions such as Asia and the Middle East, it is considered bad form to ask questions about employees, performance, standards, and financing. Sometimes, the solution is just to reframe the question in a less sensitive format. Rather than ask, "How old are you?" ask, "In what year were you born?"

Pay careful attention to the translation of questions. One of the authors of this book, for example, once used the phrase "group discussion" in a questionnaire for Russian executives only to learn that it translated to "political indoctrination session." It helps to use a translation-retranslation approach, when the researcher writes the question, has it translated, and then has a second translator return the question to the original language. This technique helps identify potential missteps.

Another recommended safeguard is using alternative wording. This lets the researcher use questions that address the same issue but are worded differently and that resurface at various points in the questionnaire in order to check for consistency in how respondents interpret the question.

It is also important to categorize respondents appropriately in the regions so that there is data equivalence with other regions. For example, a white collar worker in one region might be considered middle class, while in another that person is categorized as upper class. Also, the terminology needs to be evaluated in terms of its connotation. An "engineer" in one nation might indicate someone who uses his hands to fix broken things, while in another region the same term might designate a person with a specific advanced academic degree.

The underlying key is to keep questions clear by using simple rather than complex words, by avoiding ambiguous words and questions, by omitting leading questions, and by asking questions in specific terms. This is good advice in any survey development situation, but is particularly important when formulating questions for international market research.

The sampling plan will also be influenced by factors that might differ from the home country environment. Address directories might not exist. Multiples families might live in one dwelling. Differences in population groups – those in the highlands versus those in the lowlands, for example – might require segment differentiation. The international researcher needs to keep the market complexities in mind when developing the sampling plan. Samples might need to be stratified to reflect different population groups or to use innovative sampling methods to assure representative and relevant responses. It is a complex process, but it is usually doable. Remember, the idea is to improve decision-making. This happens not by getting answers from many (who might not know or not be relevant), but by getting fewer responses from those who know and accurately reflect reality.

Execution can vary from market to market. In some cultures, questionnaires and their administrators are not taken seriously by the population. Therefore, it is important to check the quality of the data. Reality checks that compare the data collected with secondary research or information gathered in analogous markets often helps marketers uncover any issues which need more exploration. For example, research on store-bought spaghetti in Italy indicate low consumption, but the reality check shows everyone eats pasta. The solution is to include home-made pasta in consumption figures to get a more accurate read on the situation.

Internet and e-mail based research methods are increasingly popular in regions where there are many Internet users. E-mail research lends itself to customer research because it allows the marketer to use the customer's e-mail address specifically gathered during the order-taking process to ask questions about the customer's satisfaction with the process or products. As with other research methods, web-based research needs to incorporate an understanding of cultural differences. Those encountering pop-up or other questions on a website, or receiving an e-mailed questionnaire, should encounter a process that represents their cultural icons, values, and rituals if the process is to be relevant and effective.

Safe Maker Secures Markets with Research

Before introducing its residential and light commercial safes in international markets, the Sentry Group, a U.S. small business, conducts primary research to determine consumer usage and attitudes. Working with local researchers who know the region's customs, the company interviews safe owners about why they bought a safe, where they bought it, and how they use it. They also interview people who have expressed interest in purchasing a safe but have not done so yet to learn more about how they protect valuables without a safe. Researchers have learned, for example, that Chinese safe owners are more concerned about security than they are about protection from fire or water damage. Research findings have guided the company's entry into 80 global markets.

How to Observe Global Trends

Any company expanding into global markets needs an international information system. It helps guide ongoing decision-making and becomes a valuable strategic planning tool. Only by observing global trends and changes can a company maintain or improve its international competitive position. Much of the information that a company can acquire is quantitative in nature, but it is possible to gather essential qualitative data as well. Technology makes quantitative data analysis easier, but qualitative analysis needs to contribute to corporate research and strategic planning.

Many companies have information systems already in place that they can mine for data that guide decision-making. When those systems that track the data generated by customer orders or prospect inquiries are mined for patterns and trends, they can help marketers analyze and predict market responses in regions where they already have data. Companies often enhance this information with additional information generated by environmental scanning, Delphi studies, and scenario building.

Environmental scanning helps international companies stay on top of political, social, and economic affairs as well as monitor attitude changes among individuals and institutions. One method involves obtaining factual input on many secondary variables – similar to the research done by the U.S. Census Bureau. The type of information gathered by the Census Bureau is also available on other countries from the World Bank or United Nations. Many companies also use content analysis, too. By evaluating content of, say, annual reports or newspapers, for specific words, themes, symbols, or pictures, businesses can identify trendsetting events. These, in turn, can help marketers prepare for and cash in on new opportunities.

Typically, environmental scanning is done by groups that are both inside and outside the corporation. Subsidiary staffers often provide information and intelligence as well as analysis to a small coordinating group at the headquarters location. Those gathering information about other companies must always be careful, of course, to avoid the risk of being accused of economic or corporate espionage.

Delphi studies (see Chapter 10) gather qualitative information by tapping into the knowledge of a group of experts. They are usually carried out with groups of about 30 well-chosen participants known for their in-depth expertise. Participants receive a written request asking them to identify the major areas in the area being studied. They rank their statements according to importance and explain the rationale behind the ranking. The responses are then shared collectively with all participants, who respond to the rankings of others. After several rounds of such back and forth, the researchers usually can identify a consensus. The advantage of a Delphi study is that it provides very valuable information at a reasonable cost. The disadvantage is that it is a slow process, taking up to six months.

Some companies use scenario-building and analysis to help them plan for potential events or situations. For example, by projecting future variables such as economic growth rates, import penetration, population growth, and political stability, companies can analyze their potential impact on their international marketing strategies. Identifying crucial trend variables and the degree of their variation is essential. For this exercise to have merit, it is important to look at a wide range of potential occurrences – even the most far-fetched scenarios. One extreme response might be too far out for a forecast, but two outliers might become the basis for new directions. Managers must use the information from this process to develop contingency plans, whether the situation relates to technology obsolescence or the threat of terrorism.

BUILDING CULTURAL KNOWLEDGE

Once markets are selected, it is essential that marketers understand the region's culture and its idiosyncrasies. While most agree that nothing beats primary research in the form of personal experience, companies can also become more knowledgeable about other cultures with additional forms of secondary research.

Supplementing first-hand cultural experience

Supplement first-hand cultural experience with information gleaned from secondary resources, including:

- The U.S. Department of Commerce's *Country Commercial Guides* covering 133 regions, which are posted on the department's website at www.ita.doc.gov as they are released.
- The Economist Intelligence Unit's Country Reports covering 195 countries (www.eiu.com).
- Culturegrams detailing the customs in more than 200 countries (www.culturegrams.com/).

Analyzing the Culture

Marketers often examine a market's culture by focusing on:

- Its propensity for change as determined by the strength of cultural beliefs
- The behavior of change agents and opinion leaders
- The nature of communications about change and innovation from government, social, and commercial sources

Remember that culture is learned, not genetic, so someone's environment and experience make all the difference in the world.

One good model available for understanding cultural dimensions comes from Geert Hofstede, an influential Dutch expert on the interactions between national cultures and organizations. Hofstede identified five major dimensions of cultural difference (www.geert-hofstede.com) that help marketers understand their target customers and help multinational corporations understand their employees in other nations:

1. *Individualism* – is the emphasis on the individual ("I") or the collective group ("we")?
2. *Power distance* – the degree of equality in a society.
3. *Uncertainty avoidance* – the need for formal rules and regulations.
4. *Masculinity* – the distribution of roles between the genders.
5. *Long-term orientation* – the need, or not, for quick results.

Understanding how these dimensions apply to a market can guide strategy. (To compare a home culture with a host culture, use Hofstede's tool at www.geert-hofstede.com/hofstede_dimensions.php.) Examining all markets' positions can help produce culture-based segmentation plans that are more reliable guides for addressing cultural similarities and differences than are geographic segmentations. For example, consider risk-reducing marketing programs that offer extended warranties and return privileges in markets such as Eastern Europe and Russia that are high on the uncertainty avoidance continuum.

Cultural analysis can also provide specific guidelines for developing the marketing mix. In cultures where individualism is shunned, marketing communications should emphasize that a product is socially accepted. During difficult economic times, emphasize a message that focuses on society and groups rather than on individuals. Cultural factors also influence channel choices. Marketers in high-individualism markets are more likely to choose channels based on objective criteria while those at the opposite end of the dimension would prefer to deal with friends. This is evident in Japan, where Western companies often encounter barriers in the distribution system because the emphasis is on relationships. It is a system where the familiar is preferred over the unfamiliar.

It is just as important to be clear on the mores and expectations of another culture as it is to understand the nation's natural resources, infrastructure, income, or transportation systems. All of a company's carefully orchestrated market selection and entry planning can fail if the marketing offends or confuses because of cultural misunderstandings.

FOOD FOR THOUGHT

- What questions does the company need answered about its goods and services and the targeted markets?
- What research capability does your firm have already, either in-house or outside the company?
- Will your key decision-makers be able to secure first-hand market research by visiting targeted regions? How can they prepare for this experience?

Further Readings

Doole, Isobel and Robin Lowe. *International Marketing Strategy: Analysis, Development and Implementation*. Mason, OH: South-Western Cengage Learning, 2008.

Mooij, Marieke de. *Global Marketing and Advertising: Understanding Cultural Paradoxes*. Thousand Oaks, CA: Sage Publications Inc., 2010.

Scott, David Meerman. *The New Rules of Marketing and PR: How to Use News Releases, Blogs, Podcasting, Viral Marketing, and Online Media to Reach Buyers Directly*. Hoboken, NJ: John Wiley & Sons Ltd., 2007.

Wankel, Charles. *Encyclopedia of Business in Today's World*. Thousand Oaks, CA: Sage Publications Inc., 2009

Zikmund, William G. and Barry J. Babin. *Essentials of Marketing Research*, 4th edition. Mason, OH: South-Western Cengage Learning, 2010.

Online Resources

International Market Research Information
www.imriresearch.com/

The European Union: A Guide for Americans
www.eurunion.org/eu/index.php?option=com_content&task=view&id=34&Itemid=43

World Development Report (2010: Development and Climate Change)
Published annually, the WDR is the World Bank's major analytical publication.
http://go.worldbank.org/LOTTGBE9I0

Chapter 4

Getting There With Customers and Suppliers

While some firms expanding overseas view their distribution or marketing channels as temporary market entry systems, the veteran global marketer embraces a broader perspective of the network. This marketer sees each organization participating in the distribution system as a partner on a team that is responsible for helping to plan and implement the product's marketing strategy, ranging from its inception to its delivery to the ultimate consumer.

An intermediary – whether an outside sales force, a distributor, or a retailer – is often the de facto marketing arm of the company expanding into international markets. Because they are the ones closest to the customer, they form the distribution network which can provide feedback on everything from marketing messages to product demand changes. Their success, after all, depends on your success – and vice versa. A mutually symbiotic relationship like this works best when the approach is collaborative.

Distribution systems which incorporate partners are flexible and can adapt to market conditions. Often, companies marketing overseas tend to use channel structures that are similar to their domestic efforts. Such systems include selling directly to customers through a field sales force or e-commerce, operating through independent intermediaries at the local level, or using an outside distribution system. The goal is to have a channel that functions as one rather than as a collection of different or independent units. An effective channel will meet the requirements of its customers, accomplish the intended geographic coverage, deliver the desired quality of coverage, and offer long-term continuity.

CHANNEL STRUCTURE AND DESIGN

Distribution channels involve moving the goods, facilitating transactions, and sharing information. Getting a consumer product from the manufacturer to the consumer might involve just a retailer as the intermediary, or include a wholesaler or agent – or both – acting as intermediaries between the manufacturer and the retailer, who sells to the consumer. It might even be expanded to include the supplier of material inputs. Industrial product channels might include an agent or an industrial distributor – or both – to get the product from the manufacturer to the customer. When it comes to marketing services, there is sometimes an agent or two between the provider and the customer, whether the customer is an industrial user or a consumer.

Companies can also use several channel options, some of which may be culturally determined. For example, according to the *Journal of International Marketing*, most Canadian software companies – 40 percent – enter international markets by exporting directly from Canada, but some open their own sales offices, use cooperative arrangements with other exporters, use a local distributor or reseller, or employ a mixture of these options. British companies, on the other hand, exported directly 60 percent of the time, relying much less on the other options than the Canadian firms.

Channel configurations for the same product will vary within industries – even within the same company – because individual markets often have unique features that require adjustments. This sometimes means that companies have to deviate from policies established and accepted in one market when entering another, but global marketing requires new thinking and new options. Channels for some companies vary according to their market experience, too. For example, AMPAK, a packaging machinery manufacturer, uses locally based distributors in markets where its packaging is well-established but enters new markets by working through trading companies or by selling to larger companies that will sell AMPAK's products alongside their own. What matters is using channels flexibly and appropriately in each market.

We often define channels by their length and width. Length refers to how many levels or types of intermediaries are involved; width refers to the number of each type of these intermediaries. For example, consumer product marketing channels might be wide because the manufacturer wants to sell through as many retail intermediaries as possible, while an industrial products channel might be narrow because the manufacturer chooses to sell exclusively through a single distributor.

What will work best for the company's product or service? When designing a distribution channel, it helps to be fluent in the "11 Cs" of distribution channel design. Their individual influences vary from one market to another. They are interrelated, so one factor should not be determined without considering its effect on the others. The 11 Cs are external and internal:

External

■ Customer characteristics
■ Culture
■ Competition

Internal

■ Company objectives
■ Character
■ Capital
■ Cost
■ Coverage
■ Control
■ Continuity
■ Communication

The external characteristics are market-based and nonnegotiable while the internal characteristics are controllable to a certain extent.

External Channel Design Characteristics

Every marketer needs to understand fully its *customer characteristics* – what customers need, what and when they buy, how they buy, and so on. This basic understanding of the target customer helps the firm get its product into the customer's hands through the system that works best for them (rather than for the marketer). For example, when Suntory, a Japanese producer and distributor of alcoholic beverages, began importing Budweiser beer from the U.S., its marketing strategy targeted Japan's hip, urban, and well-heeled youth because they are more easily influenced by American culture and adapt to new situations more easily than older generations. Suntory went after the target customers where they consumed such beverages – in trendy nightspots – developing a loyal following there before expanding distribution to retail stores where it could be found by a broader audience.

Different customer groups might also require different distribution approaches. While certain products are sold to industrial customers through dealers, government purchasers might bypass intermediaries and purchase their products directly from the manufacturer. In addition, primary target audiences might vary from market to market. For example, when McDonald's entered the Japanese market, it did not concentrate its restaurants in the suburbs as it has in the U.S. It placed them in urban areas, instead, focusing on the affluent and youthful pedestrians who flood the cities and set trends.

The distribution *culture* can also vary from region to region, making it essential to study a market's distribution systems in general and the types of linkages between channel members for any product or service type. More often than not one has to adjust an existing approach to the new structures to gain distribution. This might involve changing operating expectations of channel members according to local customs, so the marketer needs to understand the functions of each channel in each market. Japanese retailers, for example, expect more from manufacturers than do other retailers. They expect to be able to return all unsold merchandise to their supplier – a practice that is similar to the way that U.S. booksellers operate, but one that is not typical of other consumer products categories.

Legislation also affects the distribution culture of a market. For example, laws might require a majority percentage of local ownership of an intermediary. This is important considering the trend toward globalization by acquiring businesses in other countries or establishing alliances. Distribution formats, including options such as department stores, mini-marts, and super centers, are also crossing borders, especially to newly emerging markets, presenting new options for marketers.

The *competition* probably uses the same distribution channels the marketer needs to use, so studying how other firms are distributing their wares already should yield some major insights quickly. Of course, it helps to be innovative, as well. A firm might decide to choose a distributor who can develop new contacts rather than working with old established ones. New developments in a region will offer new channels reaching new customers and uncover unexpected sales propositions. For example, banks and do-it-yourself chains might be able to benefit from new linkages, where customers can select new kitchen appliances and finance them at the same store.

It might also be useful to form a jointly owned sales company with a distributor to secure more control. Another option is to find a company with similar goals and objectives to one's own for complementary or co-marketing. When considering such an approach, analyze and test this option to ensure that it works with the market's cultural, political, and legal environment. In some situations, though, there will be no options. For example, in Iceland, Sweden, and Finland, laws require distribution of alcoholic beverages through state monopoly-owned outlets. In other cases, powerful domestic competitors block all feasible channels.

Internal Channel Design Characteristics

Because internal channel characteristics relate to an organization, they are more controllable than those outside the company. *Company objectives* are crucial in making such choices. Distribution channels must meet the requirements established by market share and profitability objectives. Frequently, marketers can reach these objectives only by compromise. For example, while using integrated channels owned by the company can give more control, protect knowledge-based assets, and allow the company to provide better customer service, the cost can be 15 to 35 percent of sales. This compares with using a distributor, which might cost just 10 to 15 percent. The question to analyze then is whether control is worth the cost.

The need to increase sales might require using multiple channels. For example, Starbucks uses a variety of partnership arrangements to extend the brand's reach beyond stores in its U.S. home market to nontraditional coffee venues, new global markets, and retail outlets. Its new channel arrangements brings its coffee shops into banks, bookstores, department stores, and cruise ships; licensing deals have brought the brand to Asian nations; and new products such as ice cream and bottled drinks introduce supermarket shoppers to the brand name. Starbucks has controlled its expansion so that rapid growth and adjustments to local conditions do not cause the brand to lose the economies of scale or its reputation.

The nature of the product – its *character* – has an impact particularly on the length of the channel. Perishable, specialized, expensive, and bulky products will have channels that are relatively short because of the need to get them to market quickly or because size or security issues makes it too expensive for them to pass from intermediary to intermediary. Staples such as soap tend to have longer channels. In addition, the type of channel selected must match the product's positioning or personality. A premium, luxury product, for example, is sold in an upscale environment where it can be priced accordingly and where it is surrounded by other products marketed to similar customers.

Capital refers to a channel's financial requirements. A company's financial strength is one determinant of how much or well it controls the distribution channel. Intermediaries will also have financial requirements such as beginning inventories, selling on consignment basis, preferential loans, and training. For example, an industrial goods manufacturer might learn that distributors in a targeted country cannot service the product. The manufacturer has two options – set up an elaborate training program either in the region or at headquarters, or assist distributors by establishing company-owned service centers in local locations. Both options require capital.

Cost – the expenses incurred in maintaining a channel – are closely related to capital. Costs will vary over the life cycle of the relationship and the products marketed, with greater expense involved upfront when systems are new. They can include cooperative advertising or expenses incurred in the context of shifting exchange rates. Costs often vary according to the manufacturer's power in the distribution system. In Europe, where the number of retailers accounting for 75 percent of consumer sales has decreased dramatically in the past two decades, manufacturers have less influence with retailers than in the past. Specifically, larger retailer groups are forcing manufacturers to make smaller deliveries more frequently, which increases transportation and warehousing costs for manufacturers and their distribution intermediaries.

Channel *coverage* refers to both the breadth and the quality of a product's representation in a market. The number of areas covered – the breadth – depends on demand for the product as well as how long it has been in the marketplace. Companies must decide if they want:

- Intensive coverage where the product is distributed through as many intermediaries as possible
- Selective coverage through fewer intermediaries (which could be appropriate for products positioned with a cache that suggests that they are appropriate only for people at a certain level)
- Exclusive coverage (typically used for luxury goods) with just a single entity in a market

Intensive and selective coverage generally means longer channels using different types of intermediaries, typically wholesalers and agents, because greater coverage requires more assistance. A company may enter a market with one local distributor, but as volume expands, so does the list of distributors involved in meeting that demand. But expanding distribution too quickly has pitfalls. While Italian clothing exporter Benetton originally aimed to found more than 1,000 U.S. stores, the company abandoned the plan because of concerns that included oversaturation. The company focused on fewer stores with quality customer service, resulting in just over 80 stores in U.S. markets in 2010. Similarly, expanding from specialty stores to mass distribution can have an undesirable impact on the product's image or after-sales service. For example, after Sara Lee Corp. purchased authentic athletic-wear manufacturer Champion Products, it substantially adjusted Champion's position as the isolated top quality brand for serious athletes by also opening sales channels through mass retailers.

Exclusive distribution is more conducive to direct sales. Customers for some products are concentrated geographically, which permits more intense distribution through a more direct channel.

Loss of a certain amount of *control* over the marketing of a products is a consequence of using intermediaries. The looser the relationship between a company and the intermediaries, the less control the manufacturer will be able to exert. In addition, longer channels also mean that manufacturers have less final say in pricing, promotion, and the types of sales outlets. Still, intermediaries and their specialized knowledge and working relationships are usually essential when first entering a market. As a company gains market experience and knowledge, other options offering more control often emerge.

Control correlates heavily with the product type. There is usually more manufacturer control with industrial and high technology products because intermediaries depend on the marketer for new products and service. The ability of the marketer to exercise any type of power – reward, coercive, legitimate, or expert – determines the extent of control. This highlights the need for careful communication with intermediaries about intentions as well as the need for control over specific elements. The marketer might want to be responsible for all advertising and promotion materials or in charge of all product modifications. More control typically costs more, or increases risk.

Because channel design decisions are the most long term of those in the marketing mix, *continuity* is crucial. Ensure that continuity by taking utmost care when choosing the type of channel. Consider the types of intermediaries available and review any environmental threats that might have an impact on the channel design. Occasionally, unpredictable events cause problems, but knowing that helps a company react in a way that is more productive than destructive. For example, Cockspur, a rum distiller in Barbados, had high hopes for U.S. market penetration when it negotiated a distribution contract with a U.S. distributor. Yet almost immediately after signing, another company acquired the distributor and eliminated its beverage alcohol business, leaving Cockspur without a U.S. importer.

Marketers often need to assume the responsibility for ensuring long-term continuity because international distributors sometimes have a more short-term view until they see that the exporter is in the market for the long run. Demonstrate commitment by sending in technical or sales personnel, offering training, or setting up wholly owned sales subsidiaries staffed by locals from the start. These actions help communicate that the company wants to stay in the market.

Communication is perhaps more important in international channel design than it is in domestic channels because of the potential for problems caused by distance and language differences. Distance can be social, cultural, technological, time, and geographic, but effective communication can help overcome any issues or confusion caused by the different types of distance. Good communication will help communicate goals to distributors, solve conflicts, and market products. Remember, though, that this two-way process does not involve dictating to intermediaries. It helps to be clear on channel members' needs and goals too. Design a channel and choose intermediaries that guarantee good information flow. Facilitate this with personal visits, personnel exchanges, or distributor advisory councils with members from all channel participants. Also consider offering rewards for good communications, so that intermediaries do not have to fear that the messenger will be shot.

SELECTING INTERMEDIARIES

With channel design complete, it is time to select intermediaries that will help achieve the company's global marketing goals. Start with two basic decisions.

The first involves deciding whether to work with a distributor or an agent. A distributor will purchase the product, which makes it more independent than an agent. Distributors usually organize along product lines and provide companies with complete marketing services. Agents are paid, on the other hand, on a commission basis and they do not usually physically handle the goods. This arrangement gives the manufacturer the control to make sure that the customer gets the most recent or appropriate version of the product. Doing so, in turn, helps build a quality reputation. The type of relationship selected has business implications that include how easy or hard it is to terminate the agreement.

The second decision is whether to use direct exporting, indirect exporting, or integrated distribution. With *direct exporting*, companies sell products abroad either directly to the global customer or by finding a local representative who will carry the product. *Indirect exporting* involves dealing with another domestic company that serves as a sales intermediary, often acting as the company's international arm (which you sometimes might not even know). The benefits of this option include access to established international channels – and not having to worry about the complexities of international sales. However, the downside of this approach is that it makes it harder for a firm to be active and aggressive in the global market.

Integrated distribution involves making an investment in the non-domestic market by, for example, opening a sales office, distribution hub, or manufacturing or assembly operation. Although integrated distribution indicates the longer-term commitment to the market that some intermediaries like to see, it is the riskiest option because of the financial investment required and the major cost incurred if one wishes to reverse the approach.

Global, or direct, agents are known as brokers, manufacturer's representatives, factors, managing agents, and purchasing agents. Domestic – indirect – agents include brokers, export agents, EMCs (export management companies), Webb-Pomerene associations, and commission agents. International direct distributors are generally known as distributors/dealers, import jobbers, and wholesalers/retailers. Domestic indirect distributors can also be classified as domestic wholesalers, EMCs, ETCs (export trading companies), and complementary marketers (where an exporter seeking a larger product line takes on additional products of other companies).

Where to Find Intermediaries

Treat this process as seriously as you would when filling a key management position. A bad distributor can set the company back years, so it is almost better to have no distributor than to have one that is ineffective. Marketers can be passive or aggressive, and while passive might be easier, it is in the company's best interest to be aggressive. Do not wait to be contacted – go looking for appropriate representation. Then, rather than contract with the first intermediary to show interest, research the marketplace to understand roles, expectations, and reputations. Search for the best fit for the firm's goals and needs.

Government and Private Agencies Can Help

Governmental and private agencies help marketers find intermediaries in their country or in other regions. The Japan External Trade Organization helps promote foreign direct investment in its home country by offering the Japan Trade Directory online. In the United States, the U.S. Department of Commerce offers a range of services that can help companies find representatives abroad, including some designed specifically for that purpose. Its U.S. Commercial Service offers a searchable online database of trade leads at www.export.gov/eac/trade_leads.asp. Other resources include:

- *The Trade Opportunities Program*, which provides daily trade leads from U.S. embassies. These leads are printed in the *Journal of Commerce* and other private sector newspapers. TOP leads are also available through the STAT-USA Internet site at www.stat-usa.gov/tradtest.nsf. For subscription information, call 1-800-STAT-USA.
- *Country Directories of International Contacts* provides lists by country, directories of importers in other countries, government agencies, trade associations and other organizations in countries where the U.S. Commercial Service maintains a presence. Find it at www.stat-usa. gov/tradtest.nsf.
- *International Partner Search* is a customized search for U.S. companies seeking global representation. U.S. commercial officers abroad conduct the agent or distributor search based on a firm's specific requirements. The process takes about 30 days and there is a fee. Access the service through one's regional Export Assistance Center.
- *Commercial News USA* is an online magazine produced by the Commerce Department to help American companies find buyers and distributors for their products and services. Ads from U.S. companies help them find export partners and locate export companies and related services. Available both online and in print format, the print version reaches about 400,000 readers in more than 175 countries. Get access online at www.thinkglobal.us/.

> ■   *Trade Mission Online* from the Small Business Administration allows U.S. and companies from other countries to search a database for partners matching specific criteria.
>
> Country and regional trade business directories offered by private entities are useful resources They include the worldwide *Kompass* business-to-business directory, *Nordisk Handels Kalendar* with information for firms in five Nordic countries, and *eBizFinder Japan*. The International Company Profile service helps exporters screen partners by providing a trade profile of specific international firms. Dun & Bradstreet, R.H. Donnelly, and Kellysearch provide company lists by country and business line. Yellow Page sections of telephone directories can provide distributor lists.

Many global banks, advertising agencies, shipping lines and services, airlines, and other companies have substantial international information networks that can also be helpful. Trade associations and chambers of commerce often have information about potential intermediaries. Some companies also find distributors or agents by placing ads for intermediaries in relevant industry trade publications while others meet them at trade fairs or industry conferences.

Working with Intermediaries

Once there is a list of potential intermediaries, the marketer needs a way to compare and evaluate them – just as the company would with job candidates. Criteria might vary from industry to industry and individual companies will put different amounts of weight on different characteristics, but most exporters first decide what is most important to them, then evaluate candidates using a list of qualities and functions similar to this one:

■   Goals and strategies
■   Size of the firm
■   Financial strength

- Reputation
- Trading areas covered
- Compatibility
- Product experience
- Product quality match
- Experience with competitors
- Sales organization
- Physical facilities
- Willingness to carry inventories
- After-sales service capability
- Use of promotion
- Sales performance
- Relations with local government
- Communications
- Overall attitude and commitment

The candidate's financial standing is certainly one of the most important characteristics. Is the distributor or agent making money and able to perform the necessary marketing functions? Can they extend credit to customers, especially in economically difficult times when bank lending diminishes? Because financial reports are not always complete or reliable, consider getting a third-party opinion.

Sales are another excellent indicator of stability and success. Analyze management's ability along with the adequacy and quality of the sales team and its ability to provide service when appropriate to the situation. Review existing product lines according to four dimensions: competitiveness, compatibility, complementary nature, and quality. Learning that a distributor is already handling a top competitive product will make it easy to cross that company off the list quickly. While such a firm may be willing to take on the company's products, the main purpose might be to exclude the firm from further market penetration. It might generate one or perhaps even two orders, but just when the business relationship seems well established, it turns out that the faucet has been turned off.

Complementary products can be key, especially in industrial markets where customers are looking for complete systems or one-stop shopping. The quality match for products is important for product positioning reasons, particularly when marketing a high-end product. The number of product lines handled might also offer insights when considered with the size of the organization – can they adequately represent every client well and efficiently? The intermediary's physical facilities can be particularly important, too, for products such as certain foods that need a specific type of storage environment. Study not only the organization's market coverage but also how well the markets are served. The characteristics of the sales force and the number of sales offices are often good indicators of market coverage.

Check the distributor's reputation, too. Marketing is a social science, which means that marketers must be in touch with the people who are essential to marketing success. There is no substitute for talking to customers, suppliers, vendors, and other stakeholders, and to observe the intermediary's actions when it comes to performance, reliability, and ethical behavior. Learn more about values that are important to a relationship with the company, whether it is marketing savvy or political clout. Talk to the intermediary's management about its goals to make sure that they are a good fit. Learn more about its business strategy and how the firm's product line will fit into it. Discuss the company's expectations for the product line as well as the details of the relationship – pricing, credit, delivery, sales training, communication, personal visits, any necessary product modifications, warranties, advertising, warehousing, technical support, and after-sales service. Uncovering weaknesses now will prevent problems later.

Finally, assess the intermediary's overall attitude and commitment to the relationship. One effective way to do this while weeding out the less interested candidates is by asking the firm to assist in developing a local marketing plan. In addition to helping identify which organizations are most interested in working with the firm, this exercise will help identify potential problems. After the initial screening and once the list is narrowed down, visit the top candidates. Inspect their facilities and interview their constituents. Use the local bank and credit reports to verify financial stability before making a decision.

When there is a decision, sign a sales agreement (see Figure 4.1 for a checklist of elements to include). Such agreements tend to be very detailed. Be careful to take local laws and stipulations into account. Contract duration and termination processes are key elements; there

A. Basic Components

    1. Parties to the agreement
    2. Statement that the contract supersedes all previous agreements
    3. Duration of the agreement (perhaps a three- or six-month trial period)
    4. Territory:

        a. Exclusive, nonexclusive, sole
        b. Manufacturer's right to sell direct at reduced or no commission to local government and old customers

    5. Products covered
    6. Expression of intent to comply with government regulations
    7. Clauses limiting sales forbidden by U.S. Export Controls or practices forbidden by the Foreign Corrupt Practices Act

B. Manufacturer's Rights

    1. Arbitration:

        a. If possible, in the manufacturer's country
        b. If not, before international Chamber of Commerce or American Arbitration Association, or using the London Court of Arbitration rules
        c. Definition of rules to be applied (e.g., in selecting the arbitration panel)
        d. Assurance that award will be binding in the distributor's country

    2. Jurisdiction that of the manufacturer's country (the signing completed at home); if not possible, a neutral site such as Sweden or Switzerland
    3. Termination conditions (e.g., no indemnification if due notice given)
    4. Clarification of tax liabilities
    5. Payment and discount terms
    6. Conditions for delivery of goods
    7. Nonliability for late delivery beyond manufacturer's reasonable control
    8. Limitation on manufacturer's responsibility to provide information
    9. Waiver of manufacturer's responsibility to keep lines manufactured outside the United States (e.g., licensees) outside of covered territory
   10. Right to change prices, terms, and conditions at any time
   11. Right of manufacturer or agent to visit territory and inspect books
   12. Right to repurchase stock
   13. Option to refuse or alter distributor's orders
   14. Training of distributor personnel in the United States subject to:

        a. Practicality
        b. Costs to be paid by the distributor
        c. Waiver of manufacturer's responsibility for U.S. immigration approval

C. Distributor's Limitations and Duties

    1. No disclosure of confidential information
    2. Limitation of distributor's right to assign contract
    3. Limitation of distributor's position as legal agent of manufacturer
    4. Penalty clause for late payment
    5. Limitation of right to handle competing lines

FIGURE 4.1 continued

6. Placement of responsibility for obtaining customs clearance
7. Distributor to publicize designation as authorized representative in defined area
8. Requirement to move all signs or evidence identifying distributor with manufacturer if relationship ends
9. Acknowledgment by distributor of manufacturer's ownership of trademark, trade names, patents
10. Information to be supplied by the distributor:

    a. Sales reports
    b. Names of active prospects
    c. Government regulations dealing with imports
    d. Competitive products and competitors' activities
    e. Price at which goods are sold
    f. Complete data on other lines carried (on request)

11. Information to be supplied by distributor on purchasers
12. Accounting methods to be used by distributor
13. Requirement to display products appropriately
14. Duties concerning promotional efforts
15. Limitation of distributor's right to grant unapproved warranties, make excessive claims
16. Clarification of responsibility arising from claims and warranties
17. Responsibility of distributor to provide repair and other services
18. Responsibility to maintain suitable place of business
19. Responsibility to supply all prospective customers
20. Understanding that certain sales approaches and sales literature must be approved by manufacturer
21. Prohibition of manufacture or alteration of products
22. Requirement to maintain adequate stock, spare parts
23. Requirement that inventory be surrendered in event of a dispute that is pending in court
24. Prohibition of transshipments

Source: Adapted from "Elements of a Distributor Agreement," *Business International*, March 29, 1963, 23–24. Some of the sections have been changed to refflect the present situation.

FIGURE 4.1 Elements of a Distributor Agreement

need to be protection provisions such as starting with a trial period of three to six months. Many new distributors would like to see exclusive contracts and territories. While such a desire is understandable, there needs to be agreement on minimum purchase requirements, and specific growth expectations, customer coverage, and customer satisfaction. To get more insights into such issue, initial contracts are generally for a short duration, usually for one or two years.

Pay close attention to geographic boundaries to eliminate conflicts when expanding – one distributor might claim rights to a region that will be served by a different company. Retain rights to distribute products independently, too, and to certain customers. Many companies maintain a dual distribution system, dealing directly with specified large accounts, and this needs to be detailed in the contract so there are no misunderstandings. Prevent parallel importation by prohibiting transshipments and sales to customers outside the agreed-upon territory or customer type. Of course, one also needs to consider legislative restraints on such rules. For example, for the sake of market unity, the European Union is likely to restrict limitations on transshipments within the EU.

Stipulate the currency to be used for payment, the payment methods, and how the distributor or agent will be compensated (discount or commission), making certain that payments do not violate the Foreign Corrupt Practices Act or OECD guidelines. Stipulate in clear terms the products or product lines covered as well as how the intermediary will inventory, promote, and service them. Conditions of sale – including credit and shipment terms – will determine which party is responsible for some of the expenses involved, which will in turn have an impact on the price to the distributor.

The contract should ensure that the marketer has access to all information related to the product's marketing, including past records, present situation assessments, and marketing research information. Provide for formal communication channels that allow the distributor to voice concerns or problems, and outline requirements for confidentiality procedures to protect intellectual property rights along with other confidential information.

MANAGING DISTRIBUTION CHANNELS AND RELATIONSHIPS

A channel relationship is similar to a marriage in that it brings together two independent entities with shared goals. And, as in a marriage, the keys to success include reasonable and clear expectations combined with good and open communication. Because any marketer wants the relationship to last, address both small grievances and larger issues quickly and effectively so they do not have a negative impact on the relationship. Harmonious relationships tend to have trust, good communication, and cooperation – all of which means there is less conflict and perceived uncertainty. As operations expand to multiple markets with many intermediaries, consider establishing a distributor advisory council to share best practices or respond to issues such as parallel importation. In addition to helping with channel management, a council will also contribute to stronger relationships between the company and its intermediaries.

Potential Problems and Solutions

The factors that complicate channel relationships fall into three categories:

1. Ownership
2. Geographic, cultural, and economic distance or separation
3. Different laws

Help ensure that they do not impede progress by acknowledging that divergent perspectives exist and taking steps to address them in a way that builds mutual trust.

Ownership problems stem from the reality that manufacturers and distributors or agents are separate, independent entities with different personalities. Because a distributor judges products by their ability to generate revenue without adding expense, offer financial incentives or psychological rewards to get more than your fair share of attention.

Bridge *geographic and cultural distances* by being excellent communicators. Some companies assign distributor-related communications to a single individual to ensure consistency and to help build a long-term relationship and trust. Others exchange personnel so both organizations better understand the other company's systems, processes, and personalities. In all cases it is important to dedicate one's best people to the task, rather than using the joint activities as a dumping ground for unwanted personnel. In all situations, it is important to understand, acknowledge, and respect the other country's belief systems and behavior patterns and to adjust behavior accordingly.

There will be *economic distance* in exchange rates. Their instability can create serious difficulties for distributors in their trading activities, not only with suppliers, but also with domestic customers. Develop with distributors mutually acceptable mechanisms that allow for some flexibility in interactions when unforeseen rate fluctuations occur. Harley-Davidson handles this by sharing the risk. The company maintains a single international currency price as long as the spot exchange rate does not move beyond an agreed-upon rate. If that happens, Harley-Davidson and its distributors share the costs or benefits of the change. It is important to anticipate these kinds of economic issues and have agreed-upon contingency plans in place.

Laws and regulations in other countries might restrict control. In the European Union, for example, a firm cannot prevent a distributor from re-exporting products to customers in another member country, even though there might be another distributor there. EU law insists on a single market where goods and services can be sold throughout the area without restriction. Even tracking such parallel imports might be considered a trade restriction. The solution is to always comply with the law while working to build strong intermediary relationships.

Evaluating Channel Relationships

We have mentioned before that selecting a channel partner is much like recruiting a key employee, and the evaluation process is not much different. A company's performance reviews probably involve communicating employee expectations upfront, then reviewing performance according to those defined and communicated expectations. Employees, in turn, usually have an opportunity to participate in the review process, evaluating their own performance and expressing their workplace or job description needs. This applies to intermediary evaluations, too. As with employees, an evaluation that is not conducted in a fair and transparent way will generate conflict. Distributors and others have a right to know from the beginning how they will be evaluated and to participate in the assessment process.

Focus the approach on mutual benefits. For example, it is important that a company receive detailed market and financial performance data from a distributor. But because distributors realize that knowledge is power, they might be reluctant to part with it. Both rewards and punishments for performance need to reflect and encourage the ability and willingness of information exchange. The exchange of this level of data is often a good indicator of a successful relationship.

Sometimes channel evaluations will lead to adjustments. These might involve channel shifts that force a marketer to eliminate a particular type of channel, channel modifications, or changes in roles or relationships. Because of the impact these steps have on the marketing and distribution process, it helps to approach potential changes cautiously, without haste.

There will be situations when a company has to end a relationship with an intermediary, usually because the distribution approach has changed (perhaps by opening a local sales office), product growth requires support at a level the distributor cannot provide, the intermediary fails to perform, or because there has been a breach of contract. Open and honest communication will help smooth the process. The marketer might need to compensate the intermediary for investments made on the company's behalf or make joint sales calls to major customers to assure them that service will not be interrupted.

Grounds for termination are a key consideration in a contract with the intermediary and must be detailed and agreed upon. Just cause includes fraud or deceit, damage to the other party's interests, or failure to comply with contract obligations. In some countries, though, termination just is not possible and in others, it is a challenge. In the European Union and Latin America, terminating an ineffective intermediary is time-consuming and costly. In Austria, termination without just cause and/or failure to give proper notice of termination can result in damages amounting to average commissions for between one and fifteen years. As a minimum, plan on giving the intermediary three to six months notice when terminating the agreement.

Dealing with Gray Market Imports

Distribution channels can be disrupted when products are imported or diverted to a market by bypassing the assigned distribution channel. In the high technology industry alone, manufacturers are losing up to $10 billion in profits annually to this "gray" market, with as much as $58 billion of technology products passing through it each year, according to the Alliance for Gray Market and Counterfeit Abatement. Gray market products vary from inexpensive consumer products to expensive industrial equipment.

A range of conditions allow unauthorized resellers to exist, with the most important being price segmentation and exchange rate fluctuations. Competitive conditions might require a marketer to sell the same product at different prices in different markets or to different customers. For example, because many products are priced higher in the U.S., due to income differences, a gray marketer can buy them in Europe or the Far East and offer substantial price discounts when selling them in the U.S. on the gray market.

Exchange rate fluctuations can cause price differentials that present opportunities for gray marketers. During one Asian financial crisis, gray marketers imported Caterpillar, John Deere, and Komatsu construction equipment that was no longer needed for halted projects in Asian countries, paying as little as 60 percent of what U.S. dealers paid wholesale. Product shortages also present opportunities. At one time, many U.S. computer manufacturers had to turn to gray market sources for key supplies to keep their production lines from stopping. Apart from uncertainty and lack of manufacturer tie in, these firms had to pay a premium price as well.

Gray market goods can severely undercut local marketing plans, erode long-term brand images, eat up costly promotion funds, and sour manufacturer–intermediary relationships. Proponents argue for their right to free trade by pointing to manufacturers that are both overproducing and overpricing in some markets. They say that consumers benefit from lower prices and discount distributors. Consumers, on the other hand, have begun to have concerns about obtaining a counterfeit version, a deficient warrantee, or no product service.

For the most part, the solution lies with the contractual relationships that link businesses together. In almost all gray marketing cases, someone in the authorized channel violates the agreement by diverting the product. The standard response to this action is disenfranchising the violator. In addition, some of the gray marketers can be added to the authorized dealer network if all parties can agree on the terms. Still, a one-price policy can eliminate one of the main reasons for gray markets. This might mean choosing the most efficient distribution channel options and selling at the lowest price to all customers regardless of location and size.

Other strategies have included producing different versions of products for different markets. Some Hewlett-Packard printers, for example, will not print if ink cartridges purchased outside the original region are used. The power adapters for Nintendo's hand-held games do not work in Europe. Some companies have promoted the benefits of dealing only with authorized dealers while others have conducted educational and promotional campaigns to educate consumers about the pitfalls of gray market goods.

Channels Online

E-commerce is growing worldwide and presenting many companies with growth opportunities abroad. Some companies sell through their own sites, but many are taking advantage of e-commerce portals created by others. These hub sites – sometimes known as virtual malls, e-marketplaces, or digital intermediaries – bring together buyers, sellers, distributors, and transaction payment processors in a single marketplace created around a product or category type. Examples include Quadrem (www.quadrem.com/) for supply chain solutions and Eat-Japan Trade Directory (http://trade.eat-japan.com/) for Japanese food ingredients or equipment. Companies such as bearings manufacturer Ducasse Comercial use the electronic marketplaces of these services as well as their ancillary support to streamline operations.

E-commerce requires 24-hour order-taking and customer service, customs-handling expertise, appropriate shipping options, and an in-depth understanding of global marketing environments. Many of these challenges can be handled with outsourcing to a company such as Quadrem, which has expertise in remote and developing markets. Air express carriers such as DHL, Federal Express, and UPS have complete structures to support this type of business, handling fulfillment, customer support, warehousing, and inventory management. Some U.S. companies, including television retailer QVC and Amazon.com, have overseas distribution centers so they can serve international customers effectively, affordably, and efficiently.

LOGISTICS AND SUPPLY CHAIN MANAGEMENT

In an era of new trade opportunities in regions that might have logistical infrastructure shortcomings, competent logistics management is more important than ever before. The basic goal of international logistics management is effectively coordinating the materials management and the physical distribution of the product to customers. Companies want maximum cost effectiveness while maintaining service goals and requirements.

Supply chain management encompasses planning and managing activities linked to sourcing and procurement, conversion, and logistics. It includes coordinating and collaborating with channel partners, including customers. It essentially integrates supply and demand management within and across companies. Globalization has opened up supplier relationships for companies outside the buyer's domestic market, but the supplier's ability to provide satisfactory goods and services plays the most critical role in securing long-term contracts. Close collaboration with suppliers is required for a just-in-time inventory system, which could be crucial to maintaining manufacturing costs at a globally competitive level.

This level of collaboration requires technology, which is typically available in advanced economies, but issues related to the business infrastructure – accounting and inventory tracking or partners' willingness to share information – often get in the way. This is a particular issue in China, which is struggling to get demand and supply in line.

The long-term survival of international activities depends on a solid understanding of the differences inherent in the international logistics field. One of the most basic is distance – global marketing frequently requires goods to be shipped farther to reach final customers. This, in turn, leads to longer lead times, more opportunities for things to go wrong, larger inventories, and greater complexity. Currency variation is another significant difference, requiring the manufacturer to adjust planning according to currencies and changes in the exchange rate.

Border crossings bring their own issues, with the need to conform to national regulations, participate in customs inspections, and provide proper documentation. These processes bring new intermediaries to the process – freight forwarders, customs agents, customs brokers, and so on.

Transportation modes might differ, too. While the company might be accustomed to shipping domestically by truck or rail, when going international, air or sea freight are required.

Transportation Varies by Region

It is not unusual for global marketers to encounter major transportation infrastructure variations. Some countries might have excellent inbound and outbound systems but weak links within the country. It is important, then, to learn about existing and planned infrastructures abroad. In some regions, for example, railroads surpass trucking options while in others, using railroads for freight is risky. Investigate methods used to carry cargo to seaports or airports, too. Mistakes made when evaluating transportation options can be costly, as many companies have learned.

There are three types of vessels available for ocean transportation:

- *Liner* service offers regularly scheduled passage on established routes
- *Bulk* service provides contracted services
- *Tramp* service is available for irregular routes and is scheduled only on demand

In addition, different types of vessels carry different types of cargo. Conventional cargo vessels are useful for oversized and unusual cargoes but might be less efficient in their port operations. Because of this, there has been a sharp increase in the use of container ships, which carry standardized containers that can be loaded and unloaded easily. Roll-on-roll-off (RORO) vessels reduce the time a ship spends in port because they are essentially ocean-going ferries – trucks can drive on and off. Lighter aboard ships (LASH) hold barges that are lowered at the destination and used on inland waterways.

The greatest constraint in ocean shipping remains the lack of ports and port services, though. Modern container ships cannot use some ports because the local equipment cannot handle the traffic. This is more of a problem in developing economies, where there are not funds to develop the necessary facilities. Good research will uncover these issues and details.

Airfreight is available to and from most regions, including developing economies. High value items and those with a high density tend to be shipped by air. Airfreight might be the best choice, too, for a product that is perishable or requires a short transit time. International shipments include multiple transportation modes, of course. The cargo arriving in a market by ocean or air still needs to hop on a truck or train to get to its ultimate destination.

When selecting transportation mode, take into account transit time, predictability, cost, and noneconomic factors. The transit time difference between ocean shipment and airfreight is 45 days versus something more like 12 hours. With products such as fresh flowers or produce, airfreight is the only option. Airfreight is more predictable than ocean delivery, and offers advantages that include an ability to maintain lower inventories and more reliable delivery dates to customers. Cost is a key factor, too, with faster airfreight costing more. Bulky products might be too expensive to ship by air while high-priced items are a good fit for air travel because they can absorb the extra cost of shipping. When comparing costs, take into account overall logistical considerations, the competition, and the environment, as well. Noneconomic factors include government involvement in shipping, when carriers are owned or heavily subsidized by governments. In these situations, the government puts pressure on organizations to use "national" carriers, regardless of the economics.

Daunting Documentation

Documentation for international shipments is so universally conceived as complicated that it can actually be a trade barrier, especially for smaller companies. But as countless companies show, it is not necessarily as challenging as anticipated. In the most simple form of exporting, the only documents needed are a bill of lading and an export declaration. In most countries, these documents are available from either the government or the transportation company. (U.S. documents and procedures are explained at www.census.gov/foreign-trade/aes/index.html.)

Most exports fit under a general license, a generalized authorization consisting simply of a number to be shown on the documents. Certain goods and data require a special validated license for export. Imported products require a bill of lading and an invoice. The following box lists the main documents used in international shipping.

Documentation for an International Shipment

Documents required by the U.S. government

- Shipper's export declaration
- Export license

Commercial documents

- Commercial invoice
- Packing list
- Inland bill of lading
- Dock receipt
- Bill of lading or airway bill
- Insurance policies of certificates
- Shipper's declaration for dangerous goods
- Vessel loading observation inspection

Import documents

- Import license
- Foreign exchange license
- Certificate of origin
- Consular invoice
- Customs invoice
- Customs notification

Of these, the bill of lading is the most important document to the shipper, carrier, and the buyer. It acknowledges receipt of the goods, represents the basic contract between the shipper and the carrier, and serves as evidence of title to the goods for collection by the purchaser. The inland bill of lading is a contract between the inland carrier and the shipper. The shipper's export declaration states proper authorization for export and helps the government collect data. The packing list includes the contents, gross and net weights, and the package dimensions. Corrosives, flammables, and poisons require a shipper's declaration for dangerous goods. When moving the goods to a port of export, the marketer is issued a dock receipt or a warehouse receipt (when goods are stored). Collection documents include the commercial invoice, often a consular invoice or pro-forma invoice, and a certificate of origin. Insurance policies or certificates are included when required by the transaction.

In certain countries, particularly those in Latin America, shippers also need an import license for certain types or amounts of specific goods or a foreign exchange license that allows the importer to secure the hard currency needed to pay for the shipment. The exporter has to provide the importer with the data needed for these licenses and should make sure they are obtained before products are shipped.

Help is available for a fee through international freight forwarders and customs brokers. Freight forwarders will act as an agent and advise on shipping documentation and packaging costs, even preparing or reviewing the paperwork to make sure it is in order. Forwarders will also book the space on a carrier, arrange for customs clearance, and forward the documents to the customer or the paying bank. A customs broker will serve as the agent with authority to clear inbound goods through customs and ship them on to their destination.

Managing Inventory Overseas

While just-in-time inventory is often the goal, the ability to achieve that goal often depends on the order cycle time, desired customer service levels, and how inventory is used as a strategic tool. In international marketing, the order cycle is frequently longer than it is in domestic marketing. Packing and shipping require more detailed attention, a lack of familiarity with the marketplace might make it harder to anticipate and prepare for orders, and transportation time increases with the distance involved. Consistency is often hard to maintain, as well. To decrease the order time and increase consistency, change transportation methods, change inventory locations, or improve any of the other components, such as how orders are transmitted.

Consider adjusting customer service levels for international market conditions. While a marketer might fill 95 percent of the domestic orders within a designated timeframe, that level of service is probably unrealistic in global markets. In addition, it might not be necessary. Different regions or industries have different needs and expectations, making domestic benchmarks inappropriate. Set new standards for global markets by learning more about customer needs, then establish inventory levels and fill orders accordingly.

International inventory can also be used as a strategic tool when dealing with currency valuation changes or hedging against inflation. Increasing inventories before an imminent devaluation of a currency, instead of holding cash, reduces exposure to devaluation losses. Similarly, in the case of high inflation, large inventories can provide an inflation hedge. Balance the cost of maintaining high levels of inventory with the benefits accruing to the company from hedging against inflation or devaluation. When doing this, though, keep in mind that many countries will charge a tax on stored goods. If the tax increase outweighs the hedging benefits, it would not make sense to increase inventories before a devaluation.

One of the biggest issues related to inventory management is deciding how many distribution centers to have and where to locate them. Because the availability of facilities and their quality might differ from those in the home market, the storage decision might require a large-scale, long-term investment. Carefully analyze storage options because they can vary from market to market. In some countries, warehouses have low ceilings which have an impact on how products should – or should not – be packed for stacking. Automated warehousing is often available, making proper bar coding and acceptable packaging dimensions for that system essential.

To optimize the logistics system, analyze international product sales and then rank products according to warehousing needs. Classify those that are most sensitive to delivery times as "A" products and stock them in all distribution centers. Products for which immediate delivery is not urgent are classifed as "B" products and stored only at selective distribution centers. "C" products are those that do not need a short delivery time and are not in great demand. Stock them only at headquarters. This "ABC" approach will let the firm substantially reduce total international warehousing costs while still maintaining acceptable service levels.

Consider whether it is possible to take advantage of foreign-trade zones, too. These are considered to be outside the customs territory of the country within which they are located. They are special areas that can be used for warehousing, packaging, inspection, labeling, exhibition, assembly, fabrication, or transshipments of imports without the burden of duties. Trade zones can be found at major ports of entry and at inland locations near major manufacturing facilities. They are designed to help a company exclude the impact of duties from the location decision by exempting merchandise in the foreign-trade zone from duty payments. Get a list of U.S. trade zones at www.trade.gov/ia.

With transportation determined and storage facilities selected, make sure certain products are packaged appropriately for the shipping mode and warehousing situation. Take into account differences in environmental conditions either during shipping or at the destination. While the packaging must be strong enough to protect the product, a heavy packaging material can add to the total cost since duties might be assessed on total weight of shipments, including packaging. Some products packaged for display need to be packaged in a second box for protection during shipping. Some shippers benefit from lower transportation rates by using intermodal containers – those large metal boxes that fit on trucks, ships, railroad cars, and airplanes. They also provide greater ease of transfer and help prevent pilferage. Regardless of the package or method used, the goal is to get the product to the customer on time and in good condition. Failure to do that will lead to dissatisfied customers and lost sales.

Managing and Securing Logistics

The best way to generate system synergy is by managing logistics at headquarters with a centralized approach. In this situation, avoid problems by requiring headquarters staff and local logistics managers to report to the same person, who is the final arbiter on the company's priorities. On the other hand, if the company serves many diverse markets with little in common, decentralization will make it more responsive to local needs. The down side of this is that decentralization deprives the local logistics function of the benefits of economies of scale.

Some companies prefer to outsource logistics to a third-party source. The services offered by logistics providers vary. Some might use their own assets for physical transportation, while others might subcontract that part of the job. Others develop the systems and databases required or consult on administrative management services. One of the greatest benefits of contracting with an outside provider is the ability to take advantage of an existing network, complete with resources and experience. This local expertise with business formats, languages, and customs can be crucial when entering a new market.

Today's global realities also mean companies might have to protect the logistics network from terrorist attacks, in spite of government efforts to improve security. Logistics systems are often the targets of attacks because they are vulnerability points for countries and companies. Because there is almost always potential for high-profile disruptions in a transportation network or for attacks on supply sources, all companies moving materials overseas must have a contingency or "what if?" plan in place so that there other options.

In addition, when shipping cargo, security will need to ensure that nothing goes missing and that nothing is added to the shipment. Increased inspections of containers used in international shipping, new security programs to protect ports, and other new protective policies are decreasing the efficiency and effectiveness of international shipping and logistics. This means that supply chain costs have increased, and there is more uncertainty and less control over the timing of arrivals and departures. Security measures have an impact on distribution systems and timing, but they are necessary. Some companies are hedging their bets by increasing their inventory holdings in the hope of protecting against delays.

Surprisingly, pirates are still roaming the open seas. The twenty-first century bandits we read about constantly in the news are highly organized and heavily armed. Their shenanigans account for annual international cargo losses of $30 to $50 billion. The International Chamber of Commerce Commercial Crime Services (www.icc-ccs.org/) unit warns that the highest risk areas include Southeast Asia and the Indian subcontinent and Africa and the Gulf of Aden (location of the headline-grabbing Somali pirates). Companies doing business in these and surrounding areas face higher costs because of increased security measures that include installing electric fences on cargo ships.

Creating Green Logistics

In addition to all of these issues, pressure to function in an environmentally responsible way extends to global logistics. Environmental laws, expectations, and the company's goals for functioning in a "green" manner are difficult to meet without a logistics orientation that systematically takes these concerns into account. One approach involves a reverse distribution system that lets companies retrieve products from the market for subsequent use, recycling, or disposal. The ability to implement a system like this is increasingly important in market acceptability and profitability.

The boom in consumer Internet sales has generated a staggering volume of returns that need to be processed, with most coming back to publishing, catalog retailing, and greeting card companies. Customers do not want to wait weeks to have charges removed from their credit cards, and returned goods lying idle in warehouses cause higher carrying costs and the risk of obsolescence. Idle electronic and computer parts in inventory lose 12 percent of their value every month. Conversely, efficient management of returns can reduce annual logistics costs by as much as 10 percent.

As with forward logistics, reverse logistics require quality information and processes, and the ability to track both at all times. Reverse logistics, however, is also a complex customer service, inventory control, information management, cost accounting, and disposal process. The objectives are to recover the greatest value possible from returns while maintaining customer loyalty, controlling costs, and securing information that will help reduce future returns. Reverse logistics management is highly specialized but doing it successfully has an impact on a company's bottom line.

Product retrieval is no longer limited to unwanted products sent back to the seller or bottle returns for recycling. As interest in recycling continues to grow, global companies will need systems that allow for retrieving and disposing of long-term capital goods such as cars, refrigerators, air conditioners, and industrial goods. Governments are starting to establish rules related to product retrieval that outside marketers will need to tune in to. Germany, for example, requires car manufacturers to take back their used vehicles for dismantling and recycling. The design of such long-term systems worldwide could end up being one of the key challenges and opportunities for logistics specialists.

Global businesses will also need to be environmentally responsible in other ways, always working to reduce their carbon footprints. This is necessary not only because it will protect the environment from further destruction, but also because consumers will demand it. There is an international tidal wave of change as individuals, corporations, and governments look for ways to function in more "green" ways. The impact on marketers, whether changes are voluntary or mandated, will be significant for some. Packaging will change, as buyers reject wasteful containers used solely for aesthetics rather than product protection or as manufacturers opt for materials that can be recycled after use.

Pressure to reduce the toxic impact of emissions from transportation modes will influence how far products are shipped, as well. At some point, transporting produce from one part of the globe to another so that people worldwide can enjoy fruits and vegetables off-season will be unrealistic. The selection in stores will be limited to locally produced and seasonal produce – a small price to pay in exchange for clean air and water.

With distribution channels in place using the right intermediaries that work together as team members, products getting to customers as quickly and efficiently as possible through a logistics network, and the security to protect goods as they enter or leave a market, the company is on track to see the impact of thoughtful planning in a very tangible way.

FOOD FOR THOUGHT

- What are your company's three external channel design characteristics?
- Will you use direct or indirect exporting, or will you use integrated distribution when getting your products into new markets?
- What are the most important characteristics of a distribution or sales intermediary for your firm?
- How will your company manage its logistics and supply chain needs?
- What does your company do now to be environmentally responsible and how can that translate to its global marketplace?

Further Readings

Benfield, Scott and Stephen D. Griffith. *Disruption in the Channel: The New Realities of Distribution and Manufacturing in a Global Economy*. Camby, IN: Power Publishing, 2008.

Dent, Julian. *Distribution Channels: Understanding and Managing Channels to Market*. London: Kogan Page Ltd., 2008.

Friend, Gil. *The Truth About Green Business*. Upper Saddle River, NJ: Natural Logic Inc., 2009.

Rangan, V. Kasturi and Marie Bell. *Transforming Your Go-To-Market Strategy: The Three Disciplines of Channel Management*. Boston, MA: Harvard Business School Press, 2006.

Online Resources

Logistics Management
Editorial coverage offering information on the role of logistics in today's business practices
www.logisticsmgmt.com/

Logistics Today
An all-digital publication that provides current news and knowledge for logistics managers
http://logisticstoday.com/

Logistics World
Offers service and contact information for companies in the logistics and supply chain industry
www.logisticsworld.com/

Chapter 5

Creating a Global Presence

Globalization reflects a belief that the world is becoming more homogenous and that distinctions between national markets are not only fading but, for some products, will eventually disappear. As the inefficiencies of duplicating product development and manufacturing in each country become more apparent, the pressure to leverage resources and coordinate activities across borders becomes more urgent.

This chapter will help marketers better understand the key issues facing global enterprises, the factors that should drive strategy, and the options available for executing the company's vision in international markets.

IT BEGINS WITH EXPORTING

Typically, companies experiment with exporting before making direct investments in overseas markets. The decision to reach beyond exporting is usually based on market factors, barriers to trade, cost factors, and the investment climate, with market factors playing the biggest role. Global investments can vary in commitment and control and range from creating or purchasing wholly owned subsidiaries to joint ventures. While many organizations prefer full ownership because it comes with full control, government regulations sometimes make this option impossible. In some situations, it is not even desirable. A joint venture with partial ownership is sometimes the best alternative.

Other options include strategic alliances or partnerships that allow companies to align with businesses that have complementary technologies and skills. Strategic alliances, often encouraged by governments, are on the upswing. In addition, as countries develop service-based economies, some businesses expand through contractual arrangements in lieu of equity investments.

The global appliance industry is a good example of how and why manufacturers in that category embraced globalization. Facing increased competition in the U.S. from imports, American appliance manufacturers looked overseas for growth. In Europe, they found a market with rapid expansion, breakdowns in trade barriers within the European Union, and a less saturated market than in the U.S. Appliance giants that included General Electric, Whirlpool, Electrolux, and Bosch-Siemens took advantage of the opportunities by acquiring regional manufacturers or forming strategic alliances with them. Whirlpool bought the appliance arm of Dutch electronics concern N.V. Philips, acquiring ten European plants, popular regional brands, and a third-place market share ranking.

Regional preferences in appliances show the challenges of implementing a global strategy for this industry. The French prefer top-loading washing machines while the British prefer front-loaders. When it comes to stoves, the French like cooking at high temperatures that cause grease splatters, making self-cleaning ovens popular. Because Germans cook with lower temperatures, the self-cleaning feature is not in such demand. While taking these variations into account, manufacturers have had to be careful not to create a one-size-fits-all product that simplifies manufacturing but, in the end, appeals to no one.

Companies in other industries face increasing global competition and challenges similar to those in the home appliance industry. Even large companies that dominate their domestic markets cannot survive on domestic business alone when they are in industries that are increasingly globalized. They must be in all major markets to survive shakeouts or risk being niche market specialists.

WHAT DRIVES GLOBALIZATION?

Globalization is driven by four factors:

- Cost
- Market
- Environment
- Competition

Cost

Maximizing their investment is a motivator for many global companies. Single-nation markets might not be large enough to offer a company's country subsidiaries all possible economies of scale and scope, especially given the dramatic changes in the marketplace. The goal, then, is to get the most mileage from the investment cost. At the same time, advertising and promotion can bleed across borders, so it makes sense to make the product available where people are going to hear or learn about it.

A realistic, objective assessment of global opportunities and costs will probably lead to tough decisions about which markets, customer segments, or product positioning to focus on and which ones to bypass as well as appropriate strategies. In pursuing price leadership, for example, the global marketer offers a product or service that is nearly identical to the competition's, but at a lower price. This often means investing in scale economies and controlling costs that typically include overheads, research and development, and logistics.

The alternative strategy, product differentiation, takes advantage of the marketer's real or perceived superiorities on value elements such as design or technical support. Cost leadership and differentiation are not mutually exclusive, of course, and should be balanced appropriately. For instance, product components manufactured to one worldwide standard on one production line can be assembled into different final products backed by unique positioning and brand differentiation to meet local customer tastes. And the "mass customization" product design movement that emerged two decades ago still permits low-cost tailoring of manufactured goods to individual customer specifications. Most global marketers combine high differentiation with cost containment so their global activities contribute to economies of scale in production and marketing.

Marketers who opt for high differentiation cannot forget to monitor costs, though, because customer value perceptions rely at least in part on the price paid for the quality obtained. Knowing this, Nissan introduced the sub-$10,000 Versa in the U.S. in late 2008, as the economic recession was just being acknowledged. The small vehicle lacks frills – there is no air conditioning or power steering – but its target market does not expect luxurious touches in a car in that price range.

Market

Consumers in advanced economies are becoming more similar in terms of education, income, lifestyles, aspirations, and their use of leisure time. Marketers of certain products find ready buyers in countries with high purchasing power and well-developed infrastructures. Still other products might fare best in markets that are less sophisticated.

Having a global strategy does not mean that a company should serve the entire globe. Critical choices include deciding where to spend resources and where to hang back. The usual approach is to start by picking regions and then countries within them. Regional groupings might follow the organizational structure of existing multinational management or export offices, such as splitting Europe into northern, central, and southern regions that have similar demographic and behavioral traits. Market data might be more readily available in situations where the firm is grouping markets according to existing structures and frameworks.

Environment

Increasing consumer wealth and mobility, rapid information transfer across borders, publicity about the benefits of globalization, and technological revolutions continue to accelerate demands for global products and services. Newly emerging markets are benefiting from advanced communications by leaping over economic development stages that others slogged through in earlier years.

A new group of global players is taking advantage of the increase in trading regions and newer technologies. These "mini-nationals" or "born globals" serve world markets from a handful of manufacturing bases rather than building a plant in every country as was the procedure in earlier years. Their smaller bureaucracies also allow these companies to move quickly to conquer new markets, develop new products, or change directions when the situation calls for it.

Competition

To remain competitive, global rivals have to intensify their marketing everywhere by attempting to sustain advantages that, if weakened, could make them susceptible to market share erosion worldwide. Competitive companies introduce, upgrade, and distribute new products faster than ever before. A company that does not remain ahead of the competition risks seeing its carefully researched ideas picked off by other global players.

Leading companies drive the globalization process. There is no structural reason why soft drinks should be at a more advanced stage of globalization than beer and spirits, except for the opportunistic behavior of Coca-Cola. Similarly, German beauty products maker Nivea is driving its business in a global direction by creating global brands, a global demand for those brands, and a global supply chain that helps the company meet those demands.

Nonetheless, the four global drivers have affected countries and industrial sectors differently. While some industries, including paper and soft drinks, are truly globally contested, some others, such as government procurement, are still closed. Commodities and manufactured goods are already in a globalized state, while many consumer goods are accelerating toward more globalization. Similarly, the leading trading nations display far more openness than low-income countries and that openness is advancing the positive state of globalization in general.

PLANNING YOUR GLOBAL SUCCESS

Global strategy planning starts with a multi-functional team led by the executive with the most experience in global or regional markets. Team members should include managers from marketing, production, finance, distribution, and procurement. Their first task involves working to understand the success factors that are common to the company's various markets. Identify the profitability and competitive drivers by analyzing the structure of the global industry. Add the common features of customer requirements and choice factors. Avoid planning global strategy on a country-by-country basis – it can result in spotty performance. Success tends to come from a portfolio-based planning process that focuses simultaneously across a broad range of markets to help balance risks, resource requirements, competitive economies of scale, and profitability.

Every company gets a reality check when it examines its resources for global expansion. While industrial giants with deep pockets might be able to establish a presence wherever they want, others with shallow pockets will have fewer options. And money is not the only issue – a survey of multinational corporations revealed that people with certain types of knowledge or skills were particularly difficult to find. The shortage is even worse when looking for people with cross-cultural experience to run regional operations.

Portfolio-Based Planning

Some marketers favor a portfolio model for their analysis. They typically use two dimensions to describe the relative characteristics of a product, company, market, or other entity. How the dimensions compare suggests certain strategies, such as whether to invest more, divest, or hold steady. This matrix approach shown in Figure 5.1 has become quite popular.

Global marketing portfolio models usually involve two measures:

1. The company or business unit's strengths as measured by relative market share, product fit, contribution margin, market presence, or other metrics.

2. Market attractiveness according to metrics such as size, growth rate, number and type of competitors, governmental regulation, or economic and political stability.

If a business unit is a "star" in a strong position in an attractive market, it will typically attract more investment and attention. If a business is in a weak position in an unattractive market, the typical model-based decision will lead to abandoning the market. But those are the easy decisions. What is the wise decision when the situation is more ambiguous? Does the company invest in attractive markets and challenge better-established players there? Does the company harvest profits in relatively unattractive markets where the company or unit is strong? The strategist must also assess the competition and anticipate its reactions to these types of potential challenges when making decisions.

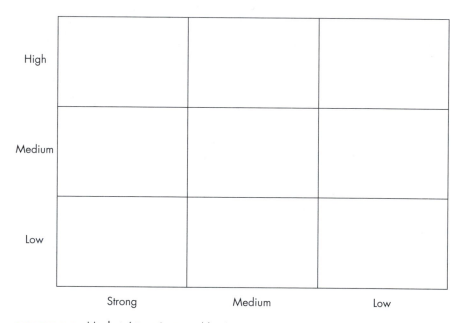

	Strong	Medium	Low
High			
Medium			
Low			

FIGURE 5.1 Market Attractiveness Matrix

Diversify or Concentrate?

There are often questions related to diversity versus concentration when a company looks to allocate finite resources among various markets. Choices involve concentrating on a small number of markets or diversifying by growing in a relatively large number of markets. The path taken is determined by a mix of factors that include:

- *Market attractiveness*. When there are high and stable growth rates in only certain markets, the company will likely opt for a concentration strategy. This is often the case with innovative products early in their life cycle. If demand is strong worldwide, as it might be for consumer products, then diversifying might make sense.
- *Concentration or saturation*. This will occur in markets that are responding to marketing efforts at marginally increasing rates. But when the cost of acquiring additional market share points goes too high, marketers tend to look for opportunities to diversify.
- *Product uniqueness*. While unique product attributes that are in demand might offer a significant lead time over competitors and make diversifying less urgent, it is hard to sustain the advantage for long.
- *Marketing mix and its spillover*. The expanding reach of media outlets makes it increasingly difficult to confine advertising messages to one country. In Europe, for example, ads on satellite channels now reach most Western European markets simultaneously, even if the company does not want to reach all of them. The more a marketer can standardize marketing mix elements, the more likely the company is to achieve economies of scale and diversification. While on the one hand, the marketer can benefit from the spillover, the downside is that if the marketing message in one region varies from the marketing message in the neighboring region, the marketer is losing some control.
- *Objectives and policies*. If the unit must maintain extensive interaction with intermediaries and clients, it will need to concentrate its marketing approach.

The conventional wisdom of globalization requires a presence in all of the major triad markets – North America, Europe, and the Far East.

Some of the markets in those regions may not be attractive but may have some other significance, such as hosting the headquarters of the most demanding client or being the home market of a significant competitor. That is why three factors should determine country selection:

- The *stand-alone attractiveness* of a market, such as China for consumer products because of its sheer size
- *Global strategic importance*, such as Finland for shipbuilding because of its technological lead in vessel design
- *Possible synergies*, such as entry into Latvia and Lithuania after success in Estonia because of the market similarities.

Segment Choices

With some market segments, political boundaries are less important in the market selection process than similar customer characteristics. That is because those similarities let the marketer customize its approach to highlight different product features to different segments. The teenage market segment is a good example. Thanks to computer literacy, travel abroad, and financial independence, teens from country to country often share common tastes in sports and music. The media plays a large part in this, with global networks such as MTV not only helping to create the commonalities, but also helping international marketers reach this audience worldwide. Still, despite intrasegment similarities, marketing mix adjustments are often necessary for subsegments, as Levi Strauss learned when European teens reacted negatively to the urban realism of Levi's U.S. ads for its jeans.

Similarly, two other distinct segments prime for an across-region approach include wealthy and well-educated trendsetters and Europe's affluent business people. Trendsetters universally value independence, refuse consumer stereotypes, and appreciate exclusive products. Europe's businesspeople regularly travel abroad and enjoy luxury goods.

Choosing segment bases is one of the biggest challenges for global marketers. The objective is to identify groups that are substantial enough to merit individual attention and can be reached efficiently by marketing tools. Teens, for example, are a large enough group to target and can be reached easily through their electronic and print media favorites. Most marketers let creativity and a solid understanding of market segments and product benefits guide their selection and testing of segment bases. They go beyond the obvious; knowing, for example, that using household income alone might not be enough because household income is a poor gauge of class and behavior. Take Chinese consumers, who spend less than 5 percent of their total outlays on rent, transportation, and health, while a typical U.S. household spends 45 to 50 percent on these needs. In addition, income distinctions do not reflect education or values, which are two increasingly important indicators of status and buying behavior.

Marketers have traditionally used environmental bases – geographic proximity, political system characteristics, economic standing, or cultural traits – for segmentation decisions. But each of these alone might not provide relevant data for decision-making. Combining them might generate more usable information.

Attitudes and lifestyles often provide robust segmentations that differentiate purchasing behavior. The middle-class family is one segment pursued by marketers worldwide, but defining the composition of the global middle class is tricky considering the varying levels of development among nations, particularly in Latin America and Asia. Some marketers further define this market using comprehensive models that categorize individuals by deep-seated interests and attitudes.

Barack Rocks with Data

Barack Obama's 2008 presidential campaign segmented its database successfully to appeal to attitudes and lifestyles of voters of all ages and income levels. Campaign workers sent text messages to the cell phones of younger voters and made certain the e-mails sent to older voters were short and concise. In addition, when a voter visited an Obama website, "cookies," or Internet tags, from the Obama site let the campaign follow the user's Internet trail. This knowledge of any individual's Internet patterns and usage would then allow the campaign to select the most relevant ad for that person to see on the next visit to an Obama site.

Companies often rely on the information provided in international consumer surveys conducted by GfK Roper Reports Worldwide. The company's annual studies give a range of global, national, and local perspectives.

Product-related bases include the degree to which products are culture-oriented, their stage in the product life cycle, consumption patterns and infrastructure, and attitudes toward product attributes. Marketers might be surprised, for example, by the growth of microwave ovens in low-income countries, where they might appear to be a luxury. The reality is that these products have become status symbols, making the purchase more of an emotional issue. Many consumers in developing countries also want to make sure they have access to the same products that are available in developed markets, which can eliminate the need to create market-specific products. Adjustments might still be needed, though, depending on market idiosyncrasies. In Australia, for example, soft drink bottles are sized and shaped differently than in other regions, while freezers in Bangladesh have to be larger because of the way fish and meat are stored there.

Promotional bases might require local, rather than regional, solutions. The availability or scarcities of media vehicles and government regulations also have an impact on promotional campaigns.

Pricing bases such as price sensitivity might lead a company to target segments that insist on high quality despite high price in markets where overall purchasing power might be low, just to ensure global or regional uniformity in the marketing approach. Affordability is a major issue for customers whose buying power might fall short for the time being. Offering only one option could exclude potential future customers who are not yet in the targeted segment. Some companies offer an array of products at different price points – similar to the variety of Apple iPod – to attract these customers and to keep them as they move up the income scale.

Distribution bases become more important as distribution systems converge and global retailers and purchasers proliferate. For example, mattress manufacturers might look at markets not only in terms of retail outlets, but also in terms of global hotel chains that might purchase their products.

EXPANDING INTO GLOBAL MARKETS: EXPORTING

While some companies are founded intentionally to serve a market outside its domestic boundaries, most expand internationally in a gradual way. The first step typically involves exporting, which might be followed by direct investment overseas. Companies become aware of international sales opportunities, perhaps from that first order from another country, then start answering international inquiries, participating in export counseling sessions, attending international trade fairs and seminars, and, of course, filling those unsolicited export orders.

Export Options

Firms with a track record of domestic market expansion are often prime candidates for export opportunities. In the exploratory stage, a company begins to export systematically, usually to psychologically close countries. After some export activity – typically around two years – management evaluates the effort from both an expectation and a financial perspective. Are the products as unique as they thought? Is the company making enough money on the effort? It might withdraw or continue and even explore the possibility of exporting to other countries that are psychologically farther away. This level of export expansion is usually reached when export transactions comprise about 15 percent of the company's overall sales volume.

They are focused on different issues at different levels of export experience. Those just starting out face operational questions – the mechanics of shipping orders to other countries, for example – while those that have tackled and solved those problems begin thinking about marketing and sales issues. Companies that have been through the adaptation process worry about longer-range issues such as delivering service and regulatory changes. The more they become active in international markets, the more they recognize that international marketing is just as important as its domestic counterpart.

While companies can export directly, as their export operations become more sophisticated, they often rely on e-commerce, use the services and assistance of intermediaries known as export management companies and trading companies, sell to a domestic firm that in turn sells abroad, or license or franchise their products or concepts.

E-commerce

As e-commerce continues to grow thanks largely to the global accessibility of the Internet, it is an attractive option for companies large and small. Much of the marketing is done through a company's websites, with country-specific sites using translations into the native language and a mechanism for accepting international payments – but companies also take advantage of business-to-consumer and business-to-business online forums. Online auction site eBay (www.ebay.com) is one example of a site enjoying success with an incredible range of products while China's Alibaba (www.alibaba.com) attracts businesses that want to sell products in that country. Alibaba, in particular, attracts small and medium-size businesses looking to export to China as well as its domestic businesses looking to expand in their home country.

Companies selling through the Internet must be prepared to provide 24-hour order-taking and customer support services, have the requisite regulatory and customs handling expertise, and an understanding of the global marketing environment to succeed. Many use the global shipping services of companies such as Federal Express and UPS because they will provide support services that include order fulfillment, delivery, customs clearance, and supply chain management.

Legal considerations include export control laws, especially for strategically important products or software; privacy, security, and intellectual property regulations; and identity theft protection. It is worth noting that the European Union's privacy measures are much more stringent than those of the U.S. and might impact on U.S. companies looking to do business in that region.

Intermediaries: Export Management Companies and Trading Companies

Export market intermediaries such as export management companies and trading companies specialize in bringing the products or services of others to the global market. They often have detailed information about competitive conditions and personal contacts with buyers in specific industries. They can evaluate credit risk, make sales calls, and manage a product's physical delivery.

Export management companies (EMCs) are domestic firms that perform international marketing services as commissioned representatives or as distributors for several other businesses. They tend to be owned and operated by one or two individuals with experience in international marketing in particular industries or in specific geographic regions or countries. They operate in one of two ways – they either take title to the goods and operate internationally on their own account, or they perform services as agents. EMCs acting as agents usually have contracts specifying exclusivity arrangements and sales quotas along with any price arrangements and promotional support. It is not unusual for an EMC to act as an agent for one of its clients and as a distributor for another.

Working with Export Management Companies

Working with an EMC is a major channel commitment for an exporter. EMCs often differentiate themselves with market intelligence and flexibility – options that allow them to compete during an age of e-commerce.

A successful EMC relationship requires that both parties recognize that responsibilities are delegated, that there are costs associated with these activities, and that they must cooperate and share information. Thoroughly investigate all options, cooperate once the firm has committed, and be prepared to reward appropriately.

Trading companies can import, export, counter-trade, invest, and manufacture. The best known are the *soga shosha* of Japan, which gather, evaluate, and translate market information in a way that often gives them a strategic information advantage. Their vast transaction volume gives them cost advantages that include an ability to negotiate favorable shipping rates. They also have access to capital. While trading companies were originally unique to Japan, they now exist in Brazil, South Korea, Turkey, and other countries.

An export trading company (ETC) allows small and medium-sized businesses to join together to export or offer export services in a way that lets them share facilities, resources, expertise, and talent. The Bank Export Services Act of 1982 permits U.S. commercial banks to own and operate export trading companies, a move designed to allow better access to capital. While they seem to make good business sense, there were fewer than 80 listed as export trade certificate holders on the U.S. Department of Commerce's Export Trading Company Affairs website at http://ita.doc.gov/td/oetca/ in 2009.

Export trading companies do best when participants collect, share, and respond to information on the needs and wants of global companies. Too often, though, there is a tendency to use them to dispose of existing merchandise rather than uncovering needs and providing the products or services that meet those needs.

Licensing and Franchising

Licensing is an international marketing strategy that lets a company test new markets without a capital investment or marketing knowledge of the regions. The royalty income generated by a foreign licensing agreement lets a company earn additional income from existing research and development investments. It is a proven concept that reduces the risk of R&D failures, the cost of designing around the licensor's patents, or the fear of patent infringement litigation. In addition, ongoing cooperation and support lets the licensee benefit from new developments. NaturalNano, a U.S. developer of extended release technologies and supplier of polymer additives based on naturally occurring nano materials, granted a worldwide exclusive license to its processes to Fiabila, S.A., a global cosmetics supplier. The deal lets NaturalNano generate sales from its joint development agreements and leverage its intellectual property portfolio in markets far from its domestic base.

Because the licensee is typically a local company, licensing reduces the exposure to terrorism and government intervention. It can also provide the licensor with a partner in the protection of intellectual property rights when the licensee becomes a local force with a distinct interest in uncovering unlicensed activities. The disadvantages of licensing for the licensor include a lack of first-hand knowledge that can be further leveraged in the market. Licensees, on the other hand, might end up directly competing with the licensing company.

Key issues in licensing negotiations include the scope of the rights offered, compensation, compliance, dispute resolution, and the term and termination of the agreement. It is important to define the scope of the product and/or patent rights by specifying the technology, know-how, or show-how to be included; the format; and guarantees. When negotiating compensation, the licensor wants to cover transfer, R&D, and opportunity costs through a share of the profits generated from the use of the license. Compensation can take the form of running royalties and/or upfront payments, service fees, and disclosure fees (for proprietary data). Licensee compliance should address export control regulations, confidentiality, and record-keeping and provisions for licensor audits.

In franchising, a parent company (franchiser) grants another company (franchisee) the right to do business in a specified manner. The typical reasons for the international expansion of franchise systems are market potential, financial gain, and saturated domestic markets. Franchising is attractive to the franchisee because it reduces risk – the company is implementing a proven concept. In Malaysia, for example, the success rate of franchises is 90 percent versus a 20 percent rate for nonfranchise new businesses. From a government perspective, franchising is appealing because it does not replace exports or export jobs. Host countries see franchises as requiring little outflow of their currency with the bulk of the profit generated remaining locally.

A franchise must be standardized if it is to be recognized no matter where it is located. Standardization includes a common business name, brand image, and similar production or service processes. People expect their experience with a franchise in one locale to be similar at a franchise elsewhere. Standardization does not always mean 100 percent uniformity, though. Adjustments usually take local market conditions and preferences into account. For example, in order to enter India, where cows are sacred, McDonald's had to create a nonbeef burger.

Selecting and training franchisees can present concerns. Although the franchisee knows the local market best, the franchiser still needs to understand the market to adapt the product and operations. There could also be complications selecting local advertising media, effective copy testing, translating the franchiser's marketing message, and the use of sales promotion tools. Because of this, some companies use a master franchising system that allows partners to be awarded the rights to a large territory in which they in turn can sub-franchise. The franchiser gains market expertise along with an effective screening mechanism for new franchises while reducing expensive mistakes.

EXPANDING INTO GLOBAL MARKETS: DIRECT INVESTMENT

Some companies find that they cannot meet their global marketing objectives by continuing to export, so they make direct investments in international markets to gain access to manufacturing facilities, supplies, or labor, among other reasons. They become multinational corporations, which the United Nations defines as "enterprises which own or control production or service facilities outside the country in which they are based." While this definition makes all foreign direct investors "multinational corporations," large corporations are the key players.

Building and managing operations outside the domestic market requires skills and resources beyond those used for exporting. Multinational firms with subsidiaries and other investments in other countries also deal with issues ranging from local versus headquarters control, to product or service standardization versus customization for individual market needs. At the highest level of marketing globalization, companies integrate their international and domestic operations into relatively seamless enterprises that have portfolios of nations that they market to with unified strategies.

Putting products into the hands of customers overseas involves some degree of direct financial investment, whether it is done by acquiring assets in other countries or gaining access to another company's assets through contracts. International marketers invest directly via full ownership, strategic alliances, or joint ventures to create or expand a permanent interest in an enterprise. It typically requires substantial capital and an ability to absorb risk, so the most visible players in this arena are large multinational corporations who invest either to enter new markets or to ensure reliable supply sources.

Foreign direct investment is defined by the United Nations as "enterprises which own or control production or service facilities out of the country in which they are based." U.S. firms have significant investments in the developed world as well as in some developing countries. It is a major avenue for global market entry and expansion.

The top multinational companies come from a wide range of countries and depend heavily on their international sales, with their original home market accounting for only a fraction of total sales. Some have revenues larger than the domestic output of some countries. Many operate in more than 100 countries and do not even reference "global" and "domestic" anymore. Through their direct investment, these companies bring economic vitality and jobs to their host countries, often paying higher wages than the average domestically owned firms. At the same time, though, trade follows investment, and companies that invest in other nations often bring with them imports that could weaken a nation's international trade balance.

Reasons for Direct Investment Versus Export/Import

Direct investment can help secure growth, more revenue, and greater profit by bringing a product or service to new markets in a more cost-effective and government-approved way. Acquiring companies in other countries that are already creating similar products or with the capability to manufacture yours, for example, is the fastest way to grow internationally. This approach also gives a global marketer significant political advantages, including local management with political know-how and expertise, better intelligence about the players and opportunities, and easier access to and skill dealing with politicians and business leaders.

It also lets companies circumvent trade barriers and operate abroad as a domestic company in the host nation, unaffected by duties, tariffs, or other import restrictions. This approach also satisfies customers who insist on buying only domestic goods and services or local buyers who prefer to purchase from those companies they perceive to be reliable, which often means "local." Other significant incentives include access to low-cost resources, reliable supply, and market stability with strong growth potential.

In general, companies that invest in international markets are looking for resources, markets, or efficiency. Resource seekers search for either natural resources such as water for power or human resources in the form of low-cost of highly skilled labor. Their needs might change over time as their labor changes or the natural resources they seek become scarce. Market seekers look for better opportunities and expansion options, while efficiency seekers are searching for the most economic production. They often have affiliates with highly specialized product lines or components in multiple markets and exchange their production to maximize efficiency.

Many suppliers to multinational companies overseas expand because their large customers ask them to. Elliott Group International, a suburban Detroit-based manufacturer of pressure-sensitive tape used in the auto industry, began manufacturing in Asia for U.S.-based customers, but also used its overseas presence to become a significant supplier to Toyota, Nissan, and Honda there. Advertising agencies often expand abroad to serve global affiliates of their domestic clients. Similarly, engineering firms, insurance companies, and law firms – among others – are often invited to provide their services abroad in the same way that they open up new offices in their home country to serve large clients in cities or regions outside the headquarters location. Sometimes the supplier expands internationally without being asked or invited simply to make certain the client does not find a new vendor in the overseas location.

Government incentives from host countries often encourage foreign direct investments, too, as a way to provide jobs and income. Fiscal incentives to global companies might include tax allowances; advantageous funding and loan guarantees; and nonfinancial incentives that include guaranteed purchases, infrastructure investments, or special protection from competition through tariffs, import quotas, and local content requirements. Incentives alone are not usually likely to spur investment decisions if proper market conditions do not exist, though. In addition, the new investor's arrival could have a negative effect on established domestic firms, which do not benefit from incentives created to attract new investment.

Investment Options: What Will the Overseas Presence Look Like?

International investors have a variety of investment options ranging from total ownership of a company, strategic alliances, joint ventures where partners share risks and rewards, government consortiums, and contract arrangements. Each option offers different levels of investment, risk, and control. Typically, "rich" firms needing only gradual penetration and wanting full control will have full ownership. Companies seeking rapid penetration – such as multiple markets at the same time – tend to use joint ventures. Management often sees full control as the only option whereas, strategically speaking, full control is not necessary and joint ventures make the most sense. When there is strong inter-dependence between different units, then strong control is wise. Strategic alliance is the option when there are multiple partners, a good deal of money is needed to move forward, and complementary capabilities are required.

This section will explain and define each and help marketers better understand which option is a reasonable choice for their global marketing goals.

Full Ownership

How much control is really needed for success? Sometimes full ownership is desirable, but not essential, while other times, it might be necessary – particularly when strong linkages exist within the corporation. Interdependencies between and among local operations and headquarters might be so strong that anything short of total control will not be acceptable. This might be the case if the company needs centrally controlled product design, pricing, or advertising to maintain consistency across markets. But that should be decided carefully to be sure that other ownership options are not more appropriate.

There are reasons to avoid full ownership. One is increasingly hostile attitudes from host country governments or consumers toward ownership by multinational firms. Host governments have been known to exert political pressure to obtain national control of nondomestic operations and to limit ownership options through legal restrictions. In addition to government concerns, general market instability can interfere with full ownership. While instability can be seen in political upheaval or regime changes, more common political risks come in the form of threats of political action, complex and drawn-out bureaucratic procedures, and the prospect of arbitrary and unpredictable changes in regulations after the investment decision has been made.

Strategic Alliances

Strategic alliances, also referred to as strategic partnerships, are formal or informal arrangements between two or more companies with a common business objective. These companies can actually be fierce rivals in other markets outside the scope of their business alliance, but need the talents and resources of each other in unique situations. They are more than the traditional customer–vendor relationship but less than an outright acquisition. Designed to pool partners' complementary strengths, their great advantage is their ongoing flexibility. Partners can adjust agreements easily as market conditions change.

Strategic alliances include:

- Informal cooperation involving exchanging information such as research or data
- Contractual agreements for licensing, manufacturing, or management contracts
- Joint ventures involving equity exchanges

Strategic alliances are increasing because of growing global competition, rapid increases in the investment required for technological progress, and a growing risk of failure. Market development is a common focus but some alliances are designed to defend home turf. They can include nonexclusive distribution or licensing deals. Some are intended to share the cost and risk of production and development. Even though major corporations form many of the strategic alliances, they are by no means confined to giant multinational firms. Aphra Communications, for example, is the venture of two journalists, a native English speaker in the U.S. and a native Spanish speaker in Bolivia, who have joined forces to offer clients communications written in both languages. The alliance has allowed both to expand their base businesses with new opportunities they could not have acquired alone. Other examples include U.S. high-tech start-ups looking to partner with Japanese businesses to secure new markets, profits, and applications without losing equity or making risky investments.

As with any important business decision, it is crucial to study the opportunity before committing, making certain that the partner is not unintentionally being set up to become a competitor. The most successful alliances are those that join complementary strengths to satisfy a joint objective. Partners often have different product, geographic, or functional strengths that the alliance can build on. Considering the increasing costs of international competition and technology innovation, strategic alliances are likely to continue their growth.

Joint Ventures

Joint ventures are long-term strategic alliances involving two or more organizations in which participating partners share assets, risks, and profits. Partners do not need to share everything equally and their contributions can vary. Contributions might consist of funds, technology, know-how, sales organizations, or plants and equipment.

These alliances can provide governmental advantages by allowing companies to overcome barriers related to outside ownership. In fact, government-related reasons are the primary reason joint ventures are formed in developing nations. From a commercial perspective, if a corporation can identify a partner with a common goal and if the two firms' international activities are sufficiently independent from each other, joint ventures might represent the best vehicle for international expansion. "JVs" allow companies with specialized advantages – superiorities in technologies, distribution, customer access, or local supply, for example – to pool their resources in a way that benefits all parties. They also permit better relationships with local organizations such as labor unions.

Joint Venture Advantages

Advantages of joint venture partnerships include:

- Political influence from the local partner that helps make the new venture eligible for tax incentives, grants and government support
- An organization that is less vulnerable to political risks because of the local connection
- Greater ease in applying for or negotiating certifications or licenses when the venture is treated as a local, rather than outside, entity
- Enhanced ability to tap local capital markets when the local partner has strong relationships with the local financial establishment
- Strong cultural sensitivity that presents missteps and leads to greater insights into changing market conditions and needs

---

In addition, joint ventures help companies minimize the risk of exposing long-term investment capital while maximizing returns from capital already invested. As companies reduce their investment planning timeframe, this financial reason becomes even more important.

There are, of course, problem areas with joint ventures. Some involve getting the concept off the ground. For example, because governmental regulations are often arbitrary and subject to substantial interpretation, they can create unexpected roadblocks or cause the new entity to continually shift gears. These and other related governmental challenges create uncertainty, which increases the risk for participants.

Other reasons for failure include:

- Conflicts of interest
- Problems with disclosure of sensitive information
- Disagreements over profit sharing
- Poor communication
- Lack of follow-through
- Cultural clashes, both from a national and operational standpoint
- Loyalty issues
- Insufficient funding

Many of the problems encountered by joint ventures stem from a lack of careful, advance consideration of how to manage the new endeavor. Partners should discuss in advance the whole range of business decisions covering strategy, management style, accounting and control, marketing policies and practices, production, research and development, and human resources. It helps for negotiators to have a broad understanding of their companies' goals and reach, so that a desirable market identified by the joint venture is not already in the sights of one of the partners, which might end up competing against its own joint venture.

Similarly, there can be issues surrounding profit and how it is distributed. If one partner supplies the joint venture with a product, that partner might expect that any profits accumulate at headquarters and accrue 100 percent at one firm rather than at the joint venture, where profits are partitioned according to equity participation. The partner not supplying the product but making other substantial contributions might not be enthusiastic about that arrangement. Profit distribution can also cause problems when one partner wants to distribute profit as dividends while the other wants profits reinvested. Because a partnership works on the basis of trust and commitment, it is possible to increase the likelihood of success by addressing these issues at the start of the relationship.

When seeking a joint venture partner, look for an organization that shares the company's objectives but brings different and necessary skills to the relationship so that the organizations complement each other. The goal is to work with an organization that has an excellent reputation in the local market and its financial community. Negotiate an agreement that outlines the details discussed above – how the business will be managed, profit sharing, and so on – but is flexible enough to respond to a dynamic business environment. Include specifics about how the venture can be dissolved if there are significant changes in business conditions and priorities. An agreement should cover issues such as termination conditions, disposition of assets and liabilities, how to protect proprietary information and property, rights over sales territories, and obligations to customers and employees.

Government Consortium

This specialized form of joint venture involves government funding, often with subsidies. Such consortia are usually designed to cope with escalating costs in a sector where a government seeks to build or maintain global leadership. Advanced technology research consortia have emerged in the U.S., Japan, and Europe, with government assistance helping to combat the high costs and risks of research and development. Since the Joint Research and Development Act of 1984 was passed to allow both domestic and international firms to participate in joint basic research efforts without fear of antitrust action, more than 100 consortia have been registered in the U.S. These collaborative groups have pooled their resources for research into technologies ranging from artificial intelligence and electric car batteries to semiconductor manufacturing.

Contracts

Contracts allow companies to put their corporate resources to use abroad without making a significant investment. In some situations, they also allow businesses to sidestep host government ownership restrictions.

Management contracts allow a company to provide an integrated service in a new market without incurring either the risk or the benefit of owning the skills doing the work because the client company's staff executes the work under the contracting company's direction. The international marketer can use management contracts to secure joint venture participation when equity participation is not possible or must be relinquished. Depending on the terms, the contracting company might even be able to use a contract to maintain control. For example, when the company has to relinquish manufacturing to a firm in another country, a management contract could allow it to retain control over distribution. Management contracts allow any business model to rely on an outside party with specialized knowledge, regardless of the industry.

The turnkey operation is a specialized form of management contract that lets a client acquire a complete operational system with the skills required to keep it running. Contracting for a package of services eliminates the need to find and deal with individual contractors and subcontractors.

Management contracts offer benefits to both parties – the client gets ready access to specific expertise, organizational skills, and support services that would be difficult and costly to replicate locally. In addition, the project will be totally owned, controlled, and operated by the client company (unless indicated otherwise). This is why many governments allow management contracts as alternatives to foreign direct investment and control. Contract suppliers benefit from a substantially reduced risk while operating as insiders and influencing strategic decisions. It is also a way for a company to commercialize its intellectual property and experience.

There are downsides, of course. The client risks becoming overly dependent on the supplier and losing control. The contractor risks contract termination and the resulting personnel problems and expenses.

It is clear that companies looking to expand internationally have many options but will want to test the waters first before jumping into costlier options associated with direct investment. Expansion alternatives involve varying degrees of risk along with varying degrees of control. There are also legal limitations imposed by the host government. Take into account the market prospects, the budget, legal and government restrictions, and the company's personality when deciding which approach is best for the organization.

FOOD FOR THOUGHT

- What is your company's experience with global customers? Are buyers from other countries purchasing from your firm already? How about on the Internet?
- Who is on – or should be on – your company's global strategy planning team?
- Does your company have a pattern of domestic expansion? How will it guide or inform the organization's international growth? Should that pattern continue or be changed?
- Which global expansion option appears to be the best fit for your company – exporting, strategic alliance, joint venture, licensing, foreign direct investment, or something else?

Further Readings

Gibbs, Richard and Andrew Humphries. *Strategic Alliances and Marketing Partnerships: Gaining Competitive Advantage Through Collaboration and Partnering.* London: Kogan Page Ltd., 2009.

Hisrich, Robert D., *International Entrepreneurship: Starting, Developing and Managing a Global Venture.* Thousand Oaks, CA: Sage Publications, Inc., 2010.

Hollis, Nigel. *The Global Brand: How to Create and Develop Lasting Brand Value in the World Market.* New York, NY: Palgrave Macmillan, 2008.

Jagoe, John R. *Export Sales and Marketing Manual: The Bible of Exporting*, 22nd edition. Minneapolis, MI: Export Institute, 2009.

Online Resources

E-Commerce Times: E-business Means Business
The online news source for doing business on the Internet
www.ecommercetimes.com/

The Export Institute of the United States
Resources, consulting and training for exporters
www.exportinstitute.com/agora.cgi

World Investment Directory Division on Investment and Enterprise
Offers detailed information on foreign direct investment in global markets
www.unctad.org/Templates/Page.asp?intItemID=3204&lang=1

Chapter 6

Making Communication Happen

At the start of the millennium, global software giant SAP AG had an identity crisis. Years of neglect combined with inconsistent messages distributed worldwide through locally produced advertising campaigns led to a weak brand image at a time when competition was heating up. Acknowledging the problem, company leaders hired a global chief marketing officer from the consumer products industry to create a consistent and relevant global brand image. The resulting multi-year effort involving – among other things – customer and employee research, a global advertising agency, brand champions located worldwide, and a marketing communications toolkit and intranet resource for local use, had spectacular results. Six years after starting the re-branding effort, the company's profit grew by more than 200 percent. It is a testament to the power of effective global communication in today's seemingly borderless world.

As the SAP campaign helps illustrate, communicating a message globally is complicated and expensive and will not happen quickly. Marketers must take into account country-specific advertising regulations, varying cultural interpretations of messages, the strengths and weaknesses of different communications mediums from country to country, and the critical need for local input and guidance. And yet, as SAP has shown from its award-winning success, the payoff of a campaign that communicates essential corporate messages consistently and effectively is well worth the wait.

The processes involved in executing a successful international marketing communications campaign are not very different from those used domestically. The challenge, though, is to know each of the targeted geographic – and demographic – markets as well as the company knows its domestic counterparts. What is the demographic profile of the overseas target buyer? What media outlets do they read, watch, listen to? Who or what influences their purchasing decisions?

In addition, it is important to address cultural issues that might have an impact on how the company communicates with the target audience and consider whether messages will translate accurately into another language. For example, the Spanish translation of the California Milk Processor Board's successful U.S. "Got milk?" slogan is "Are you lactating?" Clearly, it is not enough to simply translate domestic materials and drop them into the new market.

Here's how to conceive and implement a successful global marketing communications campaign.

CAMPAIGN ESSENTIALS

There are six essential components of a successful international communications campaign:

- *Information.* Market research (see Chapter 3) will help identify the key benefits and features that will appeal to customers in different markets and shape how to communicate those attributes.
- *Money.* Set aside a large enough budget to maintain a superior or competitive share of voice in the marketplace.
- *Patience.* Creating brand awareness takes time – do not expect payback in fewer than two years.
- *Local input.* With so many regional differences, guidance from the local affiliate on language and cultural issues can make the difference between success and failure.
- *Control.* While local intermediaries might take a leading role, global marketers do not want to give them a free hand.
- *Consistency.* Protect the brand image by maintaining common themes, objectives, and messages in individual market campaigns.

Information

As noted in Chapter 3, good market research will help determine the global regions where a company is likely to have the most success, the competitive environment, the product or service features and benefits that will be the most appealing to buyers in specific regions, and how to shape and communicate marketing messages.

When Seagate Technology LLC created an Asian advertising campaign for its disk drive, it did not emphasize product benefits and technical excellence, as it did in a home market campaign. Instead, Seagate used market intelligence to develop a campaign targeting original equipment manufacturers that emphasized that the drives were designed in close cooperation with the company's customers. In addition, the ad that ran in China pictured bone chopsticks on black cloth, while the Japanese version featured enameled pointed chopsticks on a marble slab for a look that was similar, yet noticeably softer. This differentiation designed to appeal to local prospects was an outcome of the disk drive manufacturer's information about individual market preferences and motivators.

Money

The ideal approach is to set the budget according to campaign objectives, but it does not always happen that way because of financial or other constraints. A typical approach is to set objectives and estimate the cost of the tasks required to meet those objectives, and then compare that "wish list" of activities to the amount of money that is actually available, funding what is essential, will have the greatest impact, or is most likely to be executed well. As in any situation, it is not wise to determine the marketing communications budget as a percentage of sales. Remember: marketing programs generate sales, not the other way around.

For many marketers, financial support from the international intermediary is a critical factor. Whether a distributor is able to spend millions, rather than thousands, on a high-impact, far-reaching campaign designed to grab share of mind, makes a significant difference. Dealer participation programs for intermediaries without large budgets could involve featuring the intermediary's name in promotional material such as a sweepstakes announcement in exchange for purchasing more products.

Patience

International campaigns require patient investment; the market has to progress through awareness, knowledge, preference, and purchasing intentions before there is any payback. This patience is particularly important in markets where these products or services have never been available, but it is also essential in situations where there is already some level of awareness.

Local Input

While a company might trust the brainstorming behind the surfboard campaign to a California beach bum, it might not want him masterminding the messages targeting Maine's commercial lobster fishermen. Similarly, allies in regional markets overseas will want to help shape messages and how they are deployed – and the company will want them to, as well. Culture, economic development levels, and regional lifestyles can influence regional changes – or in some cases, totally different approaches – in campaigns. Local colleagues are aware of the issues that should prompt changes.

Watch Those Translations

Local input can help uncover the subtle nuances in a translation that might be overlooked in the U.S. or a cultural taboo that appears in an advertisement that was effective elsewhere. Language challenges are most obvious when translating themes. One of the best-known marketing faux pas comes from the translation of the Chevy Nova for the Latin American market – in Spanish, the product name means "It doesn't go." Similarly, the Ford Pinto had problems in Brazil, where "pinto" was slang for "tiny male genitals." Ad slogan translations that did not quite work include Coca Cola's, "Can't Beat the Feeling," which translated to "I Feel Coke" in Japan, "Unique Sensation" in Italy, and "The Feeling of Life" in Chile. The Coors slogan, "Turn it loose" translated in Spanish to "Suffer from diarrhea."

Some companies work around this by having little or no copy. Using symbolism instead, though, will require adequate testing to determine how the target audience perceives the message.

A region's economic development stage has an impact on the potential demand for a product or the level of awareness and could require a message variation. While developed markets might require persuasive messages that combat other alternatives, an emerging market may be ripe for an informational campaign. Programs may also have to be adjusted in dramatic ways to adjust for lifestyle differences in regions that are demographically quite similar. For example, Swedish furniture retailer IKEA's successful advertising campaigns key into the unique cultures of each country. North American ads, for example, are cleverer than those in Europe, which are straightforward.

Market quirks that local input helps uncover can cause campaign localization. Although IBM has used global campaigns, it has created major local campaigns when necessary. In Japan, for example, it used a popular television star in personal computer ads that communicated that the computer represented a class act from America. In Europe, however, where the company was perceived as "too American," an advertising campaign informed prospects of the company's factories, research facilities, and subsidiaries in the European Union, helping to underscore the European side of its personality.

Control

Even when a distributor is sharing the financial commitment required for a successful campaign, marketers want to maintain some control of the campaign rather than allow intermediaries or a sales office a free hand in various markets. Whether markets are similar or different, common themes and objectives need to be incorporated into the individual campaigns. Although many exporters do not exert pressure to conform, overseas distributors take advantage of annual meetings to discuss promotional practices with their head office counterparts and compare notes with those in other locations, too.

SAP AG, whose branding campaign was described at the start of this chapter, used a kickoff meeting for North American and overseas field employees to communicate its new long-term program. In addition, it created a marketing communications online toolkit designed to provide field sales office with consistent sales and marketing content. This was expanded to include a sales and marketing intranet with brochures, images, branding standards, and online demonstrations for customers. All materials were adaptable to meet local needs; all were corporate approved.

Consistency

Many companies want as much control as possible over international communications endeavors because they require a message consistency that protects a brand's image and reputation. This was an especially important issue in this situation, where there had been a great deal of inconsistency over time. Brand details – the precise color to use when reproducing the logo color or the tagline that describes the company – sometimes seem inconsequential to nonmarketers, but they are one of the many unifying threads in all communications related to a company's products or services outside its home market. Many companies provide image style sheets to local agents or offices, leaving nothing to guesswork.

Websites, in particular, must have a consistent appearance regardless of the region they are designed to serve. Many multinational companies use a gateway-style home page design that lets visitors first select their country before being directed to a site with the appropriate language and products for that particular region or nation. While their content might be different, the sites for all regions look the same. Companies creating new websites in the language of the country they are exporting to can eliminate any international customer confusion by making certain that the new website mirrors that of the parent site.

Similarly, all internal and external communications materials, including brochures, advertisements, sales sheets, websites and press releases, must use the same language to describe the company. This helps ensure that the loyal customer or curious prospect familiar with the company's work in one region recognizes and embraces it in another.

TOOLS AND TACTICS

The choice of marketing communications tools and tactics is often influenced by whether the marketer chooses a push or pull strategy. Push strategies focus on the distribution channels, communicating various incentives, information or offers that encourage distributors or retailers to stock the product and "push" it onto the customer. In the consumer products arena, we see this in play typically in a retailer's sales flyer, when there is an incentive of some kind – cents off or a refund, for example – for consumers to purchase a specific product. There is a push strategy behind nearly every consumer purchase incentive.

Pull strategies originate on the customer end, where the marketer creates a demand for the product so that the customer goes looking for it and "pulls" it through the distribution channel. One of the best-known examples of a successful pull strategy in the U.S. is the "Tickle Me Elmo" doll, which enjoyed nearly unprecedented retail success when introduced during the holiday-selling season – a success that has been repeated in subsequent years with product line extensions.

Personal selling and trade-oriented sales promotion play leading roles in push strategies. In business and government markets with relatively few but larger customers making complex, big-ticket purchases, personal selling with its substantially higher cost per contract is the preferred tool. This is a buying–selling situation where personal relationships have a greater impact than most promotional efforts. Advertising to business buyers generally plays a supporting role, building general awareness of a company and its brands while soliciting sales leads.

In consumer markets, one-to-one contact is possible but not always practical, so marketers generate demand among these mass markets through advertising and publicity – a pull strategy.

What Tools to Use?

Tools used in specific situations vary and are selected according to the budget and the desired end result. The international marketer's communications tool kit typically includes:

- *Advertising*. Any purchased form of nonpersonal presentation of ideas, goods, or services by an identified sponsor. It is used primarily for mass communications such as print, broadcast or electronic media. It is also used for direct communication that is pinpointed at each business-to-business customer or the ultimate consumer using computer technology and databases.
- *Personal selling*. The process of using person-to-person communications to assist or persuade a prospect to buy goods or services or to act on an idea.
- *Direct marketing*. Uses advertising via mail, e-mail, or telephone to communicate individually with a prospect or customer.
- *Publicity*. Any form of nonpaid, commercially significant news or editorial comment about ideas, products, or institutions. Publicity is considered to be as much as ten times as effective as advertising because of the implied editorial endorsement that comes with news material.
- *Sales promotion*. Direct inducements such as incentives or special pricing that add extra value to the sales force, intermediaries, or the ultimate consumer.
- *Sponsorships*. The practice of promoting the interests of the company by associating it with a specific event – typically sporting or cultural – or a cause such as a charity or a social issue.

While in the past it was not uncommon for various tools and techniques to have different looks and messages, savvy marketers have come to appreciate the value of integrated marketing communications so that they have continuity among efforts and a greater impact of the whole as a result. Coordinate promotional tools according to the target market and product characteristics, the promotion budget size, the type and length of international involvement, and control considerations.

Industrial purchasing decisions, for example, typically involve eight to eleven people. Because a sales person might not be able to reach all of them, this in-person effort is often supported by advertising designed to influence everyone involved in the decision-making process. And while the sales person might use a brochure to help inform a prospect and motivate the buying decision, an informative website is needed to enlighten the prospect reached by advertising, but not in person.

Here's what marketers need to know about each method in the global marketplace and how they might support each other.

Global Advertising Considerations

The two main concerns when selecting advertising media are reaching the appropriate target audiences and doing so efficiently as measured by the cost per thousand (CPM). If the company is in a position to define a target audience clearly in terms of demographics or product-related variables, the media choice will be easier. The more targeted you can become when describing the most likely customer, the easier it is to identify what they read, watch, or listen to or how to reach them through their key influencers.

Do not make decisions by CPM alone, though. With an integrated marketing communication mindset, media work synergistically. For example, advertisements in publications and directories might drive customers and prospects to a website, while publicity can educate about a product category and advertising provides brand-specific information.

As in the U.S., international advertising vehicles include business and trade journals, consumer magazines, broadcast media outlets, the Internet, and directories. Media availability and spending vary dramatically around the world, with the U.S. spending more money on advertising than most other advertising nations combined. According to ZenithOptimedia, the fastest growing region includes Central and Eastern Europe while Latin America is seeing more moderate growth in advertising spending. China and Russia are moving up on the list of largest advertising markets, with China estimated at fifth place in 2008 and Russia expected to be in seventh place by the end of 2009.

How and where the money is spent varies, too. Some Latin American nations have the heaviest concentration of their advertising in television, while print media dominates in some Scandinavian lands. Cable and satellite enhance TV penetration in affluent markets, while radio remains a strong medium in many developing markets. Outdoor and transit advertising, cinema ads, and the Internet also compete for a share of the marketing communications budget in many global markets. Interactive telephone and TV are on the horizon, too.

One of the challenges for the international advertiser is the need for market-specific information. A medium popular in one country might well be significantly less important in another nearby, forcing the marketer to, for example, use radio in one market and print in another, which increases production costs. Currency exchange rate fluctuations also complicate media planning and budgeting.

Follow the Code

Conflicting national regulations have the greatest impact on media availability and planning. Conditions vary from country to country, making it harder to create one ad that is acceptable according to each country's national regulations. Although one might expect it, there is no uniform standard even within the European Union. Most European countries use the *Consolidated ICC Code of Advertising and Marketing Communication Practice* (http://tinyurl.com/zzwhq) or base their guidelines on it.

The Code is available in several languages, including French, Spanish, and German. Find links to each country's advertising regulators at www.lawpublish.com/international-links.html. Most regulatory organizations offer copy advice; take advantage of it and contact every self-regulatory group in each of the countries where the ad will appear to make certain it is acceptable.

Some of the regional regulations include limits on the amount of time available for ads. In Italy, for example, the state-owned and commercial TV channels have different maximum advertising limits. Other regulations affect how content is presented. In Italy, unlike the U.S., there is a strict separation between programs and commercials. Many countries restrict gender stereotypes and comparative claims.

Thanks to cable and satellite transmissions, the media in neighboring countries is increasingly crossing global boundaries, generating significant implications for global marketers. The viewer's choices have expanded, leading to competition among government-run public channels, state channels from neighboring nations, private channels, and pan-European channels. As a result, marketers must make certain that their advertising communicates effectively not only in the region where they make the buy, but also across boundaries. This makes ad creation and media buying more challenging, frustrating marketers and their advertising agencies. Agencies often must produce several separate versions of a campaign to comply with various national regulations. As in the U.S., tobacco, alcohol, and pharmaceutical products are the most regulated in Europe.

Not surprisingly, what is and is not allowable is a reflection of the country that is imposing the rules. For example, while explicit advertisements for condoms are common in Sweden, they air less frequently in other parts of the world. In addition, a message that works well in one region might fall flat in another. Unilever discovered this in 2007 when its "real beauty" campaign for Dove soap performed well in the U.S. and Europe but fell flat in China. The campaign, which attacks the unattainable beauty of models in ads – models whose beauty is often achieved through digital manipulation of images – was applauded by feminist and advertising groups worldwide. When it did not succeed in China, the company conducted research to learn why and discovered that Chinese women felt they could attain the beauty of billboard models if they tried hard enough.

As a result, the company abandoned the Chinese "real beauty" concept and introduced an entirely different marketing campaign to Chinese customers. Unilever launched a Chinese version of the popular U.S. ABC-TV show *Ugly Betty*, negotiating exclusive ads and product placements during the show. The company tested awareness of its products after the first season of *Ugly Wudi*, and found that unaided awareness of Dove rose 44 percent among target consumers, a number that tripled among those who watched the program. In addition, after the first season ended, shipments of a specific product, Dove Shower Cream, were up 21 percent over the same period the year before.

Global media advertising is dominated by major consumer product categories such as airlines, financial services, telecommunications, automobiles and tobacco. These advertisers are looking for three important media characteristics:

- Targetability
- Compatible editorial
- Editorial quality

International advertisers can often leverage the reach of media outlets that are considered global – those targeting audiences on at least three continents and that have centralized media buying. In the past, these have been primarily print publications with regional and worldwide editions. One example is *Time*, which offers editions for the U.S., Europe, the Middle East, Africa, Asia, and the South Pacific region. Other global print publications include dailies such as the *International Herald Tribune*, weeklies such as *The Economist*, and monthlies such as *National Geographic*. Global broadcast media outlets joining the print media today include BBC Worldwide TV, CNN, the Discovery Channel, and MTV. While there is growing reach among the global media outlets, some have found that certain parts of the world are more appealing to advertisers than others, or that world economic conditions make it harder for them to offer so many international editions. In these situations, they sometimes eliminate editions that do not generate enough advertiser interest.

Global Broadcast Media Outlets

In broadcast media, pan-regional radio stations have been joined by television, thanks to satellite technology. Many pan-European satellite channels, including CNBC Europe for business and financial news and Sky1 serving the United Kingdom and the Republic of Ireland, were originally conceived as advertising vehicles. Many observers are skeptical about global broadcast media outlets, however, because of the challenges of developing a cross-cultural following in what are often highly nationalistic markets. A good example of this is STAR TV, Asia's leading media company, serving more than 300 million viewers located in more than 50 Asian countries. In 1994, Hong Kong-based STAR was forced by the government of the People's Republic of China to remove BBC World from its lineup because the government did not like BBC's coverage.

Standard Rate & Data Service (srds.com) is the premier source for international print media buyers, providing a complete list of international publications in its *International Media Guides,* a collection of five databases listing more than 21,000 titles from more than 200 countries. The databases cover business publications in Europe, Asia-Pacific, the Middle East, Africa and the Americas, and newspapers and consumer magazines worldwide. Use them for rates, circulation figures, readership descriptions, and other specific information necessary to help select media.

Trade journals can be global, regional, or country-specific – the SRDS directories can help marketers identify which is which. In addition, many U.S.-based trade magazines are published in national language editions, with some offering regional buys for specific export markets.

There are also government-sponsored publications similar to *Commercial News USA,* the export promotion vehicle published by the U.S. Department of Commerce. This particular catalog-style publication charges as little as $399 for an ad in the "U.S. Product Showcase" section of the magazine sent six times a year to more than 400,000 overseas buyers, representatives, distributors, government sourcing and purchasing agencies, government officials, and potential joint venture partners in 176 countries. View a recent issue at www.thinkglobal.us/archive.php.

Export directories that present U.S. products to the world offer similar advertising opportunities. Many markets feature exporter telephone Yellow Pages in both print and electronic forms. The Export Yellow Pages, produced in cooperation with the U.S. Department of Commerce, are designed to help connect small and medium-sized companies with overseas buyers, solve language barriers, improve market visibility, and simplify sales sourcing. It offers U.S. companies a way to promote worldwide at no cost for a simple listing and at a very low cost – no more than $85 – for one of three enhanced advertising options. A number of online directories offer advertising opportunities, too. The *Internet International Business Exchange* (www.imex.com), for example, sells exporters banner ads for $100 to $195 a month.

When making a decision about where to advertise and how often, the simplest approach is to use U.S. publishers serving overseas markets. That option could offer more confidence in terms of rates or circulation data. Consider a regional edition of a national publication if the company needs a more localized approach. But before advertising in an unfamiliar publication, analyze its content and overall quality to make sure it is a good fit for the brand and its image.

Personal Selling in an Export Market

Personal selling is the most effective of the promotional tools available. Although costs per contact are high, personal selling provides immediate feedback on marketing information and customer reactions. Overseas, personally selling is often done by the intermediary's sales force.

This tactic has a greater impact when selling directly to the end user or to government agencies such as foreign trade organizations. Companies selling high-priced products such as airplanes or selling to single-buyer markets must rely heavily on person-to-person communication, oral presentations, and direct-marketing efforts. These might be supported by corporate advertising and publicity designed to help educate prospects about the products or services or the manufacturer in advance.

In these situations, the sales effort is often linked to sales automation tools, call centers, customer service departments, and the Internet. It is essential to make certain that these customer interfaces reflect the company's image and that they do not create a negative impression. This is more likely to happen with cultures that place a high value on personal relationships. Localizing tools to reflect the market's language and culture can help prevent the potential to inadvertently alienate prospects.

Establishing direct contact with the buyer through a local sales force does not necessarily eliminate the need for intermediaries. In fact, sales people might be dedicated to supporting the intermediaries' efforts. At this stage, it is possible to use expatriate sales personnel to manage the effort locally or regionally. Expatriates are a popular option because of the knowledge of the company and its products but also for their ability to share best practices with the intermediaries' sales team. While this gives the marketer more control over the sales function, one of the key benefits is the impression it gives the local market. This level of local presence often suggests to customers that the company has a long-term commitment to the market.

The challenge lies primarily in finding the right person for the market and being in a position to afford the extra expense – expatriate staff costs about 2.5 times the domestic cost. If the organization is small, it might also be a struggle to find suitable talent.

No matter who is meeting directly with clients and prospects, provide them with the same support offered when selling domestically – basic selling materials such as product literature with specifications and data, catalogs, advertising assistance, product testing details, and information on demonstrated performance. All are designed to help the intermediaries' sales force succeed.

In order for the direct or indirect relationship to work, the exporter must:

- *Know the sales scene.* What works domestically does not necessarily work globally. This is especially true with compensation for sales representatives. Incentives and commissions motivate sales people in the U.S. but salaries are expected in most other markets. Study the salary structures and incentive plans in other competitive organizations in the market to make sure the company meets expectations.
- *Research the customer.* Because customer behavior varies from market to market, the sales effort must vary, too. ECA International learned this first-hand. The company, which sells marketing information using a membership concept that allows members to receive the data they need while also participating in the information-gathering process that helps generate that data, discovered that its membership approach did not work everywhere. In Asia, customers wanted only to purchase information as they needed it, piece by piece. Only through research and a modification of the sales effort was the company able to gain a foothold in Asia.

- *Work with the culture.* Take cultural expectations into account when setting realistic sales goals and quotas and when interacting with the intermediaries' sales force in person. In some cultures, such as those in Asia, the exporter is expected to act as a teacher and dictate how things are done – so it is extra important to do the homework first to understand how things get done in that region. In others, such as Northern Europe, training sessions should allow give-and-take and discussion in a seminar-like environment.
- *Learn from local representatives.* Listen closely to their feedback. If the sales force believes the product is not a good fit for the market and senses there is nothing it can do about it, sales representatives will not be motivated. Respond to their concerns with changes whenever possible. Because a local sales force has close contact with customers, marketers want to cultivate relationships with those people doing the selling so they can benefit and learn from their customer intelligence on a daily basis.

In addition, help create long-lasting personal connections with the company and its overseas sales representatives by allowing the sales force to visit its facilities and interact with the staff. When active in several markets in the same region, make it possible for salespeople in the various markets to interact with each other to exchange ideas, share best practices, and learn from each other's experiences. Their collective intelligence, in turn, will help marketers provide exactly what each market needs for sales success.

There are several types of structured promotional events that give overseas sales representation an opportunity to reach more people with personal selling methods. These include trade shows, trade and seminar missions, and exhibitions.

Trade shows or fairs are a long-standing European tradition and one of the most significant cost items in a global marketing budget. A trade show is typically an event at which manufacturers, distributors, and other vendors display their products or describe their services to customers, prospects, suppliers, industry associates, and the trade press. Whether or not the company should participate depends on the type of business relationships desired within a particular country. When looking only for one-time or short-term sales, the expense might not be worth it. But if the goal is a long-term investment, it is probably worth the cost.

Companies participate in trade shows because:

- They provide an excellent opportunity for introducing, promoting, and demonstrating new products to many people efficiently.
- Appearing at shows helps generate goodwill and face-to-face customer contact.
- It provides an opportunity for to "wave the company flag" in front of the competition.
- Participating helps boost sales force and distributor morale.
- It is a cost-effective way to meet with and screen potential intermediaries in a new-to-the-company market.
- Attending a show is an excellent way to meet government officials and decision-makers. In fact, the host government of the Chinese Export Commodities Fair held twice a year expects exporters to participate.
- They offer potential for market research and gathering competitive intelligence because rivals are participating in the shows, too.
- There are opportunities to obtain data that help marketers evaluate the effectiveness of a promotional campaign.
- They can reach a large number of sales prospects in a brief period of time at a reasonable cost per contact. Some 82 percent of all attendees of the average trade fair have the power to recommend or making final purchasing decisions. In addition, people are there because they have a specific interest in the exhibits.
- It can be a good place to find suppliers.

Capitalize on trade show participation by inviting key prospects to visit the booth or even better, the company's hospitality suite, where there is more privacy for negotiations. Use incentives to attract people to the booth; have systems in place to track leads generated and to evaluate show performance.

Trade Show Participation Obstacles

Companies have many reasons for avoiding international trade shows:

■ They are expensive, although events sponsored by the U.S. Department of Commerce, U.S. trade centers, or export development offices can be less expensive. It is also possible to lower costs by sharing expenses with distributors or representatives. In addition, the costs associated with closing a sale at a show are estimated to be much lower than for closing a sale through nonshow personal representation.

■ It is hard to select the right show. Many companies rely on suggestions from their international distributors, which helps. Caterpillar, for example, usually allows its overseas dealers to make the selections.

■ Large companies with many divisions sometimes struggle to coordinate their presence when several plan to exhibit at the same show. They are often required to participate together under the unified company banner. Similarly, it can be a challenge for these larger organizations to coordinate with distributors and agents, too.

Companies have the option of participating in general or specialized trade shows. General trade shows or fairs are held in Hannover, Germany; Guanzhou, China; and in Milan, Italy. There are a range of industry-specific shows, such as ISPO, the sporting goods show in Munich, Germany, and Retail Solutions, the store automation fair held in London.

In addition to registering and exhibiting independently, companies often have the option of participating as part of a national or group pavilion made possible by a government export promotion program. This is an appealing option for small and medium-sized companies because it reduces costs and simplifies coordination and logistics. Government assistance might also be available. The Japanese External Trade Organization, for example, helps non-Japanese companies participate in Japan's to largest trade shows.

Virtual trade shows have become increasingly popular as Internet technology and tools, including virtual world Second Life, make this a more interesting option. One advantage to show attendees is that they can learn about products and services without leaving their workplace. Exhibitors, on the other hand, can track what people do at the show, learning how long they stayed at their exhibit, what they looked at, and so on. In addition, the virtual show sponsor collects and forward sales leads to participating companies in the same way that exhibitors might gather them in person at a traditional in-person trade show. For a schedule of virtual and traditional international trade shows, visit:

- export.gov
- fairsandexpos.com
- siso.org
- mpiweb.org

Other exhibit opportunities include *trade missions* – group trips – designed to expand the sales of U.S. goods and services as well as to help establish agencies and representation abroad. The U.S. Department of Commerce organizes a variety of trade missions each year designed to introduce U.S. companies to qualified international buyers. They typically include individual business appointments tailored to each participating company's needs as well as meetings with government officials. Participants benefit from market reports and briefings as well as opportunities to network with representatives from other participating companies.

Seminar missions are more like conferences, where an organizer invites eight to ten companies to present general discussions on technological issues during a one- to four-day forum. They are designed to share information, with promotional efforts taking a back seat to a more soft-sell approach. Smart exporters leverage their participation in these events by following up with the representatives of government agencies, research institutions, and the end users who attend. The process for getting on the agenda to present is similar to that of industry association conferences in the U.S.: companies must submit summaries of proposed lectures along with company details and speaker credentials to the organizer, who will circulate the proposals to decision-makers. While it is an excellent opportunity for companies new to a market to showcase their expertise, the typical one-year lead time is considered a drawback for some.

Solo exhibitions hosted by a single company are generally limited to one, or at the most, a few product themes and are scheduled according to the marketer's needs. For example, in 2003, Philips introduced the Philips Electronic Circus, a 12-city tour showcasing the company's electronics technology in South America. *Video/catalog exhibitions* are a low-cost product promotion opportunity. They consist of five- to ten-minute product presentations or demonstrations on a videotape with 25 to 30 other presentations, giving prospects an opportunity to see the product in use.

The Department of Commerce also schedules *virtual trade missions* for smaller businesses. These two-hour interactive video conference calls that connect U.S. companies with potential international business partners are arranged by local Export Assistance Centers.

Country Development Level Influences Direct Marketing Method

The Internet has changed how marketers communicate with international customers and prospects. Usage varies by region, but it is trending up universally. According to Internet World Stats, Asia has the most Internet users as of 2008 because of its population size but the U.S. has the greatest Internet penetration. While the Oceania/Australia region has the fewest users, it has the second greatest penetration among the population. Europe ranks second in percentage of users and third in penetration. The lowest level of penetration is in the Middle East, Asia, and Africa. The challenges faced by exporters regarding Internet-based communications relate to the newness of the medium outside the U.S. and the degree to which they must make adjustments for individual markets.

Marketing use of the Internet can range from something as simple and basic as a web presence to using intranets to facilitate processes with intermediaries. Sophistication might vary depending on the products and markets, but all exporters need a well-designed and well-marketed website. At a minimum, it should communicate the company's personality and quality while offering more information or clarification than can be presented in advertisements or direct marketing materials.

Why Marketers Need Global Websites

As with domestic operations, a website targeting global markets offers these advantages:

- It provides 24-hour access to product and other information for customers and prospects, providing an improved level of customer service to users who have become accustomed to the "we're never closed" nature of e-commerce.
- Customers can learn from each other through product specific forums that let them ask questions and get more information.
- A company's site offers an incredibly inexpensive way to gather information about customers for research or database marketing purposes.
- E-commerce sites let the marketer close the order with a customer who might not be found any other way.
- Intranets provide detailed product and price information, marketing collateral, and other business information or materials to agents, representatives, and distributors through a system that allows for quick and easy information updates when necessary.

Demonstrate appropriate market and cultural sensitivity with local language sites. Consider dialects, too – Spanish, for example, has three – European, Mexican, and South American. Websites created for specific overseas markets should be quite similar to the main domestic site in terms of aesthetics, but will need adjustments for details such as products offered and the market presence level (customers might already be aware of the company's products by visiting the main site). Website pages modified for different regions typically include those emphasizing marketing, sales, and the corporate identity. In addition, since individuals around the world have different information needs, varying levels of company and product familiarity, and different user capabilities, adjust the company's site content to meet a range of needs.

Banner advertising on Internet sites is a global marketing communications option for products or services targeting an audience that spends a great deal of time online, too. Global Internet advertising is on the upswing; the Kelsey Group reports that while global Internet ad spending in 2007 was $45 billion, it expected that number to more than triple to $147 billion by 2012. Counter that with a 2007 study by the Nielsen Company reporting that banner, search engine, and cell phone text message advertising are the least trusted advertising options across the board, in all global regions. They are trusted the most by Latin Americans and the least by Europeans, but collectively they ranked at the bottom of the list of influential platforms. Even so, a 2008 Morgan Stanley report on Internet advertising trends reveals that search engine marketing is responsible for most – more than a third – of the new customers for online retailers. Like traditional advertising, online advertising regulations differ from region to region. Germany, for example, sued Benetton for "exploiting feelings of pity" in an online campaign.

Finally, an online communications strategy should incorporate taking advantage of mobile telecommunications technology, whether it involves messaging or creating websites that can be read by handheld devices such as personal digital assistants and iPhones.

While selling to businesses and consumers via the Internet is on the upswing, direct mail is still the dominant global direct response medium. Direct mail's effectiveness is directly related to the availability and quality of mailing lists, though. Lists might not be available around the world at the same level that they are in the U.S., but more and better lists are becoming available in Asia, Latin America, and the Middle East. In addition, newer types of mail service, including Express Mail International from the U.S. Postal Service, let companies deal with their customers more efficiently when customers buy through catalogs or the Internet.

The growing mail order segment is attracting an increasing number of international entrants to markets previously dominated by local companies. However, because consumers are understandably wary of sending money to a business they are not familiar with, a local address is key to market penetration. One example of a company succeeding with a localized approach in Japan is L.L. Bean. The U.S. outdoor clothing and accessories manufacturer uses a locally based intermediary to accept and process orders, which are then sent to the company's Maine headquarters for fulfillment.

In Europe, companies encouraging telephone orders localize their direct mail materials by using local numbers assigned to call centers. The call centers they use depend on a number of factors, including the product's distribution area, operation costs, the importance of local presence, language needs, and the ability to handle calls from multiple time zones. Top choices for Central and Latin American call centers include Argentina, Brazil, and Costa Rica. Asian choices include India and the Philippines, while Belgium, Holland, Ireland, Portugal, and some of the new European Union countries are leading locations in Europe. Centers receiving calls for several countries with different languages use a system that displays the country name when the call comes in and routes the call automatically to an operator who speaks that language.

Some exporters see the use of call centers as a preliminary step to entering an international market with a sales force or other type of presence. Their call center activity generated by direct marketing can help them create an individual relationship with each customer or prospect by recording purchasing or inquiry habits and better predicting which offers might generate a response from the individual.

Publicity is Priceless but Unpredictable

Publicity is a subset of public relations, which includes employee, investor, and community relations; corporate communications; and other situations involving an organization's communications with its publics. Publicity refers to those situations when the company, product, or service receives a free mention or more in editorial content, whether it is a product review, an interview with an executive, or an event announcement. It differs from other marketing options such as advertising or direct mail in that marketers do not – and cannot – pay for it. Because the company does not purchase it, the company cannot control it, either, but because of the implied editorial endorsement that comes from this free media exposure, publicity is a powerful element of the marketing mix.

Publicity Supporting an Advertising Campaign

Princess Lines' introduction of a new liner, the *Royal Princess*, offers a good example of how publicity can support an advertising campaign. Because of its innovative design and size, the *Royal Princess* received substantial news media coverage, especially in travel and leisure magazines. This type of exposure rarely happens serendipitously and is instead the result of a well-thought out and carefully executed publicity plan coordinated by a company's public relations department. The public relations team works closely with the marketing group to make certain that the publicity campaign incorporates key brand messages and is timed to yield the maximum impact. Often, the goal is to maximize the number of impressions on a consumer in a specific time period so the publicity efforts dovetail with advertising, direct mail, and other marketing tactics.

It is important to note that publicity in global markets is as unpredictable as publicity in U.S. markets. A marketer will never know for sure if the product or service will receive exposure and will never be able to control the exposure received. Journalists might interview a competitor for an article about the product category or even make an error. This lack of control frustrates many marketers who like to orchestrate what is said about their products – as well as where and when. Those who can see past the unpredictability to the value of the credibility that comes from a media mention, however, know that publicity is an essential and affordable component of a complete marketing plan.

Of course not all publicity is good publicity. Sometimes an unpleasant development can put a company in a position to be defensive. More often than not, these situations are centered around a perception that a particular company is not a good corporate citizen in the region where it is doing business. One classic and well-known example is Nestle's promotion of infant formula in developing countries where breast milk is a more sensible approach for mothers there, since it costs nothing and is thought to provide the baby with extra health benefits. Another is the global perception that Union Carbide did not respond appropriately in the Bhopal industrial disaster.

If not handled properly – in a timely and honest manner – crisis situations can have a long-lasting negative publicity impact. Nestlé endured a multi-year international boycott of its products resulting from public perception related to its marketing efforts in Third World countries.

Sales Promotion Has International Limits

Sales promotion directed at consumers usually involves an incentive such as cents-off coupons, rebates, sampling, premiums, sweepstakes, and point-of-purchase displays. The specific sales promotion offer is often delivered to consumers through advertising, direct mail, or at point of purchase. It is increasingly popular worldwide because it allows for more targeted outreach and often provides a way for tracking effectiveness – by the number of coupons redeemed, sweepstakes entries, and so on. As in the U.S., sales promotion campaigns in global markets will not succeed without the support of retailers.

Because of the localized restrictions, truly global promotions are rare. The products that do best with the resulting customized multi-country promotions include soft drinks, liquor, airlines, credit cards, and jeans because these categories seem to span cultural divides. Successful execution involves taking local laws and regulations into account at the planning stage so there are no surprises or problems. While these global programs might be funded centrally, they will need to be implemented differently in each market so they can be linked to the company's other regional marketing efforts.

Johnson & Johnson had success with a customized, multi-national promotion campaign for its one-day Acuvue contact lens in Europe, Africa, and the Middle East. The goal for the brand was to deliver the brand's message – "enhancing everyday experiences" – and encourage consumers to schedule a vision test. To do this, it created a road show that adapted easily to various local market conditions. Professional lens fitters offered on-the-spot trials at gyms, sports clubs, and leisure centers. Devised and tested in Germany, which is one of the more restrictive countries, it was eventually executed successfully in 18 countries.

Sponsorships Should Reflect the Brand's Image

Sponsorship funds worldwide are, for the most part, directed at sports and cultural events. Sponsorship spending is spread around the world: according to the IEG Sponsorship Report, of the nearly $43.5 billion spent in 2008, North America contributed $16.8, Europe $11.7, Asia-Pacific $9.5 and Latin America $3.5 billion. Examples range from MasterCard's multi-year sponsorship of World Cup Soccer to Volvo's new sponsorship of golf's 2009 World Match Play Championship, an annual event previously sponsored since 2003 by HSBC, and mobile device BlackBerry Bold's sponsorship of the North American leg of Madonna's 2008 Sticky & Sweet Tour.

The Olympics are perhaps the best example of a truly worldwide sponsorship, as the summer and winter games allow a company to be associated with a worldwide event that has a positive image, global reach, and a proven position as a symbol of excellence. While still popular among the limited number of global brands that can afford it, some long-time supporters have ended their sponsorships because of the rising costs and difficulty establishing a return on investment. For example, major sponsor Eastman Kodak Co. ended its relationship with the event in 2008. It was a relationship that had lasted more than a century. Sponsors of the 2012 Summer Olympics in London are expected to pay as much as $80 million each.

Because the Olympic events are so high profile, companies run the risk of suffering from ambush marketing when sponsoring this unique combination of sporting competitions. Ambush marketing occurs when marketers pretend to be event sponsors when they are not, undermining the impact of category competitors who have invested worldly sums of money to be exclusive category sponsors. One of the most blatant examples involved Nike's campaign during the 1996 Summer Olympics in Atlanta, so dominating the landscape with billboards, logo "swooshes" to wave during the games, and the Nike center erected near the Olympic stadium that many consumers thought the athletic wear company was an official sponsor.

Global Cause-Related Marketing

In addition to sports and cultural events, many marketers are investing in cause-related marketing, sponsoring events or activities that position them as socially responsible community partners. This works best when the company has a social vision and a planned long-term social policy. For example, British Petroleum has sponsored a number of community-relations programs and events in Casanare, Columbia, a region where it is developing oil interests. The company invested $10 million in activities that support its business plan while contributing to the region's development. The funding is used for an entrepreneur's loan fund, providing technical training for students, supporting a center for pregnant women, reforestation, building aqueducts, and helping to create jobs in other industries.

When investing in cause-related marketing outside the home base, use the same judgment used domestically. Does the cause fit with corporate goals? Will it provide an opportunity to position the company appropriately with its various audiences or stakeholders? Is it something the company's management can support with genuine enthusiasm or is it just window-dressing? The backlash that can follow disingenuous support will cost more in reputation and loss of customers than the financial investment required.

Word of Mouth Still Sells Best

No global marketer will rely on word of mouth alone, but the reality is that word-of-mouth-marketing still sells the most worldwide. A 2007 Nielsen Company global Internet survey showed that consumers around the world still trust other consumers the most. The survey of more than 25,000 Internet users in 47 markets from Europe, Asia Pacific, the Americas and the Middle East revealed that 78 percent still trust recommendations from consumers when making buying decisions, underscoring the value of word of mouth marketing worldwide.

Here's what fuels good word of mouth no matter where products or services are marketed:

■ A quality product
■ Topnotch customer service

- A unique customer experience that people want to talk about
- Better product selection than anyone else
- Product representatives that know more than the competition's
- Good relationships with key influencers
- An advisory board that includes customers

Unfortunately for some marketers, the explosion of consumer-generated media makes bad word of mouth much easier to generate than good word of mouth. Studies show that an unhappy customer will talk directly to twice as many people about the experience as a satisfied customer will. Many of the customers who are dissatisfied are doing their complaining online, reaching far more people with their message than they could when communicating directly. Whether it is on a blog, in a forum, on a product review or sale site, or in direct feedback on the manufacturer's website, customers are not shy about sharing their product experiences and opinions.

Savvy global marketers are using this unsolicited feedback to make product improvements and to establish relationships with the customers sharing their experiences, often turning them into product evangelists. Monitoring social networking services such as Twitter (and using the same services and tools to respond to complaints) helps marketers stay current from afar on everything from what is wrong with the products to what is right. Monitoring consumer-generated media also helps them identify new or unexpected product uses in different parts of the world and leverage that knowledge in individual global markets. Reviewing consumer-generated media for comments in specific international markets before introducing products or services there can help marketers shape marketing messages and hone brand positioning in that region.

EXECUTING THE MARKETING COMMUNICATIONS PLAN

Many multinational corporations have the personnel to oversee global campaigns, but most do not have enough people on staff to execute on a local level according to local regulations and mores. Smaller companies, in particular, will need to rely on outside assistance when planning a promotional effort to support global sales. To supplement in-house expertise, consider working with a domestic agency with extensive operations in the intended market or independent local agencies in individual markets. When working with a domestic agency with overseas offices, the agency can manage and coordinate the campaign at home while the affiliate executes in the local market. Plan to work closely with the agency's local representatives in message development and media choices so that the campaign will be embraced locally and will communicate appropriately.

If the campaign will support sales efforts in several regions, the best option is usually to work with a multinational agency with offices in those regions because coordination will be less disjointed than if marketers work with several independent agencies. If the marketing communications campaign has a strong publicity component, the company will also need a public relations firm with a local presence, whether it is a multinational agency with offices in the markets targeted or a local firm in a single region. Most global agencies offer a wide range of marketing services, including advertising and public relations.

Finding a good agency overseas can be a challenge requiring a leap of faith. Most companies expanding overseas will not have existing relationships with one of the large multinational communications firms and will either need to establish a relationship with one or find local resources. Tap into the networks of global partners for referrals and network with international marketing colleagues for recommendations. Follow the same call for proposals procedure used domestically.

When hiring any type of overseas communications firm, keep in mind that the goal is to work with an organization with a proven track record with the type of program being executed, whether it is an advertising campaign, sales promotion program, or a publicity-based initiative. While many put forth impressive new business presentations, it is especially important to stay focused on the agency's relevant case studies and successes since geography will make it difficult to monitor their performance as much as you might with a domestic firm. If interviewing agencies in person, ask to meet the people who will work on the account. When checking references with other long-distance clients, ask the questions that will ensure that the agency's work style and results are a good fit for the company's goals and expectations.

While there are unique issues, regulations, and cultural expectations to address with global marketing communications, the basics remain the same regardless of the region: the marketer must know what product or service features will resonate with targeted customers and present them appropriately using the most effective channels. Local guidance can make the difference between success and failure, but the company still needs to maintain control over the marketing communications process in all regions to protect the brand's integrity. Because of the challenges presented by distance and regional regulations and cultures, hire a trusted local vendor to implement the marketing communications tactics in various regions.

FOOD FOR THOUGHT

- How can your firm manage its reputation abroad?
- How will you communicate with intermediaries and customers across geographic and psychological distances?
- Does your company plan to work with a domestic agency with overseas offices or with individual agencies in each market?
- How can marketers in the global marketplace support each other?

Further Readings

Bower, Gail. *How to Jump-start Your Sponsorship Strategy in Tough Times.* Bower & Co. Consulting, 2009.

Musgrove, Linda. *Trade Shows.* New York, NY: Penguin Group, 2009.

Richards, Rene. *Online Marketing Success Stories: Insider Secrets from the Experts Who Are Making Millions on the Internet Today.* Ocala, FL: Atlantic Publishing Company, 2006.

Usunier, Jean-Claude and Julie Lee. *Marketing Across Cultures.* Upper Saddle River, NJ: Prentice Hall, 2009.

Online Resources

World's Largest Online B2B Marketplace
www.alibaba.com/activities/ibdm/generic_lp4.html?src-ibdm_d03p0026e02r01

Global Marketers: Global Ad Spending by Marketer
http://adage.com/images/random/datacenter/2008/globalmarketing2008.pdf

E-Business Trade Roadmap
A resource for small and medium-sized enterprises new to Internet-based international trade
www.ic.gc.ca/eic/site/dir-ect.nsf/eng/uw00242.html

Biz Trade Shows
A listing of upcoming international trade shows with the option to search by industry
www.biztradeshows.com

Chapter 7

Negotiating Cultural Chasms

We continually refer to the impact of a market's culture on overseas marketing efforts. Even companies in neighboring countries find that cultural, linguistic, or regulatory differences have an effect on every aspect of their business relationships. This is just as important in the negotiation process as it is with the advertising theme, product variations, or anything else. Failure to understand the local culture and to adjust a negotiation style accordingly can lead to negotiation failures. Even the little things make a difference. For example, using a baseball analogy during meetings in Italy, where the national sport is soccer, will fall flat. When in Rome, do as the Romans do.

The two biggest dangers facing global negotiators are parochialism and stereotyping. Americans tend to be guilty of being parochial, thinking that everyone in the international business world will behave as Americans do. While business is more global, it is not necessarily more American. As George Bernard Shaw once said, "England and America are two countries separated by the same language."

Stereotypes are used to explain those behaviors that are not like ours. They can have a positive or negative impact. For example, a negative stereotype about a region's financial stability might lead negotiators to push for a low-risk payment system, whether or not it is necessary. Stereotyping can also lull us into complacency when working with regions that share our native language, as is the case with the U.S., U.K., and Australia. That complacency is not necessarily good.

The negotiating process differs from country to country and is usually different from what Americans are accustomed to. To establish rapport, exchange information, persuade, or make concessions, adjust your style or process when working in an international market. In China, for example, the ideal negotiator is someone already known and respected by a Chinese trading partner. The prevailing business philosophy in China is one of *"guanxi"* (pronounced guan-si). This refers to relationships – particularly those in business – and the expectation that the marketer will look out for and support those with whom there are relationships. Negotiators who understand *guanxi* leverage it by first establishing trust and goodwill with a wide network in the region where they do business. They then go into negotiations either with good *guanxi* with those at the table, or the power of the *guanxi* of those in their network as it extends to the other negotiating party.

At the same time, though, Chinese or Chinese-Americans working on behalf of a company can be at a disadvantage because their Chinese counterparts have higher expectations for these people who understand the local rules. The ideal team for a U.S. company might be a non-Chinese who understands the culture and an ethnic Chinese individual who generates more trust.

In any negotiating situation, if neither party is familiar with the counterpart's culture, engage an outside facilitator.

UNDERSTANDING THE STAGES OF NEGOTIATION

International business negotiating involves four stages:

1. The offer
2. Informal meetings
3. Formulating the strategy
4. Negotiating

Culture influences which of these stages are most important and how long the process will take, which might be one session or several weeks. In Northern Europe, for example, culture emphasizes the technical, the numerical, and the tested, which leads to a need for careful pre-negotiation preparation. In contrast, Southern European culture favors personal networks, social contexts, and flair, so meetings in the south might take longer, but the decision process might be faster.

The Offer

At the offer stage, both parties assess each other's needs and commitment level. Their goals and the overall atmosphere help establish initial expectations for negotiations. Understanding the goals of the other team helps negotiators identify potential compromises that will create a mutually satisfactory outcome. For example, the other firm might be motivated by a need for more cash or to shelter money. Identifying this upfront can put the marketer in a better position to help both teams meet their goals.

Other expectations or biases come into play at this point, too. For example, if organizations in a particular country have a reputation for a lack of sales persistence or shutting down when the situation grows difficult, a company in another nation might hesitate to do business with companies from that region. When this reluctance is revealed, it can be countered – *if* it is revealed. The other party might be reluctant to be honest and say, "I don't believe you will stay with us when the going gets tough," because such directness might be viewed as impolite. Good negotiators are intuitive, sensing such unspoken objectives and shaping their approaches to address them. Be alert for unspoken issues or agendas and respond accordingly.

Informal Meetings

Informal meetings are held after the seller has made the offer. Designed as get acquainted sessions where both parties can learn more about each other and details of the offer, they often take place in casual settings that are more conducive to relaxed discussion. In regions such as Asia, the Middle East, Southern Europe, and Latin America, these informal meetings can make or break the deal. For business people in these regions, the relationship can be more important than the offer, and it is at this stage that they determine whether they want to work with a company. U.S. exporters doing business in Kuwait, for example, report that their experience has taught them that establishing a strong business relationship is more important than price in their negotiations in that country.

Impatient marketers who view "handholding" and "schmoozing" as a waste of time are not the best individuals for global negotiations. At the same time, while facilitators can be employed at this stage to move the process forward, there is no substitute for the face-to-face contact that not only helps the marketer gather important market and cultural intelligence, but that also indicates respect for individuals on the other negotiating team.

Formulating the Strategy

Begin formulating a strategy before the offer is made, using the subsequent informal meetings to help sharpen the company's approach and objectives. Strategies should take into account the marketer's priorities, goals, bottom-line requirements, and bargaining positions – and as much of this as the negotiator has learned about the other side during the preliminary and later informal meetings.

Study the behavior and patterns of clients and partners when formulating a strategy. Research has shown, for example, that competitive bargainers are able to take advantage of Americans and Canadians because they are more trusting than other cultural groups. In the case of governmental buyers, too, it is important to understand that government negotiations are different from those in the public sector because government needs or requirements are often different from those in the business sector. Factor all of this into the strategy.

Note, too, that negotiators might not behave as expected, because they might be adapting to the other style. If this happens, be prepared to refine the strategy.

Negotiating

The negotiating approach used will depend on the cultural background and business traditions in the country where the negotiations take place. The competitive and collaborative approaches are the most common. In a competitive strategy, companies are primarily concerned about getting a favorable outcome at the expense of the other party – something of an "I win, you lose" outcome. A collaborative approach focuses on mutual needs, with more of a win–win outcome that capitalizes on the strengths of each group but might involve some compromise on both parts. Anglo Saxons tend to prefer a win–lose approach while Latins opt for the win–win.

There are often difficulties when individuals from high context cultures negotiate with those from low context cultures. Cultures that rely on high context communications tend to observe and learn from nonverbal and verbal cues that supplement what is actually said. People in low context cultures are more literal, expecting others to learn what they need from what is said. High context cultures tend to value the group over individuality, and are more common in Eastern nations and those with less racial diversity. France, Japan, Saudi Arabia, and China are considered to be high context cultures. Low context cultures include those in North America. When these differences are not understood, acknowledged, and taken into account, misunderstandings or confusion can result.

When selecting the location for negotiations, common sense would suggest a neutral location as the fairest option, and this is indeed the choice favored by many, but it is not always an option. In those situations, one becomes the host. When hosting the negotiations on home turf, the host does enjoy that home court advantage with its lower psychological risk because of the familiar surroundings. But being in an unfamiliar location can create culture shock for guests. Add pressure by manipulating the situation with delays or additional demands, and the pressure felt by guests intensifies.

A host looking for the best outcome possible for all parties works to build relationships and reduce stress by putting considerate behavior ahead of speedy timelines. Global travelers understand the challenges presented by jet lag and make certain that they schedule meetings so that their traveling colleagues have time to recover from international travel before negotiating. Early morning breakfast sessions after a colleague crosses multiple time zones is rarely advisable. Some cultures believe it is essential to entertain their guests into the evening, forgetting that those guests might need rest after traveling or perhaps are not accustomed to this approach. This is not an opportunity to wear out the opponent and then take advantage. It is an opportunity to build the connections that will generate a long-lasting business partnership.

Visiting teams are, of course less likely to walk out even when the scheduling or other behavior seems manipulative; as a matter of fact, the pressure is on them to make concessions to achieve an agreement. The advantage of being the visitor, though, is that the visitor has an opportunity to see the counterpart's facilities first-hand and learn more about the operation and the culture.

NEGOTIATIONS IN OTHER COUNTRIES

We sometimes have to do things overseas that we would not do at home because what is acceptable and expected in our domestic markets might not work elsewhere – and vice versa. Bridging the cultural chasm is essential for success in negotiations, but it has the potential to offer a much bigger impact than that. The continuing efforts of marketers to understand cultural issues help them identify terminology that is persuasive, but, more than that, these efforts help secure important assimilations of value systems.

Meeting face-to-face generates a global connectedness that helps businesses on a personal level, but helps cultures on a global level. This enhanced "one world" sense can contribute to undermining support for terrorists, who polarize and alienate, rather than unite, world cultures. These suggestions regarding different styles for different regions will help negotiators adjust to the style of the host country.

Learn as much as possible about the other group's traditions and culture first. Ask consultants and local representatives to help identify the critical behaviors or details that can make or break a relationship. For example, in highly structured societies such as those of Korea, people respect age and position, so do the same.

Rituals are important and should be respected. For example, in Asia, a first encounter must include the exchange of business cards. Those who have not packed them should get replacements printed immediately. Add a translation to the back of the card so it can be read in the other group's native language. The exchange of business cards is so important that some airlines offer to print the cards as a service to their business travelers when customers make a reservation for travel to regions where it is a common ritual.

Show respect by reading cards as they are received. Demonstrate the significance of the card's symbolism by holding it with both hands before tucking it carefully away in a protected location, such as an inner jacket pocket, card holder, or wallet.

Use the company's best people. Some companies make the mistake of assigning global negotiation to their less talented players. This could indicate that the organization either is not concerned about the outcome or does not understand the significance of a successful outcome. Because of the importance of business partner relationships and the impact a successful contract has on the company's overall health, the negotiating team should feature a company's top talent.

Use a team. Bringing in specialists will strengthen the company's position and ensure that all points of view get proper attention. Expanding the team also allows less experienced participants to observe and learn more while participating less than they could without the backup. In addition, it helps a company match the firepower of the other group. While Western negotiation teams tend to have just two to four people, Chinese teams might have as many as ten.

Match titles. Negotiators will be more effective in certain regions if they make certain that the "rank" of the most senior member of their team matches the most senior member of the counterpart's team. It can be an important sign of respect. Titles sometimes offer surprising leverage abroad, as well. For example, when meeting the chairman of the U.S. Democratic Party in China, people respond with greater respect than one might expect and certainly with more respect than is offered in the U.S. This is because Mao Tse-tung, the remarkably powerful former leader of the Communist Party in China, was also a party "chairman."

Keep the team's disagreements private. Just as parents work to present a unified front with their children, negotiators need to bring a single voice to the conference room. Team conflicts will exist, of course, but they should be imperceptible and kept out of the negotiating room. Otherwise, the team could be subject to a competitive "divide and conquer" strategy.

Speak the language, even if it is just a few words. In an ideal situation, the negotiator speaks the customer's language fluently. If both teams are using English, but only one team has native English speakers, that team should be careful to avoid jargon and colloquialisms.

Making the effort to learn the language of a potential partner shows commitment, good faith, and sincerity, even if all the team masters is a few greetings or phrases. As international marketing becomes more important, companies will hire people who can speak several languages, particularly those of countries where the company plans to do business. These individuals can become part of the negotiating team, serving as translators when there are language barriers. There are drawbacks associated with using translators or interpreters, though. They impede spontaneity. Their presence can offend an executive who believes he speaks the other language fluently. The companies might be discussing confidential information they do not want to share with an outsider. On the other hand, the fact that they slow things down can provide each team with time to give more thought to what is being said.

Anyone involved with international business will want to learn at least one foreign language. This exposes the learner to new cultures, new thinking, and new ways of doing things – all of which better prepares the marketer for the global marketing experience.

Watch body language, too. Sitting in what might be considered a comfortable position might be interpreted in China as a lack of control over the body and, therefore, a lack of control over the mind.

Find out who has the final decision on the contract. While North American and European negotiators often arrive with the authority to sign a contract, their counterparts in the Far East seldom – if ever – do. Announcing that the negotiators do not have the authority to finalize the contract rarely has a positive effect but can be useful if the goal is to probe the buyer's motives. Verify who has authority and the obstacles the negotiator might face in reaching a decision.

Be patient. In China and certain other countries, negotiations can take three times as long as those in the U.S. and Europe. Showing impatience in certain countries, including Brazil and Thailand, can actually prolong negotiations, not speed them up.

Consider the first offer in context of the culture. U.S. negotiators tend to start the process close to what they believe is a fair offer, while Chinese negotiators are more likely to start with unreasonable demands and a rigid posture.

Understand the negotiating ethics of the region. Being shrewd is valued in some parts of the world but frowned upon elsewhere. While Russian negotiators might frustrate those from Western cultures with last-minute changes or requests for concessions, it is how they do business. Common complaints about ethics in negotiations center around traditional competitive bargaining, false promises, attacking the opponent's network, misrepresentation of position, and inappropriate information gathering.

Do not be afraid of silence. U.S. business people often interpret silence and inaction as negative signs, rushing in to fill the vacuum with premature modifications. Savvy counter-negotiators know to use this ploy to win lower prices or better deals. Japanese negotiators, for example, remain silent because they have learned that by not reacting, they can get their counterparts to offer more favorable terms. The Finns, on the other hand, might sit through a meeting expressionless with their hands folded. This is actually how they show respect and indicate they are listening carefully.

Avoid confrontation. Negotiating partners might view any insistence on answers or an outcome as a threat. In some markets, negotiating is seen as a way of establishing long-term commercial relationships rather than as an event with well-defined winners and losers, so forcing a conclusion can cause problems. Confrontations also might cause a counterpart to lose face, which is considered a particularly serious insult in the Far East.

Keep the big picture in mind. Do not make concessions until all issues have been discussed. Concessions traditionally come at the end of the bargaining. This is especially true when it comes to price. Agreeing on price too soon could lead to pressure to offer too many extras for that price.

Be prepared. A counterpart might reject a price at the outset in the hope of getting an upper hand or obtaining concessions later on. These concessions might include discounts, an improved product, better terms, or other demands that are not in the company's best interest. Prepare for this in advance by knowing as much as possible about the target market and customer, using that knowledge to develop counterproposals.

If a counterpart says better offers are available, request more details on those offers. This lets the marketer provide an informed analysis on why the company's product is superior. Double check competitive prices to see if they do, indeed, reflect market prices. In addition, if a first offer is accepted without comment, check the numbers to make sure there is not a mistake.

Be clear on the final work product. What constitutes a contract might vary from region to region. In many parts of the world, legal contracts are not needed and, in fact, referring to legal counsel might suggest to a counterpart that the relationship is in trouble. In some regions, an oral agreement and a handshake are considered enough, but this approach can leave both parties open to problems. The issue is not that one or the other is not trustworthy. The issue is that unless the agreement is in writing, the parties might not be completely clear on what is expected of each side.

When an agreement is reached, it is critical that both parties leave with a clear understanding of the terms. In some cases, a signed written agreement is enough but in the case of large-scale projects, companies will need a longer document outlining details that include the responsibilities of each party.

The Cultural Faux Pas

There are a number of resources available to help international marketers avoid unpleasant cultural mistakes when traveling overseas. Website ExecutivePlanet.com is a wiki-like resource featuring a country-by-country list of business etiquette guidelines. Use this site or another reference resource to become familiar with the destination country or the mores of the people being entertained. Here are a few examples of potential pitfalls to help those involved appreciate the importance of understanding the culture they are dealing with:

■ *Gifts.* It is customary to exchange gifts in Thailand on the second meeting but gift-giving is considered a bribe in China. Avoid black or white wrapping paper in India because both are considered unlucky. Do not offend the gift-giver there by opening a gift in front of them, because that would not be polite, but do give thanks.

- *Names.* Do not use first names with Japanese colleagues. Use their title or their last name and the prefix "san," as in "Czinkota san." It is the equivalent of "Mr." or "Ms." The use of san is not appropriate for spouses or children, though. In Mexico, a business card will include the surname of the individual's father followed by the mother's surname, but it is the father's surname that is used when addressing the individual. This means that Senor Jorge Raul Rodriguez Mendez is Senor Rodriguez, not Senor Mendez.

- *Touching.* Do not hug people in the Netherlands or Russia. And by all means, do not give the German Chancellor a shoulder rub, as former President George Bush did for Angela Merkel during one of his trips abroad. Public displays of affection are verboten in India, too, as actor Richard Gere discovered when he kissed an Indian actress on the cheek several times at a charity event – the government issued a warrant for his arrest on obscenity charges.

- *Hand signs.* In countries such as India, using the left hand for anything is cause for concern, so do not do it. In Indonesia, pounding the fist into the palm of the other hand could be considered an obscene gesture.

- *Social situations.* Do not bring up business topics during social engagements in Australia and Thailand. Leave it to local hosts to decide if business conversations are appropriate. In Australia, make sure that everyone takes a turn at buying a round of drinks. It is not wise to directly reject a social invitation in India. Even if it is not possible to attend, saying "I hope I can be there" is more acceptable. When doing business with a Scot, do not ask personal questions, even though that might be how to begin to establish a relationship with domestic colleagues.

- *Dining out.* In Muslim regions, people believe the left hand is dirty, so using it to eat is inappropriate and disrespectful. In all regions, never refuse to eat the local delicacy, no matter how unpleasant it might seem.

In the home country, it is wise to approach the negotiation process with as much market intelligence as possible so that the negotiation team is not caught off guard, surprised, or taken advantage of. When negotiating with international partners, the team needs this same information as well as cultural knowledge, awareness, and sensitivity. In international situations, there is greater risk of undermining a position by committing a cultural faux pas but at the same time, counterparts face that risk, too.

FOOD FOR THOUGHT

■ How does your company currently gather data on markets and consumers? How can you improve this process?

■ What are some ways to get to know individuals and consultants who know the state of the market and the competitive environment?

■ Language familiarity is one of the best ways to demonstrate commitment and sincerity. How can your company encourage language learning?

■ What is your company's perspective on concessions? How do you ensure that the big picture is not lost?

Further Readings

Axtell, Roger. *Essential Do's and Taboos: The Complete Guide to International Business and Leisure Travel.* New York, NY: John Wiley & Sons, 2007.

Jolles, Robert. *The Way of the Road Warrior: Lessons in Business and Life from the Road Most Traveled.* New York, NY: John Wiley & Sons, 2006.

Martin, Jeanette, and Chaney Lillian. *Global Business Etiquette: A Guide to International Communication and Customs.* Westport, CT: Praeger Publishers, 2006.

Requejo, William H. and John Graham. *Global Negotiation.* New York, NY: Palgrave Macmillan, 2008.

Online Resources

Tips for Business Travel Abroad
www.bizmove.com/export/m7i.htm

Going Global: A New Era in Cross-Cultural Communications
www.going-global.com/articles/a_new_era_in_cross-cultural_communications.htm

US-China Business Council: Chinese Business Etiquette
www.uschina.org/info/china-briefing-book/section6a.html

World Biz: Country-specific reports on doing successful business worldwide
www.worldbiz.com/index.php

Chapter 8

Positioning the Product and Brand

Products and services marketed in other parts of the world often need to be adjusted or modified to meet the needs of global customers and local regulations or requirements. The challenge when looking to maximize export performance is to maintain a balance between the advantages of standardized products and those of localization. Manufacturers do not want to spend so much money on changes to meet local needs that global exporting or manufacturing is no longer profitable enough to be worth the effort. In addition, it is not wise to view product adaptations in the context of a single market, because modifications for one region might also apply in others, including the domestic location.

ADAPT, REMAIN THE SAME, OR STANDARDIZE?

Once a company has decided to go global, the first question concerns whether product modifications are needed and if so, which ones. Certain products are good candidates for standardization while others are not. Consumer nondurables, including food products, are the most sensitive to differences in national tastes and habits, making them more likely to need changes for various markets. Consumer durables such as cameras and home electronics are less subject to regional issues. Industrial products tend to be shielded from cultural influences, but government regulations or restraints often force substantial modifications.

There are four product options when approaching international markets:

1. Selling the product as is
2. Modifying products for different countries or regions
3. Designing new products for global markets
4. Incorporating all market differences into one flexible product design and introducing a global product.

Many companies use several of these options simultaneously. A large consumer products company might have in its product line global, regional, and purely local products. They can later introduce some of the products developed for one market into others. For example, the Levi Strauss line of Dockers casual wear originated at the company's Argentine unit and was applied by its Japanese subsidiary before being adopted in the U.S. and becoming that country's top-selling brand in the category.

There are pluses and minuses for both standardizing and adapting. The advantages of standardization include cost-savings in production and marketing. Economic integration is often a driving force behind standardization, especially in Europe, as marketers are standardizing many of their marketing approaches. These include unified branding and packaging that products use across many markets, which also contributes to better branding in global regions where people travel from market to market. Just as an American expects a drink purchased at a Starbucks coffee shop in San Diego to taste like one from his home Starbucks in Boston, the Italian tourist visiting London has similar expectations. At the same time, food is regional, not global, so the food sold in the San Diego Starbucks might differ from what is available in a Venice shop.

Similarly, facing the same competitors in the world's major markets will add to the pressure to have a worldwide approach to marketing. Coca Cola and Colgate toothpaste have universal products and marketing strategies. Still, the argument that the world is becoming more homogenized might actually be true for only a limited number of products that already have universal brand recognition combined with minimal requirements for use – most anybody can figure out how to open a bottle or can of Coke and drink the contents. For most marketers, demand and usage conditions will vary enough to require some changes in the product or service.

Products such as steel, chemicals, and agricultural equipment tend to be less culture sensitive and require fewer modifications than consumer products. Similarly, scientific instruments or medical equipment are generally universally accepted as is. Within the consumer products sector, people typically accept luxury goods and personal care products such as the Colgate toothpaste just mentioned without changes, while food products are less standardized. Consumer goods generally require more product adaptation because of their close connection to the culture. The level of change needed depends not only on culture but also on economic conditions in the target market. Low incomes might require offering a simplified version of a product so that it costs less to make and buy.

Unilever Customizes for India

Unilever saw an opportunity among low-income consumers in India who wanted to buy the company's high-end detergents and personal care products, but could not afford them. The company responded by developing low-cost packaging and other options that allowed it to offer dramatically less expensive options. This flexibility not only opened a new market for the company, but also allowed it to develop brand loyalty that consumers could take with them when their income increased and they could afford higher-end products from the same manufacturer.

Regional norms have an impact on products such as detergent, too. For example, while in the U.S. people are accustomed to using both hot and cold water for laundry, some regions use only cold water and require detergents that will get clothing clean in those conditions.

Even companies with standardized global products have regional versions. Coca Cola offers many beverages that are sold only in their country of origin, Colgate sells a spicy-flavored toothpaste in the Middle East, and McDonald's offers mutton burgers in India. In addition, companies often create entirely new products to meet local tastes. For example,

IKEA makes sleeper sofas specifically for the U.S. market, where that type of furniture is in demand.

By contrast, firms are also working more to develop global products that incorporate regional differences and needs into one design. Rather than take a product created in one market and try to sell it as is in all other markets, these marketers gather information from the markets it wants to serve, and incorporates the features or attributes needed into one product that will work well in all target markets. This also allows them to standardize certain elements of the product's marketing and branding while emphasizing regional product attributes in different markets. They are beginning to take regional preferences into account with their marketing, too. Studies of facial features have shown that people in different cultures have preferences with regards to cheekbone levels, nose sizes, or eyebrow thickness. As a result, companies are starting to use different computer-generated faces in their advertisements to appeal to customers in different regions.

For most companies, the key question involved in whether and how to adapt a product is whether the effort is worth the cost involved. Studies show that the majority of products require some amount of modification. Most companies need the costs for these changes to be moderate. Required changes typically affect packaging, measurement units, labeling, product features, instructions, and, to a lesser degree, logos and brand names. All products have to conform to the marketing environment so that the product is competitive. Conforming usually includes matching competitive offers, catering to customer preferences, and meeting demands of local distribution systems.

Many apply the "principle of postponement," delaying customization as far into the production and marketing cycle as possible for a variety of reasons. Paint sold at the retail level is one example. Rather than offer a limited number of standard paint colors or warehouse cans offering many colors, shades, and variations, stores stock only one color – white. Varying amounts of colored pigments are added when the customer is ready to purchase to get the range of options that consumers expect and appreciate.

It is easier to decide how to adapt after the company has experience in the international market involved. The more the company learns about local market characteristics, the more it is able to identify similarities in various markets and to determine ways to standardize both the product and its marketing.

UNDERSTANDING MARKET FACTORS THAT HAVE AN IMPACT ON ADAPTATIONS

There are three categories affecting adaptation and several factors within each category that have an impact, as shown in Table 8.1. It helps to understand each of the categories and characteristics in a global context.

Regional, Country, or Local Characteristics

Government regulations often generate the most rigid product requirements. Companies have no choice but to obey them, but they can work

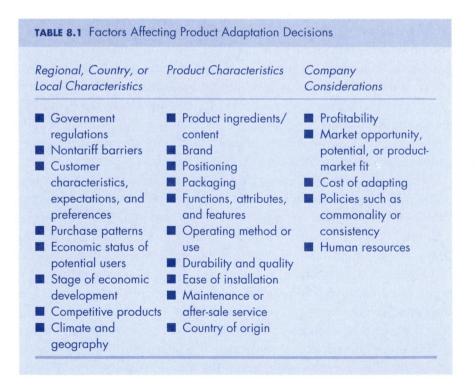

TABLE 8.1 Factors Affecting Product Adaptation Decisions

Regional, Country, or Local Characteristics	Product Characteristics	Company Considerations
■ Government regulations	■ Product ingredients/content	■ Profitability
■ Nontariff barriers	■ Brand	■ Market opportunity, potential, or product-market fit
■ Customer characteristics, expectations, and preferences	■ Positioning	■ Cost of adapting
■ Purchase patterns	■ Packaging	■ Policies such as commonality or consistency
■ Economic status of potential users	■ Functions, attributes, and features	■ Human resources
■ Stage of economic development	■ Operating method or use	
■ Competitive products	■ Durability and quality	
■ Climate and geography	■ Ease of installation	
	■ Maintenance or after-sale service	
	■ Country of origin	

to generate changes by lobbying, either directly or through industry associations. Government regulations are probably the single most important factor contributing to product modifications and, because of the red tape involved, are often the most cumbersome and frustrating to deal with. Google found this out in China, when the government there forced the U.S. company to establish a new site, Google.cn, with contents censored by the government. It helps to monitor trendsetting markets such as Sweden because other countries might adopt their restrictions or regulations in the future.

Nontariff barriers are usually in place to keep nondomestic products out or to protect domestic producers. They usually concern elements outside the core product – product standards, testing or approval procedures, subsidies for local products, and bureaucratic red tape. For example, some countries require all product marketing and promotion to use the local language, whether it is in an advertisement, the instructions, or on an invoice. Japan's product testing and certification requirements have made entry into that market difficult, if not impossible. Globally, an international trade agreement announced in 2000 requires genetically modified food to be labeled as such, which means that farmers have to separate these increasingly controversial foods from the overall supply. The cost of compliance with regulations that often seem arbitrary or unnecessarily difficult can be high, so small companies with limited resources often simply give up.

Customer characteristics, expectations, and preferences are as important as governmental influences, but usually easier to understand. Often, even when the benefits sought by customers are the same, the product needs changes. Tefal, a world leader in cookware, accommodates the smaller storage spaces in Japanese homes by selling pans with detachable handles. Product decisions made by marketers are especially affected by local behavior, tastes, attitudes, and traditions – all reflecting the product's need to secure customer approval. This group of variables is the most difficult to quantify but is essential to the decision to sell in a given market. Sometimes, it is adopt or perish – the U.S. Mint has been unable to penetrate the Asian market with its gold coins, because they are 22-carat products in a market that values 24-carat gold.

Consumption patterns, psychosocial characteristics, and general cultural criteria determine product expectations. Answer all of the 23 questions in the three categories in Figure 8.1 to help analyze the situation. They will ensure that the company addresses all necessary points. This type of review and analysis helped Dunkin' Donuts to position its products as snacks and desserts in Brazil, where people tend to skip breakfast. Adding local fruit fillings such as papaya and guava add to the appeal of the snacks in that region.

Sometimes, all that is needed is a change in a product's positioning. Diet Coke has been renamed Coke Light in many markets to take the focus off losing weight and place emphasis on the idea that the product helps people look and feel their best. It is a subtle shift, but one that is important. On the other hand, sometimes the positioning remains the same while the product changes. Unilever's shampoo brand, Timotei, is positioned in all markets as a natural and gentle alternative, even though the formulation is changed for the hair types of different markets.

Purchase patterns refer to specific and repeated behaviors of customers which are useful to be analyzed by suppliers in preparing the product offering.

Economic station of users addresses the relative position of those who actually engage in the consumption process with a particular good or service. Given varying income levels and subsequently, varying prices around the globe, the economic station of a user may well be quite different dependent on location. For example, in a highly industrialized nation, the user of a bicycle may typically be a middle-class executive who seeks a work out on weekends, while in a developing nation the same bicycle may well be the principal means of transportation for the family.

It is also important to take a region's *economic development* into account. Advanced economies have buyers who are in a better position to buy and demand more sophisticated products and product versions. Keeping the economic realities in mind helps determine the potential for selling certain types of products and services. Products that are affordable will be more accessible. Swedish apparel manufacturer H&M proved this when it successfully entered the U.S. market in 2000 with trendy women's clothing priced low enough for the typical teenager's budget.

Developing markets sometimes require backward innovation to meet the region's lower income level by providing a simplified version of a product. In emerging economies, products often need to be simple and

I. Consumption Patterns

   A. Pattern of Purchase
1. Is the product or service purchased by relatively the same consumer income group from one country to another?
2. Do the same family members motivate the purchase in all target countries?
3. Do the same family members dictate brand choice in all target countries?
4. Do most consumers expect a product to have the same appearance?
5. Is the purchase rate the same regardless of the country?
6. Are most of the purchases made at the same kind of retail outlet?
7. Do most consumers spend the same amount of time making the purchase?

   B. Pattern of Usage
1. Do most consumers use the product or service for the same purpose or purposes?
2. Is the product or service used in different amounts from one target area or country to another?
3. Is the method of preparation the same in all target countries?
4. Is the product or service used along with other products or services?

II. Psychosocial Characteristics

   A. Attitudes toward the Product or Service
1. Are the basic psychological, social, and economic factors motivating the purchase and use of the product the same for all target countries?
2. Are the advantages and disadvantages of the product or service in the minds of consumers basically the same from one country to another?
3. Does the symbolic content of the product or service differ from one country to another?
4. Is the psychic cost of purchasing or using the product or service the same, whatever the country?
5. Does the appeal of the product or service for a cosmopolitan market differ from one market to another?

   B. Attitudes toward the Brand
1. Is the brand name equally known and accepted in all target countries?
2. Are customer attitudes toward the package basically the same?
3. Are customer attitudes toward pricing basically the same?
4. Is brand loyalty the same throughout target countries for the product or service under consideration?

III. Cultural Criteria

1. Does society restrict the purchase and/or use of the product or service to a particular group?
2. Is there a stigma attached to the product or service?
3. Does the usage of the product or service interfere with tradition in one or more of the targeted markets?

Source: Adapted from Steuart Henderson Britt, "Standardizing Marketing for the International Market," *Columbia Journal of World Business* 9 (Winter 1974): 32–40. Copyright © 1974 Columbia Journal of World Business. Reprinted with permission.

FIGURE 8.1   Analyzing Cultural and Psychological Factors Affecting Product Adaptation

easily operated in harsh environments. India's TVS Electronics recognized this when designing its all-in-one business machine for retailers in developing markets. Part cash register and part computer, it tolerates heat, dust, and power outages, making it an appealing and practical product. Buying power in developing economies also has an impact on packaging – companies often sell products such as cigarettes and razor blades individually so that those with limited incomes can afford them. On the other hand, companies also sell food mixes in larger packages that contain more servings per container in these regions because it is economical and suits family needs.

Monitoring *competitive products* is just as important in international markets as it is domestically. Analyzing competitors' offerings can help identify holes in the market or segments to avoid. It will also help establish baselines for market penetration and spending. In many markets, a marketer will be competing with global players and local manufacturers while overcoming traditional purchasing patterns and the security they provide. Address these issues by offering a niche-breaking product adjusted to local needs.

Climate and geography usually have an effect on everything from the core product to its packaging and special features. Chocolate products are a good example of this. Because chocolate melts so easily, many companies prevent melting or waste by either making product adjustments or controlling how retailers display their candy. While one manufacturer provides its own display cases, another only distributes to air-conditioned outlets. When vendors sell a product on street corners, as is common in countries in developing economies, marketers use special varnish on the wrappers so the coloring does not fade in the sun and create an unattractive package.

Product Characteristics

Manufacturers sometimes need to adjust *product ingredients and contents* according to local tastes or needs. Always make sure that products do not contain ingredients that might violate legal requirements or social or religious customs. Formaldehyde, for example, is banned in Japan, so DEP Corporation, a U.S. maker of hair and skin products using that ingredient, has to be certain that products shipped to Japan contain no traces of it. In Islamic countries, manufacturers of products made with animal fats replace those fats with alternatives. Technology assists with marketing, making it easier for entertainment companies to provide movie product placements that reflect those that are available locally so the films are more relevant to local viewers. For example, the Dr. Pepper logo in the U.S. version of *Spiderman 2* was replaced overseas with the logo for Mirinda, a fruit-flavored soft drink that is more common outside the U.S.

Brands are one of the most easily standardized elements in the product mix. Standardized *branding* is strongest in culturally similar markets. For the U.S., this means Canada and the United Kingdom. Establishing a worldwide brand is difficult, but globalizing brands presents significant opportunities to cut costs and achieve economies of scale. Brand loyalty translates into profits, even when the branded product is not superior.

Global Product Name Tips

Brand names do not always travel well; semantic variations can hinder a product overseas. To avoid problems, NameLab, a company that develops and tests company and product names, suggests the following:

- *Translation.* For example, Little Pen Inc. would become La Petite Plume, S.A.
- *Transliteration.* Test the existing brand name for connotative meaning in the language of the intended market.
- *Transparency.* Use this to develop a new, essentially meaningless brand name to minimize trademark issues, transliteration problems, and translation complexities.
- *Transculture.* Give the product a foreign language name. For example, no matter where they originate, many vodkas have Russian sounding names while perfume names often sound French.

Product positioning reflects the focus of a good or service on a specific market group, offering to fulfill specific wants or needs. The positioning often depends on the minds of consumers, who are the ones ultimately deciding what purpose the product serves for them.

Packaging is responsible for getting a product to the international markets in the product's intended form – undamaged and appealing. While one might be able to keep the same packaging used in domestic markets, the ultimate package will depend on transportation modes as well as transit time and conditions. Exporters of food products usually need to use more expensive packaging and transportation modes because of the time and distance involved. Theft is another issue, so some shippers use nothing but shipping codes on outside packaging so thieves will not know from the outside what is on the inside. Reduce damage during rough handling by including handling instructions in the destination language on the shipping container.

Packaging also has a promotional role, with the biggest issue involving labeling. Several countries require bilingual labels – including Canada (French and English), Belgium (French and Flemish), and Finland (Finnish and Swedish). Even when the market has a single language, there are still nuances involved when translating from the domestic market language to the global market. Some governments require more information on labels than others. For guidance, review government guidelines and study competitors' labels to see what they are doing.

Usability and aesthetics are ongoing concerns everywhere. In times of austerity, consumers who might have to cut back on the quality of products purchased often like to make up for it by buying items with a better aesthetic value as indicated by the packaging. When it comes to appearance, African countries prefer bold colors, but flag colors are either preferred or not allowed, making local market research essential. Red is associated with death or witchcraft in some countries while black is seen as suggesting quality in others. Size varies according to purchasing patterns and market conditions. For example, some countries use soft drink four-packs instead of six-packs because of difference in storage capacities. Some numbers have negative connotations – in Japan, the ideogram for the number four can also be read as "death" – so marketers avoid using four-packs there.

Some marketers find solutions for packaging challenges while monitoring packaging innovations in other parts of the world. The widely accepted aseptic Tetra Pak container for juices and milk was created in

Sweden and is now used in more than 160 countries worldwide. The increasing trend to make packaging more environmentally friendly is having an impact now on global products, as consumers demand less waste and manufacturers find ways to be responsible. Germany has the toughest regulations in this area, requiring that all packaging be reusable or recyclable.

Functions, attributes, and features might need to change according to customer requirements. Marketers often make sophisticated products more affordable and appropriate for emerging markets by offering product versions with fewer bells and whistles – think of the iPod classic versus the iPod touch. Product characteristics valued in one market might be worthless in another. When Snapple beverages were introduced in Japan, for example, the bottle had to be smaller to fit with local preferences, the sweet taste needed reformulation, and the manufacturer had to address the negative connotation of the characteristic sediment in the bottom of the bottle.

Sometimes local conditions have an impact on a product's *operating method or use*, as in the case with products that use electricity. While local government representatives and industry resources can be helpful in this area, the best options include observing competitive products and having local individuals use and test the products. Products that rely heavily on the written or spoken word, including books, have to be adapted so they are usable in countries where a different language is used.

The environment in which they are used also often prompts product changes. French subway ticket vending machines have to be waterproof because they are hosed down. Marketers often benefit from watching how their products are used in global markets. Turbo Tek Inc. uncovered new markets for its hose attachment originally intended for washing cars when it saw Dutch customers using it to wash windows and siding on their homes and the Japanese used it for cleaning bamboo.

Durability and quality often come into play when a company cannot compete on price alone. Government and consumer panel endorsements often provide an important competitive advantage. Auto manufacturers exporting to the U.S. have boosted sales in part by scoring well in the J.D. Power and Associates rankings, then using the results in their advertising and promotion. Exporters are also realizing that they have to meet international quality standards to compete for business abroad and to win contracts from multinational corporations. European buyers are increasingly requiring compliance with international ISO 9000 quality standards. German electronics giant Siemens pushes for this type of compliance because the company saves money when it does not have to test parts provided by vendors.

Ease of installation can depend on the skills of the installers and the resources available to them. Products sold in some markets might need alternations to accommodate the tools most readily available for installation or the installation environment. Test the product and its needs by observing potential end-users as they attempt installation and make adjustments accordingly.

Maintenance or after-sales service can be challenging with products sold overseas. Manufacturers offering products that need regular maintenance or service often have to train personnel and operate overseas repair centers capable of upholding the company's standards. This is essential because ineffective repairs can tarnish a brand's image. Other challenges include situations when customers use the product overseas in new and unintended ways. For example, Saudi Arabia imports snowplows from the U.S. to remove sand, not snow, from driveways. This can create interesting maintenance challenges on products made to withstand moisture, not grit, and the manufacturer must meet those challenges if it wants to continue exporting to that market.

A product's *country of origin*, identified on the label as "Made in (country)," has a considerable influence on product perceptions. This is good news for products made in some countries and bad news for others, as that perception can either help or hurt sales. When a home country has a good reputation, leverage that by displaying the country name prominently on the label. When the country name will hurt a product's reputation, downplay the origin by using a brand name that is reminiscent of a nationality with a better reputation in the product category or by finding a prestigious partner with a shining image that will overshadow the country of origin. When the country of origin does matter to customers, monitor perceptions on an ongoing basis. These country-of-origin effects lessen as customers become more informed and as countries work to help exports by improving their images.

Company Considerations

Product adaptation is an international marketing tool that serves a variety of strategic requirements. In addition to the need to cater to market differences and compete effectively with others in these markets, product adaptation also helps a company reach its internal goals more effectively. Companies usually end up asking, "Is it worth it?" The answer depends on the company's ability to control costs, accurately estimate *market opportunities*, and secure *profitability* in the long term. It is possible to recoup adaptation costs through export performance, but there is no question that the decision to adapt – even the decision to export – has risks. Some handle this by taking the stand that sales of a standard product might be small to start but grow over time.

However, the decision that was once "Can we afford to do it?" is now "Can we afford not to do it?" Before making changes, conduct a thorough market analysis with formal market research and product testing. From the financial standpoint, some organizations have a policy of requiring specific return-on-investment levels when calculating the *cost of adapting*, while others let the requirement vary as a function of the market and the amount of time there. Regardless, most companies aim for *consistency* in their marketing efforts, which requires that all products fit in terms of quality, price, and user perceptions.

Marketers want to remember that since people make the decisions, having the right people – the *human resources* to both lead and execute – is important to the adaptation decision. Companies dealing with these issues need to develop or hire people who are willing to take calculated risks and who know about existing market conditions. Global companies usually benefit from having managers from different countries. This brings to the decision-making process a depth and breadth of experience and expertise that is needed to make informed decisions regarding standardization and adaptation.

GLOBAL PRODUCT AND BRAND MANAGEMENT

As global retailers gain more power, marketers might feel more pressure to have brands for customers who are often more global themselves, sharing increasingly similar tastes, preferences, and consumption habits. While some believe that global brands add value by making the consumer feel more cosmopolitan or sophisticated, the reality is that the marketer needs to get something from the relationship, too. Companies with global brands should benefit from the scale and scope that having a presence in multiple markets offers. Benefits to the company can include a more focused and profitable product portfolio, "best practice" sharing among regions, and manufacturing economies.

During market entry, the firm has to ensure that the brand is known abroad – the fact that a brand is soaring at home does not mean it will automatically enjoy global acceptance. At the same time, it is important to consider the wide footprint of all brand-related impressions. For example, a Turkish audience might be well informed about German products because they have been watching German television for years. While this type of brand knowledge transfer might make entering a new market easier, it might also make it harder to develop independent strategies for new markets.

Developing and managing a product portfolio in the global marketplace is both a challenge and an opportunity. Market conditions might require changes in individual product features, but companies want to manage products and product lines for the greatest possible effect globally, regionally, and locally. It is important to understand how the product development process can take into account the globalization of markets without compromising features considered essential by local markets. At the same time, marketers should know how to use worldwide resources to exploit opportunities in product markets. Many strategic product decisions, including branding, benefit from worldwide experience applied in a local context.

How to Develop Global Products

Global product development is similar to domestic product development. It starts with ideas. While in the past these ideas might have come strictly from people in the home market, global product thinking draws on input from intermediaries, franchisees, and overseas competitors. Examine competitive concepts from abroad with an eye toward modifying and improving them to meet the needs of another market – even the domestic market.

For a number of companies, especially those that manufacture industrial goods, customers are their best idea sources. Chat rooms and comments on social networking sites have become increasingly interesting sources of fresh thinking, as customers talk to each other about how they use products or about features they would like to see added. Government procurement requests can trigger ideas for product modifications that will make it possible to apply for a contract.

With a list of products in mind, screen them on market, technical, and financial criteria just as the company would domestically. Is the market large enough? Can it be penetrated? Can the product be mass produced? Can the company produce and market it profitably? Sometimes, a company can achieve the same goals by adjusting its view of the existing product line. For example, cereal manufacturers still sell their products in countries where people do not eat breakfast simply by repositioning their products as snack foods. Do not toss ideas that are not feasible at the moment – keep them in a searchable idea database because they might be marketable later.

All development phases – idea generation, screening, product and process development, scale-up, and commercialization – should be global in nature with input from all affected markets. Original product designs can be adapted for individual markets easily and inexpensively later on if necessary. Computer-aided design facilitates this by making it possible for companies to design products so that they meet most standards and requirements around the world, with only minor modifications on a country-by-country basis. Consider assigning product development to the part of the organization that has special market and technical knowledge. When a major U.S. copier company was losing ground in Europe because of competition from Japanese products, its market-savvy Japanese subsidiary assumed responsibility for developing an addition to the company's product line.

Everyone Must Participate

At the very beginning of product development, take multiple markets into account by asking, "How will this play in Nigeria?" While product development will initially take place in the parent country, all affected units need to participate actively in the development and market planning. Companies are doing this increasingly by taking advantage of clusters of innovation worldwide. For example, a company looking to design innovative sportswear can leverage the resources and talent in the Pacific Northwest of the U.S., home of sportswear innovators such as Nike.

To facilitate communication and maximize productivity, consider transferring people from one location to another to work on the project. That is what Fiat did when it wanted to build a car specifically for emerging markets. It gave the task to a team based in Italy but comprised of members from five countries. Sometimes this can be accomplished virtually with video conferencing and sophisticated project management tools and software, but even when using a virtual approach, the process benefits from in-person team meetings.

Corporate Role in Product Development

Product development responsibilities should be clearly defined for both the managing unit and those affected by the product development. The managing unit is responsible for:

- Single-point worldwide technical development and design of a product that conforms to the global design standard and to global manufacturing and procurement standards
- Transmitting the completed design to each affected unit
- All other activities need to plan, develop, originate, introduce, and support the product in the managing unit
- Directing and supporting the affected units so that the product can be introduced concurrently in all markets
- Integrating and coordinating all global program activities.

The affected units, in turn, are responsible for:

- Identifying unique requirements to incorporate in the product goals and specifications
- Activities needed to plan, originate, introduce, and support the products in the units
- Identifying any conflicts with the managing unit's plans and activities.

During the early stages, emphasize the need to identify and evaluate the requirements of both the managing unit and the affected units and incorporate them into the plan. In later stages, the emphasis shifts to developing and designing a global product with minimum configuration differences and to developing support system capabilities in each of the participating units. The result is a global product development system. This approach cuts through the standardized-versus-localized debate and offers a clear way to determine and implement effective programs in several markets simultaneously. At headquarters, a marketer has the opportunity to standardize certain aspects of the product but can also allow maximum flexibility for differing market conditions.

Time is money, of course, so most companies want to streamline this process as much as possible. To cut down on development time, some use multidisciplinary teams that stay with the project from start to finish, using a parallel approach to the product launch. Some software companies, in particular, have found that using the agile method shortens development time and lets them get a product that meets their customers' needs to market more quickly than other methods. Because the agile method involves customers in the product development, it helps overcome some of the issues that develop with internal-only R&D efforts, including an inability to predict, evaluate, and cover all possible configurations. With customer input, they at least know which features are in greatest demand.

Companies that use worldwide product management are in a better position to create products they can introduce into any market. The amount of time involved will depend on the product (industrial products may take less time because they are more likely to be standardized), how new the concept is, customer characteristics, geographic proximity, company-related variables such as the number and type of international affiliates or the company's global experience, and how much of its resources it can commit to the process.

If new product development will be an ongoing process in the firm's global marketing efforts, the company needs to be open-minded about the R&D department's location. With most functions based at the home operation, many companies assume that is the best place for R&D, too. Many operations, though, have started using globally based product development resources to improve their ability to compete internationally. A survey of more than 200 multinational organizations in Europe, Japan, and North America showed that this trend is growing, with European companies ceding more product development responsibilities to units in other countries. The Campbell Soup Company also discovered that overseas R&D efforts had applications in domestic markets. Its Hong Kong R&D center was established to adapt the company's products to the Chinese markets, but eventually took on the role of transferring product concepts developed for that region to the Americas and Europe, where there was growing interest in Asian foods.

Companies usually have four reasons for investing in R&D abroad:

- Aiding technology transfer from parent to subsidiary
- Developing new and improved products expressly for global markets
- Creating new products and processes for simultaneous application in the company's international markets
- Generating new long-term technology.

In truly global companies, the R&D function resides wherever the appropriate talent resides. Placing R&D abroad provides access to foreign scientific and technical personnel and information available in businesses or universities. Non-U.S. companies that have invested in R&D facilities in the U.S. have concentrated their attention in California's Silicon Valley, New Jersey, and North Carolina's Research Triangle Park. Sometimes a market's unique features drive the location decision. For example, most of the major auto manufacturers have design centers in California so they can monitor and observe the technical, social, and aesthetic values of the world's trendsetting fifth-largest car market.

Companies with a stake in emerging and developing markets often install R&D facilities in those regions so they can achieve a better understanding of these "new" consumers. These R&D centers are, in turn, seen as desirable investments by host governments. Developing countries are increasingly requiring R&D facilities as a condition of investment or continued operation.

While most product development teams include representatives from marketing, engineering, manufacturing, finance, and other relevant disciplines, the global product development team must add an international team member. Some multinational companies also provide product development support with additional teams of international employees who have both product and geographic responsibility. In addition to providing input to overall planning efforts, these team members gather customer input by visiting key customers throughout the product design and development process to get their reactions. Cultural and language barriers can get in the way of this global team approach, but many companies solve these problems by increasing communication and exchanging personnel.

The rising costs of basic research and shorter product life cycles have encouraged many companies to join forces in R&D. In the U.S., R&D consortia have developed technologies ranging from artificial intelligence to semiconductor manufacturing methods. A group of consumer goods manufacturers and technology firms formed a consortium to speed up the movement of goods in supply chains. The European Commission often supports similar consortia in the European Union. As long as participants work on core technologies that each can then apply in their own way in their own fields, these consortia can work very effectively.

Test and Launch the Product

Depending on the product, testing procedures range from reliability tests in the pilot plant to mini-launches used to estimate the product's performance in world markets. Any testing prolongs full-scale commercialization and increases the possibility of a competitive reaction. It is also expensive. Still, because of the high rate of new product failures, most companies want some level of testing to make sure the target market accepts their product. International product testing might involve introducing the product in just one of the intended markets and basing the go-ahead decision for the rest of the more global region on the outcome. Some countries, including Brazil and Thailand, have emerged as good test markets. Procter & Gamble has tested in Brazil before rolling out into Latin America, while Unilever has used Thailand as its test region for the Asian market.

Product Testing Issues

Companies often make the mistake of relying on their instincts and hunches too much when marketing abroad. Although they might do a great deal of research in their home markets, some marketers might be too stingy on research in other regions. They often mistakenly assume that other markets have the same priorities and lifestyles as the domestic market. Other test problems include lack of product distinctiveness, unexpected technical problems, and conflicts or confusion between the engineering and marketing functions or within the marketing functions as well. Engineering, for example, might design product features that distribution channels cannot leverage, while advertising might promise the customer something that cannot be delivered.

In addition to testing the products, companies also tend to test all elements of the marketing mix, including packaging, advertising, and pricing. Marketing mix testing is recommended because all testing up to this point has revolved around what people say they will do rather than what they will actually do. With the product in the market, the marketer will know if what users say about the products matches what they do with it. Reduce test marketing financial risks by confining the testing to a limited area using localized advertising media.

Test marketing in Europe and elsewhere is risky because of competitive exposure of new ideas, but researchers have found ways around this:

■ Laboratory test markets are the least realistic in terms of consumer behavior over time, but this method lets researchers measure customer responses to TV ads.

- Micro-test marketing uses a continuous panel of consumers served by a grocery store operated by the research agency. The agency exposes panelists to new products through print ads, coupons, and free samples before monitoring their willingness to buy and buy again.
- Forced distribution tests use a continuously reporting panel of consumers who find the products in normal retail outlets. For this to be successful, the manufacturer needs the cooperation of key retailers in the market. And, while this is a real world test, it also alerts the competition.

When the company is ready to take the product to market, the impact of an effective global product launch can be great, but so can the cost of one that is poorly executed. High development costs and competitive pressures often force companies into many markets as quickly as possible, but few companies can afford new products that are not introduced, marketed, and supported in their markets. Inter-country coordination of the rollout preparations will ultimately determine the level of success for the introduction.

Localize and translate messages before the launch. Get feedback from key internal and external audiences. Make sure that support materials reflect both cultural and technical differences among markets. Share all of this information with the sales channels, too, as those in foreign markets usually require more education and support than their domestic counterparts.

Most global marketers recommend introducing in all markets simultaneously. Setting a single date for the launch forces the entire organization to gear up for the event while it solves the "lame duck" dilemma when there are old models available in some markets. Customers appreciate knowing that a new version is on the way when they are contemplating buying the older product – and welcome attractive pricing on those lame duck products the company wants to move out of inventory. In addition, a worldwide launch offers better publicity opportunities than a launch staged according to a wide-ranging schedule across all markets.

MANAGING THE GLOBAL PRODUCT PORTFOLIO

Most companies have a considerable number of items in their product portfolios or groupings. In expanding markets, any company not growing rapidly risks falling behind for good, so the focus is on bringing out new items or lines or adjusting existing products. A portfolio's options include expanding geographically to new markets or segments and adding to existing market operations through new product lines. The goal is a balanced product and market portfolio – an appropriate mix of new, growing, and mature products that provide a sustainable competitive advantage in multiple markets. Many marketers assess their portfolio and its opportunities by using a quadrant model that lets them analyze the products in the mix according to growth rates and market share positions.

Another approach used to assess a product portfolio is the market-product-business model. This approach helps uncover interconnections in common target markets, shared R&D objectives, similar technologies, and shared marketing experiences. By exploring interlinkages between these three areas across global markets, it is possible to exploit increasing market similarities by setting up appropriate strategic business units or standardizing product lines, products, and marketing programs.

There are a number of advantages to using a product portfolio approach. This concept provides:

■ A global view of the competitive structure, especially when including longer-term considerations
■ A guide for formulating a global marketing strategy based on the suggested allocation of scarce resources between product lines
■ A guide for formulating marketing objectives for specific markets based on an outline of the role of each product in the market served – for example, to generate cash or block competitive expansion
■ A convenient visual communication goal that can be achieved by integrating a substantial amount of information in an appealingly simple format that includes assessment of interlinkages between units and products.

Before making strategic choices based on a portfolio, consider the risks related to variables such as entry mode and exchange rates, management preferences for idiosyncratic objectives such as concentrating on countries with similar market characteristics, and marketing costs. For example, the entry cost in one market might be less if the company already has a presence there in another product category and there is a chance that distribution networks can be shared. Similarly, when there are similarities in market characteristics and the company's position in those markets, it is often possible to leverage one market's ideas for new products and marketing programs in another.

There are disadvantages to the product portfolio approach, too. International behavior does not always follow the same rules as the firm's domestic market, which can make market assumptions tricky. For example, the major local competitor in a foreign market could be a government-owned firm in business not so much to make money but to keep people employed. A number of factors in the marketing environment can blur the relationship between market share and profitability, while local content laws will affect the product lines a company can offer. In addition, the fact that global companies produce the same products in different locations could have an impact – good or bad – on consumer perceptions of product risk and quality.

Still, branding benefits from a thorough portfolio analysis. Brands shape customer decisions and create economic value. In many situations, the brand itself is the key purchasing factor for both consumer and business-to-business customers. For example, according to research from the National Textile Center in the U.S., brand image is often the most important consideration in U.S. apparel purchases, allowing some companies to charge a premium price, too.

Brands offer benefits to consumers, as well. They simplify everyday choices, reduce the risk of complicated buying decisions, provide emotional benefits, and offer a sense of community. In technology, where products change at an ever-increasing rate, branding is critical and is in fact far more important than in packaged goods, where a product might be more understandable because it stays the same or very similar over time. The "Intel Inside" campaign for Intel's personal computer chips is an example of the importance of a brand in technology marketing. The computer buyer appreciates the reassurance that comes from knowing that the Intel chip will – according to the brand's image – make the product more reliable.

A strong brand will also open doors in new markets. In a global marketplace, customers are often aware of brands before they are available to them. Starbucks has relied on the strength of its brand when breaking into new markets including Vienna, Europe's café capital.

Global marketers can create brands with the corporate name, have family brand names for a wide range of products or product variations, or have individual brand names for each item in the product line. More and more companies are also capitalizing on shared target audiences by co-branding. One example of this is the new Sony Style Comcast Labs retail store and technology lab – a collaboration in Philadelphia between Sony Electronics Inc. and Comcast Corp. to showcase the latest innovative products and services from both companies and preview future Comcast technology, products and services. In Canada, one of the country's top food retailers, Sobeys, teamed with Disney to create a co-branded food line for children, Compliments Junior Disney.

Brand-name companies with market power have to determine the most effective use of this asset across markets. The value of a brand name is evident every time we see an acquisition where prices are many times over the book value of the company purchased. Nestle, for example, paid five times the book value for the British company Rowntree, owner of brands that included Kit Kat and After Eight. Many of the world's leading brands enjoy high-brand equity values – the price premium the brand commands multiplied by the extra volume it moves over what an average brand commands.

Business Week Top 100 Global Brands

Business Week magazine and brand consultancy Interbrand team up annually to determine the top 100 global brands. To qualify, a brand must get at least one-third of its earnings outside its home country, be recognized by those outside its customer base, and have marketing and financial data that is available to the public. Interbrand ranks individual brands, rather than brand portfolios, and uses a process that helps it calculate how much of a company's earnings come from the power of the brand. It considers market leadership, stability, and the ability to cross both geographic and cultural borders. In 2009, the top ten brands were:

1. Coca Cola
2. IBM
3. Microsoft
4. GE
5. Nokia
6. McDonald's
7. Google
8. Toyota
9. Intel
10. Disney

Global brands such as these help manufacturers and other companies create consistency and impact – a process that is easier with a single worldwide identity. While some of the global brands are completely standardized, some elements of the product might be adapted to local conditions. Changes can include product positioning, versions or formulations, or names – for example, Tide is sold as Ariel and Clairol as Wella in Europe.

Consumers worldwide associate global brands with three characteristics and evaluate their performance in these three areas when making purchasing decisions:

■ Quality
■ Emotion related to aspirations
■ Involvement in solving social problems

This information offers lessons for marketers. First, do not hide the brand's global nature. Creatively, this might mean referring to the brand's global leadership position or its level of innovation and reach made possible by its global position. Second, because one key marketing mantra is "be local on a global scale" and many regions favor home-grown brands, it is important to localize some features of the marketing approach. One approach might be to use a consistent global positioning but to vary the name according to the country's language. Mr. Clean, for example, uses the same recognizable bald man in a white shirt on the brand's French packaging, but the product name in that country is translated to Mr. Propre. Third, satisfy the basics. A brand needs to create differentiation and familiarity while providing the company with the necessary margins and growth.

Global brands need to deliver customer service that has a high degree of consistency and to communicate this across all customer touch points. For this reason, global brand management is usually a centralized function that takes advantage of all the brand's assets while making sure the brand's power is not diluted by inappropriate line extensions. The headquarters staff, business unit management, and global teams or managers are responsible for providing brand guidelines without hampering local initiative. To achieve the "glocal" dimension, regional and local managers need the power to interpret and express the marketing message.

In addition to using a global brand name from the beginning, some companies apply a global name to existing products with different names. Mars, for example, replaced the name of its Marathon British candy bar with Snickers, the name used in North and South America so the company could enjoy the marketing economies and higher acceptance of products by consumers and intermediaries. The drawback to this approach, of course, is that the brand loses its local identity, especially when a regional or global brand name takes its place. In these situations, internal marketing helps instill ownership of the global brand in the country organization.

Assess the brand portfolio on a regular basis to make sure the company continues to use resources appropriately. Increasing numbers of global marketers are focusing their attention on the brands with the greatest potential and disposing of noncore brands. Focusing on the top-tier brands lets companies reduce international production, marketing, storage, and distribution costs while increasing the potential for success.

Before disposing of a brand, assess its sales, loyalty, and potential alongside current market trends. When retaining local brands, a penetration price approach can position the product as a true defender of local culture. Another local brand option is to use a chameleon approach in which the brands tries to blend in innocuously. A third choice is to position the brand as one that brings the fantasy of life in a far away, glamorous world closer to home by trying not to look local. The best-selling chewing gum in France, for example, has a decidedly American name: Hollywood.

Private Label Products: Competition or a New Opportunity?

Branded products are facing increasing competition worldwide from private label goods from intermediaries. Thanks to an increase in price sensitivity and a decrease in brand loyalty as consumers look to save money, private label products are enjoying significant penetration in many regions. A study of seven countries by the Private Label Manufacturers Association revealed that private label market share has exceeded 40 percent in the United Kingdom, Germany, Belgium, and Switzerland. Market share for retailer brands is at an all-time high in France and Spain, where one of every three products sold carries a private label.

While private brand success is known to be strongly affected by economic conditions and the self-interest of retailers who want to improve their bottom lines, other factors contributing to the growth include improved quality and the development of segmented private brand products. Some private label brands even have a premium category now. Emboldened by the success of private label brands, manufacturers have expanded this "privatization" to new product categories, hoping to expand the success.

European supermarket chains in particular have had enormous success with private brands because of the chains' power over manufacturers. While the five largest operators in the U.S. command only 21 percent of supermarket sales, the figure in the United Kingdom is 62 percent, and in Finland the four leading wholesaler-led chains control more than 90 percent. As new types of intermediaries such as mass merchandisers and warehouse clubs emerge, this phenomenon will expand as these players exercise their procurement clout over manufacturers. Supporting this is a belief among many retailers that strong private label brand programs such as Loblaw's President's Choice in Canada can help them differentiate their outlets and solidify shopper's loyalty. This strengthens their positions vis-à-vis manufacturers and results in increased profitability.

There are also international retailers that either carry or focus on their own private label brands, such as the German discount supermarket chain Aldi, which sells only Aldi private label goods in stores throughout Europe, the U.S., and Australia. Aldi cuts costs instead of sacrificing quality, allowing it to drive out low-quality brands that trade only on price.

The increasing popularity of private label brands forces marketers to make critical strategic choices. When operating in an environment where consumers prefer brand names and product innovation is a success factor, a marketer can refuse to participate. The argument for participation, though, uses the "if you cannot beat them, join them" philosophy. If private label popularity is not going to disappear, get involved by becoming a private label manufacturer as well as a source of brand name goods. Before doing this, take into account not only whether it will be a profitable venture, but also whether it will dilute management attention, raise questions about quality standards, and affect consumer perceptions of the main branded business. Many marketers factor market conditions into their decision. While H.J. Heinz does little private label work in the U.S., most of its U.K. production is for private brands.

The Impact of Counterfeiting on Brands

Intellectual property theft is a critical problem for many industries and companies as they expand globally. The Organization for Economic Cooperation and Development reports that counterfeit and pirated goods that are traded internationally account for about $176 billion, or 2.5 percent, of world trade in manufactures, imports, and exports. While counterfeiting of global and successful brands is a global phenomenon that strikes every industry sector and businesses of all sizes, the most innovative, fastest-growing industries are hardest hit – computer software, pharmaceuticals, and entertainment. In the past, the only concern was whether others were counterfeiting a company's product, but today manufacturers have to worry about whether the raw materials and components purchased for production are themselves counterfeit.

How a company deals with counterfeiting problems depends on the product origin and where counterfeiters market it. About 75 percent of counterfeit goods are manufactured outside the U.S., and 25 percent are made either in the U.S. or imported and then labeled there. Customs should stop those products brought into the U.S. from other regions, but enforcement is a challenge because of a lack of staff and the increasingly high-tech character of the products. To effectively prevent counterfeits from entering a market, property holders often need to be actively involved, helping customs officers identify fakes. Firms might have to develop software programs that customs agents can use to better identify fakes during spot checks. When there is an infringement, the violated company can take action under the laws of the country in which it occurs. The largest numbers of counterfeit goods come from China, Brazil, Taiwan, Korea, and India. Countries in Central America and the Middle East are typically not sources but rather markets for these goods.

The first task in fighting intellectual property violation is to use patent application or registration of trademarks or mask works (for semiconductors). The rights granted by a patent, trademark, copyright, or mask work registration in the U.S. offer no protection in a foreign country and these U.S. protections have no foreign counterparts. Although there is no shortcut to worldwide protection, treaties and other international agreements do offer some advantages. Several treaties under the World Intellectual Property Organization as well as regional patent and trademark offices such as the European Patent Office will grant international protection throughout member countries to applicants.

After securing property rights, the global marketer has to enforce these rights through legislative action, bilateral and multilateral negotiations, private sector action with others, and individual measures. When companies in victimized industries unite, they can generate results. The pharmaceutical industry lobbied to make sure that the NAFTA agreement included meticulously detailed patent protection provisions. The manufacturers of Nutella and Ferrero Rocher chocolates fought a four-year battle in Chinese courts to protect their products from local look-a-like competitors. Governments can help with legislation, as the U.S. did when requiring that the designation of Generalized System of

Preference benefits to countries be limited to countries with strong enforcement of intellectual property laws.

Companies are increasingly taking more aggressive steps to protect themselves, including incorporating product details that are difficult to duplicate. Some companies, including Disney, have tried to legitimize offenders by converting them into authorized licensees, which in turn converts these new allies into soldiers fighting the counterfeiters who are having a negative impact on their profits. Many businesses maintain close contact with the government and other agencies charged with helping them. For example, computer-makers loan testing equipment to customs officers and company attorneys lead seminars on how to detect pirated software and hardware. Others use outside investigators to work with law enforcement officers to conduct raids. For example, when the maker of WD-40 worked with Chinese authorities to raid retailers selling a counterfeit version of the lubricant, the retailers of the bogus product led authorities to the manufacturer.

While counterfeiting and intellectual property theft are problems faced by companies or brands that have achieved a certain level of success, the potential for the incursions need to be factored into a product's development. Predicting and preventing this challenge to a brand becomes part of the overseas marketing discussion, alongside issues of standardization or customization and brand development and management.

FOOD FOR THOUGHT

- What international market has the highest growth potential for your activities? What is your likelihood to succeed in such a market?
- What changes do you need to make to adapt your existing products to the international market?
- Is there inter-cultural human capital in your organization to carry out the expansion?
- What is the regulatory environment for intellectual property protection in your targeted international market?

Further Readings

Dinnie, Keith. *Asian Brand Strategy: How Asia Builds Strong Brands.* New York, NY: Palgrave Macmillan, 2007.

Morley, Michael. *The Global Corporate Brand Book.* New York, NY: Palgrave Macmillan, 2009.

Rotheaermel, Frank T., Michael A.Hitt, and Lloyd A Jobe. *Balancing Vertical Integration and Strategic Outsourcing: Effects on Product Portfolio, Product Success and Firm Performance.* New York, NY: Wiley InterScience, 2006.

Stark, John. *Global Product: Strategy, Product Lifecycle Management and the Billion Customer Question.* New York, NY: Springer, 2007.

Online Resources

Business Week: The 100 Best Global Brands 2009
http://images.businessweek.com/ss/09/09/0917_global_brands/index.htm

The Federation of International Trade Associations: International Trade Webcasts
www.fita.org/webcasts.html

TradePort
Offers free information and resources for businesses that seek to conduct international trade
www.tradeport.org/

World Intellectual Property Organization (WIPO)
www.wipo.int/

Chapter 9

Making Money

Because price is the only element of the marketing mix that generates revenue, it is a major strategic tool when making marketing decisions. Global marketers use price to attract customers, communicate about quality, and influence competitive behaviors. The objective with pricing is to create demand for the products while maintaining profitability. Pricing and costs, after all, will determine the long-term viability of a global marketing initiative. Different dynamics come into play when setting prices in other markets, so it is important to understand factors that influence international pricing and how to respond.

Consider all marketing mix elements when setting prices. For example, JLG, the leading designer, manufacturer, and marketer of access equipment such as aerial work platforms and stock pickers, leverages the eco-friendly product positioning of its self-propelled platforms used at construction sites. The company charges premium prices because the products use nonpolluting hydrogen fuel cells for power – an attractive feature for the increasing numbers of builders seeking equipment for "green" construction sites.

Demand, competition, costs, and legal considerations all contribute to a reasonable product price range. The range might be narrow or wide, as is seen with a commodity product versus an innovation. Regardless of how narrow the gap allowed by these factors, pricing is never a static element. It can change as costs increase or competitive prices decrease, but the marketer's goal is to have a customer who will pay the price, even at a premium level.

Pricing must also take into account other functions of the company, particularly those related to financing. Companies often win or lose sales because of the availability – or lack of availability – of favorable credit terms for the buyer. As overseas competition continues to increase, financing packages – often put together with government support – can have a significant impact. Customers abroad might be willing to accept higher prices in exchange for better credit terms.

Pricing challenges are the same as those faced in domestic markets. They include pricing a new market entry, changing price as an attack strategy or in response to a competitor's actions, and multiple-product coordination. When pricing a product for its first entry into a market, the general alternatives are:

- Skimming
- Following the market price
- Penetration pricing

Price *skimming* involves setting the price high in the beginning, then lowering it later. Companies skim to get the highest possible income in the shortest amount of time. This works only if the product is unique and if some market segments are willing to pay the high price. Its success depends on the speed and quality of the competitive reaction. *Market pricing* works when similar products are already in the marketplace. In these situations, the final price is determined by competitive pricing. The company then adjusts production and marketing costs so it can afford to sell at the competitive price. It is a reactive approach that could lead to problems if sales volumes never reach a point where they generate satisfactory returns. When using *penetration pricing*, marketers offer the product at a low price intended to generate volume sales and achieve high market share. The volume helps compensate for a lower per-unit return. This approach needs mass markets, price-sensitive customers, and decreasing production and marketing costs as sales volume increases. It can also be used to discourage others from entering the market.

Prices often need to change when a competitor launches a new product, when there is a change in market conditions such as an adjustment in the value of the billing currency, or when the exporting company's internal situation changes. An increase in production costs, for example, will often encourage a manufacturer to charge a higher price to keep profits up. Changes in the product's stage in the life cycle stimulate price changes, too. As the product matures, there is more pressure to keep the price competitive in spite of decreased differentiation because of increased competition.

With multiple products, the pricing often distinguishes products in the line as good, better, and best. When pricing one of the products in the line to protect against competition or gain market share, marketers often price the others to make up for the lost contribution of the "fighting" brand.

This chapter addresses how to price exports, "foreign" products made in facilities outside the home country, and those sold from one company unit to another. It also outlines financing options so customers can afford to make the purchase at the price point.

HOW TO PRICE EXPORTED PRODUCTS

Internal and external factors influence export pricing. Internal factors include the product characteristics and costs, the distribution system, the company's export experience, and management attitudes. External factors include customer, regulatory, competitive, industry, and financial characteristics. Interactions of all factors create pricing opportunities or constraints. For example, when management wants to challenge a competitor in the competitor's home market, regulations in that market might require product adaptation that creates costs that need to be absorbed.

The target customer will establish the basic pricing premise. Key customer factors include the importance of price in decision making, perceptions of product price versus value, and reactions to marketing mix manipulations. Pricing will have a significant impact on the desired brand image as well as the product's distribution levels and promotional support.

Pricing policies generally flow from the exporter's overall objectives, which typically include maximizing profits, securing a predetermined market share, and generating a specific return on investment. Corporate pricing policies might also include copying competitors' pricing or pricing to discourage competitors from entering the market. For example, an exporter entering a new market can allow wholesalers and retailers above normal profit margins to encourage the greatest sales volume possible, widespread geographic distribution, and distributor and retailer loyalty. Industrial adhesives manufactured by Loctite Corporation, for example, require a sales process that is highly technical. Because of this, the manufacturer offers a higher-than-usual compensation package for distributors.

These types of requirements are typical in the early stages of a company's export initiative but are phased out later when the brand achieves the targeted sales penetration level. Whether pricing decisions are made at the corporate or local level also has an impact on pricing. Companies prefer to keep most of the decision making local when markets are dissimilar or uncertain.

Identifying an Export Pricing Strategy

There are two general price-setting strategies in international marketing: standard worldwide pricing and dual pricing. The latter has different prices for domestic and export markets. Marketers use standard or uniform pricing when customers worldwide have access to prices charged elsewhere and when there is little chance of differentiating the product or the service enough to warrant price differences.

Dual pricing can use a cost-driven or a market-driven approach. Cost-driven pricing is easy to establish and implement while market-based pricing requires intelligence on customer demand and product competition. There are two options with cost-driven pricing – the cost-plus method and the marginal cost method. With the cost-plus approach, exporters calculate the true cost, including domestic and international costs. This method ensures margins, but the final price could be so high that the product is not competitive enough. Because of this, some use a flexible cost-plus strategy so they can vary the price according to circumstances.

The marginal cost method uses the direct costs of producing and selling products for exports as a base level for prices. It disregards fixed costs for plants, R&D, domestic overhead, and domestic marketing. This allows the company to lower export prices to be competitive in markets that might otherwise have been beyond access. At the same time, in certain situations, this approach can open a company to dumping charges because the price level considered for dumping is usually based on average total costs, which are typically considerably higher.

Market-driven pricing uses export pricing based on the dynamic conditions of the market. The marginal cost strategy provides a basis, but prices might change frequently because of changes in competition, exchange rates, or the marketing environment. With this approach, the marketer needs information and controls. Marketers will use this approach when pricing to gain entry or better penetrate a new market.

While many exporters, especially in the early stages of global expansion, use cost-plus pricing, it does not usually lead to the performance they want. Instead, it generates pricing that is too high in weak markets and too low in strong markets because it does not reflect current market conditions. The process does become more flexible and market-driven as the company gains global marketing experience.

Exporters often differ in pricing approaches according to nationality. For example, Korean companies price more competitively in international markets than they do domestically, while U.S. businesses seem to consider costs and profits more when setting export prices.

Exports costs include the typical domestic expenses plus those involved in:

- Modifying the product for additional markets
- Running the export operation, including personnel, market research, additional shipping and insurance costs, communications with overseas customers, and promotions
- Entering global markets, including tariffs and taxes, those associated with commercial credit and political risks, and foreign exchange risks

When marketers factor in these expenses, export prices far exceed domestic rates. Complicating price escalation is the fact that price increases can be in different amounts in different regions or markets. When customers are willing to shop around before purchasing, the price differentials create problems for distributors and can lead to companies abandoning markets.

Overcoming Price Escalation

Global marketers often overcome price escalation by developing creative strategies based on the market situation. Typical methods focus on cost cutting. Some include:

- Reorganizing and shortening the distribution channel, often by cutting out intermediaries
- Adapting the product by using less expensive ingredients, removing features, or changing packaging
- Using new or more economical tariff or tax classifications, sometimes by looking for alternative categories or by lobbying
- Assembling or producing overseas.

SETTING PRICES FOR FOREIGN OPERATIONS

The process involved with price setting for products or services manufactured in nondomestic locations and sold to customers outside the corporation is similar to that used when setting export prices. Marketers set prices according to the company's overall objectives, product costs, market conditions and structure, customer patterns, and environmental constraints. Because these factors vary from country to country, uniform pricing is challenging.

What Will the Market Bear?

Multinationals tend to base pricing decisions on each market's prevailing conditions, with pricing strategies varying according to the market situation, consumer purchasing power, and product positioning decisions. The basics of first-time pricing, price adjustment, and product line pricing still apply. Price changes could depend on whether the company's goals at the time include underselling a major competitor or meeting profit goals when foreign exchange rates change.

Overseas manufacturing can allow a company to seek out the least expensive labor, natural resources, or raw materials but also brings potential cost challenges that can have an impact on pricing. These include determining how to allocate overhead, R&D, and other indirect expenses to the product. Currency inflation also impacts global operations pricing, especially because it is usually accompanied by host government controls. Environments with ongoing inflation require constant price adjustments. Manufacturers in markets with hyperinflation often quote pricing using a stable currency such as the euro, then translate it daily into the local currency. In deflationary markets, pricing strategies might include target pricing, value pricing, stripping down products, and adding value.

Consumer perceptions have a powerful impact on pricing decisions. Price sensitivity is a critical factor, as a status-conscious market insisting on products with established reputations is more elastic, allowing more pricing freedom than a market where price consciousness drives demand. As buyers learn more about prices through Internet searches, though, a more practical consumer sensibility takes over, with customers demanding top quality at competitive prices. Intermediaries also have an impact on prices charged. Close channel coordination helps ensure necessary intermediary margins. At the same time, increasingly global retailers are putting pressure on manufacturers' margins by demanding low-cost, direct supply contracts.

As with exports, a company manufacturing overseas might respond to competition by choosing to compete directly on price or select nonprice options. When responding on price, it can bundle products and prices, offer loyalty programs, make selective price cuts, or offer new products. When responding in nonprice ways, it might add benefits or services, such as warranty repairs or liberal credit terms.

Government Impact on Pricing

Sometimes subsidiaries encounter a local competitor who receives government protections aimed at foreign-owned subsidiaries, making it harder to compete in that market. Host governments also influence prices and pricing with tariffs, taxes, and price controls. Some set maximum prices as a way to stop inflation and an accelerating wage-price spiral, but operating in that environment is difficult, especially if the company has to petition to raise prices.

Multinationals fight price controls by demonstrating that they are not getting an acceptable return on investment. This, in turn, means that they will not be able to invest in the future and might have to end current production. Cadbury Schweppes sold its plant in Kenya because price controls made operations unprofitable. In addition, price controls often hurt consumers by forcing manufacturers to charge more for their products. The best way to avoid price controls is to work collaboratively with governments, especially in developing countries.

Reasons to Coordinate Pricing in Multiple Markets

Coordination among various markets served by overseas manufacturers is necessary as regional markets consolidate. But while global and regional brands require intermarket price coordination, local subsidiaries need pricing latitude. Studies have shown that foreign-based multinational corporations allow their U.S. subsidiaries to set prices because of the market's size and unique features. Recent experience shows, however, that pricing coordination has to be worldwide because parallel imports will surface in any markets with pricing discrepancies. Parallel imports will force prices to the lowest level as buyers simply buy from the least expensive source.

Companies protect against this by implementing a pricing corridor – a range within which national prices vary. The company sets the maximum and minimum prices that subsidiaries can charge, giving them enough flexibility to manage price elasticities, competition, and positioning, but not enough to attract parallel imports. The corridor is more narrow for portable products such as cell phones than for more immobile products such as industrial machinery. This approach takes pricing authority away from the country managers and moves it to regional management, which often requires changes in systems and incentive structures.

Leasing may be the only way to penetrate certain markets for products such as printing presses, heavy equipment, or machine tools. Balance-of-payment problems have forced some countries to prohibit or hinder purchasing or importing equipment, but they make exceptions for leased products. The main benefit for the lessor is that total net income, after charging off repair and maintenance expense, is often higher than it would be if the unit was sold.

SETTING TRANSFER PRICES

Multinational corporations also need to develop pricing strategies for products sold between their units or subsidiaries. This is known as transfer pricing; there are similarities to the approaches used for export pricing, but there are differences, too.

Industry sources report that up to two-thirds of world trade takes place between related parties such as company affiliates or alliance partners. Transfer or intra-corporate pricing, then, needs to accommodate different tax and foreign exchange rates and varying government regulations. As with export pricing, companies want to be competitive while reducing taxes and tariffs, managing cash flows, and minimizing foreign exchange risks. When viewed from a company-wide perspective, transfer pricing enhances operational performance, minimizes the tax burden, and reduces legal exposure. Multinational corporations recognize this; an Ernst & Young survey revealed that almost three-quarters of corporations surveyed believe that transfer pricing will be critical or very important in coming years. In addition, 40 percent of the respondents identified transfer pricing as the most important tax issue facing their group.

Transfer Price Factors Vary

When setting transfer prices, manufacturers consider everything from costs to competitive pricing to market conditions. When using a cost-based approach, the price includes a markup. The market price method usually incorporates a discount to the buying division. The arm's length method, or the price that unrelated parties might have reached in the same transaction, is a third approach. In most cases, cost-plus markup is used, requiring every affiliate to be a profit center.

The effect of environmental influences in overseas markets can be reduced by manipulating transfer prices in principle, at least. High transfer prices on goods shipped to a subsidiary and low ones on goods imported from it will minimize the tax liability of a subsidiary operating in a country with a high income tax. On the other hand, a higher transfer price might have an effect on the import duty. Adjusting transfer prices for the opposite effects of taxes and duties is a delicate balancing act. Environmental influences include fluctuating currency rates, particularly when one partner is operating in a low-inflation environment and the other in the opposite situation. Environment variations require detailed intracompany data for decision making. In the end, many companies adopt a "good citizen" philosophy, recognizing their liability to pay taxes and duties in every country where they are operating. They believe that the primary goal of transfer pricing is to support and develop commercial activities.

Because companies sometimes struggle to match corporate pricing goals with those of subsidiaries, they implement policies that motivate subsidiary managers to avoid making decisions that will conflict with corporate goals. E-commerce is causing concern, too, because there is a lack of clear understanding and agreement regarding taxes. Companies engaged in e-commerce are particularly explicit on these issues to avoid transfer-price audits.

Problems arise when manipulating transfer prices complicates internal control measures. Companies sometimes need an adjustment mechanism so divisions receive appropriate credit for their actual contributions. This is particularly important when transfer pricing has an impact on a subsidiary's apparent profit performance versus its actual performance for example, when there is a need to subsidize less efficient members of the corporate family.

The Impact on Taxes

Transfer prices involve the tax and regulatory jurisdictions of the countries where the company does business. Sales and transfers of tangibles and intangibles are closely reviewed to determine whether the seller received adequate or appropriate compensation. For example, one country might think a transfer price is too low while the other – especially if it is an emerging economy – might think it is too high. Section 482 of the U.S. Internal Revenue Code gives the Internal Revenue Service (IRS) vast authority to reallocate income between controlled global operations and U.S. parents and between U.S. operations of nondomestic companies. The organization wants to stop U.S. companies from shifting U.S. income to their overseas subsidiaries in low- or no-tax jurisdictions. To this end, it supports the arm's length pricing method as the principal basis for transfer pricing. This is because unrelated parties usually sell to each other in a way that gives the seller a profit.

Section 482 offers six methods for determining an arm's length price:

- Comparable controlled price
- Resale price
- Cost-plus
- Comparable profits
- Profit split
- Any other reasonable method

U.S. companies have to disclose the method used so the IRS can decide if it is an acceptable arm's length approach. The Office for Economic Cooperation and Development guidelines are similar, even though some argue that the arm's length method is only useful for commodity businesses.

It is possible to test transfer prices by comparing them with those in comparable transactions involving unrelated parties. In some cases, marketers have generated third-party trading they could use as a benchmark for transfer pricing. Another approach is the resale method, which is most useful in situations involving transfers to sales subsidiaries for ultimate distribution. They subtract the subsidiary's profit from an uncontrolled selling price. The appropriateness of the amount is determined by comparing it with a similar product being marketed by the multinational. The cost-plus approach is most appropriate for transfers of components or unfinished goods to subsidiaries. Companies secure the arm's length requirement by adding an appropriate markup for profit to the seller's total cost of the product.

The comparable profits and profit-split methods measure the profits of each of the related companies. They compare them with the proportionate contribution to total income of the corporation or similar multinationals. This functional analysis approach addresses the question of profit that would have been reported if the transactions had been between unrelated parties. Such comparisons, though, are not always possible.

The IRS has worked in recent years to secure APAs – advance pricing agreements – with multinational corporations to reduce unpaid income taxes. These agreements eliminate court challenges and costly audits. The most difficult pricing situations involve intangibles because it is often difficult to find comparables. As a result, many of the analyses are subjective, especially in cases involving the transfer of intellectual property.

DEFINE SALE AND PAYMENT TERMS

After establishing prices, marketers address the terms for both sales and payments. To minimize misinterpretations or misunderstandings, the International Chamber of Commerce (www.iccwbo.org) advises companies to use its "Incoterms," the standard trade definitions most commonly used in international sales contracts. Translated in 31 languages, Incoterms have been endorsed by the United Nations Commission on International Trade. Correct use of the 13 Incoterms, which include EXW (Ex Works), FOB (Free on Board), CIF (Cost, Insurance and Freight), DDU (Delivered Duty Unpaid), and CPT (Carriage Paid To), helps provide mutual confidence between business partners because they are all familiar with the language and structure of the terms.

Incoterms Categories

The International Chamber of Commerce groups its standard Incoterms into four categories:

- ■ *E.* The seller only makes the goods available to the buyer at the seller's own premises.
- ■ *F.* The seller delivers the goods to a carrier appointed by the buyer.
- ■ *C.* The seller has to contract for carriage, but without assuming the risk of loss or damage to the goods or additional costs due to events occurring after shipment or dispatch.
- ■ *D.* The seller bears all costs and risks needed to bring the goods to the place of destination.

These terms are powerful competitive tools when the exporter knows what importers prefer in a market and what the specific transaction might require.

Marketers are increasingly quoting more inclusive terms. There are several benefits associated with taking charge of the transportation on either a cost, insurance, and freight (CIF) or delivered duty paid basis defined by the Incoterms. They include being able to offer buyers an easy-to-understand delivered cost, using volume purchase of transportation services to cut costs for both the exporter and the importer, better control transportation quality and the condition of the product upon arrival, and fewer administrative procedures all around.

When taking control of transportation costs, be clear on the impact these additional costs will have on the bottom line. Mistakes or misunderstandings can lead to volatile shipping rates, unexpected import duties, and unhappy customers. Most exporters are reluctant to expand past the CIF quotation because there is too much that is unknown or uncontrollable in the destination country. Freight forwarders can help with this. They determine costs, prepare quotes, keep costs down, and make sure that unexpected changes do not cause the seller to lose money. They can also usually pass along reduced rates because of their higher volume and provide value-added services, such as handling duty-drawback receivables.

Factors that Impact Payment Terms

Contracts also include payment terms, which can provide a competitive advantage in certain situations. When negotiating terms, sellers typically take into account:

- The amount of the payment and the need for protection
- Terms offered by competitors
- Industry practices
- The company's capacity for financing international transactions
- The financial strength of all involved parties

Because each party has its preferences or issues, payment terms should be put on the negotiating table at the beginning of the relationship.

Payment methods vary by situation and range from cash in advance to open account or consignment selling. Neither extreme works well for a long-term relationship but might be necessary for situations where there is financial turmoil. Typical terms include:

- Consignment
- Open account
- Documents against acceptance
- Documents against payment
- Letter of credit
- Confirmed letter of credit
- Cash in advance

Cash in advance is the most favorable for the seller but reflects the least amount of trust. It is usually limited to smaller, first-time transactions or situations when the global marketer has reason to doubt the importer's ability to pay. Letters of credit issued by banks at the buyer's request are common. They are classified as irrevocable or revocable by the seller, confirmed or unconfirmed by the bank, or revolving or nonrevolving. The single best method of payment for the marketer in most cases is a confirmed, irrevocable letter of credit.

A letter of credit substitutes the credit of the bank for the credit of the buyer and is as good as the issuing bank's access to the dollars. In situations where orders are custom-made, an irrevocable letter of credit might help the manufacturer secure pre-export financing. Technology expedites document transfers, with much of the work done now online. For example, TradeCard, an online hub for business-to-business transactions, automates the process for users. They can view invoices, settlements, and adjustments online in real time. Services like this make it easier for exporters and importers alike to easily see the flow of money, information, and products.

The letter of credit is only a promise to pay, though. Importers pay with a draft, which is similar to a check but more like a cashier's check or money order in the U.S. It is an order by one party to pay another. Most drafts used are "documentary," which means that the buyer must have possession of the shipping documents first. The seller ships the goods; the shipping documents and the draft requiring payment are presented to the importer through banks acting as the seller's agent.

The draft, also known as the bill of exchange, is classified as a "sight" or "time" draft. A sight draft is payable when it is presented to the party to whom it is addressed. A time draft allows for a delay such as 30 days or even 120 days for payment. When a time draft is drawn on and accepted by a bank, it becomes a "banker's acceptance," which is sold in the short-term money market. Time drafts drawn on and accepted by a company become trader's acceptances and are not normally marketable. Bankers' acceptances allow companies who extend credit for competitive reasons to get paid immediately by selling the acceptance at a discount. Even if the draft is not sold in the secondary market, the exporter might convert it into cash by selling it to a bank at a discount from face value. If the discounting is with recourse, the seller is liable even if the importer does not pay the bank. Discounting without recourse, when the exporter is not liable, is also known as factoring. When there is a higher credit risk and longer-term receivables, it is called forfaiting.

Companies doing business domestically usually use the open account method, but this can present problems when exporting. When there is no written evidence of the debt and collection becomes a problem, the manufacturer's options are limited. In emerging countries, exporters will usually need proof of debt in the application to the central bank for hard currency. It often makes more sense to send the documents through a bank via direct collections, which shortens the time involved by days or weeks.

Consignment selling is the most favorable option for importers, since they can defer payment until goods are sold. There can be situations when the international marketer wants to enter a particular market through specific intermediaries and has to use this method because it is the only one the intermediaries will accept. It is undesirable for a number of reasons, including the costs of returning unsold goods back to the domestic market or elsewhere.

GETTING PAID

The goal is always to make sure one gets paid but there is usually commercial risk. While it is important to assess a buyer's creditworthiness, this can be complicated by unreliable credit reports, no audited reports, government reporting requirements that artificially inflate the value of assets, or financial reports that are harder to use because of an unfamiliar format or because the statements reflect the local currency. In addition, the buyer might have financial resources in the local currency but be unable to convert it to another currency because of exchange controls or government restrictions. This is often the case when governments restrict foreign currency transactions because of a global financial crisis.

Countertrade is another option when world debt crises and exchange rate volatility make typical trade financing risky. According to the Global Offset and Countertrade Trade Association, countertrade is often used to create financing and investment solutions or to reduce political and commercial risk. Countertrade involves exchanging goods or services for other goods or services. Similar to bartering, it allows nations to swap goods instead of cash or goods for cash plus other goods. It is one way for heavily indebted nations to be able to afford imports.

Markets with little cash can provide significant opportunities for companies willing to accept countertrade. U.S. companies are more inclined to use countertrade when they need to meet requirements established by other governments or customers. They recognize that it is often an effective way to gain entry into new markets.

Using Credit Reports

Unless there is a long-term trust relationship, get more than one credit report and be certain that the reports do not come from the same agency (see box below for international credit sources). In addition to establishing the importer's creditworthiness, it helps to match payment terms to the customer. While short term it is best to establish payment terms that guarantee payment, in the long run, it is better to establish a relationship of mutual trust that ensures payment even when complications arise.

International Credit Sources

Here are a few sources of international credit information:

- Dun & Bradstreet, www.dnb.com
- Foreign Credit Interchange Bureau/National Association of Credit Management (FCIB-NACM), www.fcibglobal.com
- www.cofacerating.com
- International Company Profiles, www.ita.doc.gov
- Local credit agencies or trade councils
- Bank reports

State payment terms clearly; follow up effectively. If a default situation occurs, the customer is the first recourse. Sometimes it is as simple as a misunderstanding or an error. If the customer has financial concerns or other objections, consider changing the payment terms. When third-party intervention is needed, a collection agency can often help. Total Credit Management Group is a global alliance of debt collection agencies with representation in more than 150 countries. An attorney is the last resort.

Managing Foreign Exchange Risk

When the seller and importer use different currencies, exchange rate movements can cause problems. Companies try to either shift the risk or modify it. When invoicing in foreign currencies, the seller cannot protect itself from currency fluctuations, but it can know how much it will eventually receive by using the forward exchange market mechanism. In essence, the exporter gets a bank to agree to a rate at which it will buy the foreign currency the seller will receive when the buyer pays. The rate is either a premium or a discount on the current spot rate. If the exchange rate does not move forward as anticipated, the exporter might be worse off. Although these forward contracts are the most common foreign currency contractual hedge, other financial instruments and derivatives, such as currency options and futures, are available.

An option gives the holder the right to buy or sell foreign currency at a specified price on or up to a pre-specified date. The difference between the currency options market and the forward market is that the transaction in the currency options market gives the participant the right to buy or sell, whereas a transaction in the forward market is a contractual obligation to buy or sell. As a result, with the forward market, if the marketer does not have the foreign currency when the contract comes due, it would have to buy the currency in the foreign exchange markets. If the currency has appreciated, the company could be exposed to losses. The greater flexibility in the options method makes it more expensive, though.

The currency futures market is conceptually similar to the forward market. To buy futures on the British pound sterling implies an obligation to buy in the future at a pre-specified price. The minimum transaction sizes are considerably smaller, though. Forward quotes apply to transactions of $1 million or more, whereas on the futures market, transactions will typically be under $100,000. The market, therefore, allows relatively small companies engaged in international trade to lock in exchange rates and lower their risks. Forward contracts, options, and futures are available from banks, the Chicago Mercantile Exchange, and the Philadelphia Stock Exchange.

When the seller's domestic currency is weak, strategies should include stressing the price advantage to customers and expanding the scale and scope of the export operation. Shift sourcing to weak currency markets and the export price can be reduced. When the exporter's currency is strong, minimize the price dimension as much as possible. Reduce costs by any means possible, including investing abroad and boosting productivity. Manipulate leads and lags in export and import payments or receivables in anticipation of either currency revaluations or devaluations.

In general, global marketers need a plan that lets them adjust prices according to a more favorable or unfavorable domestic currency rate. The strategic response depends on market conditions and could result in different strategies for different markets. When creating a plan, consider the reactions of local competitors, who might keep their prices stable or increase them along with the imports to increase profits.

Some companies prefer price stability and allow mark-ups to vary in maintaining stable local currency prices. Harley-Davidson, for example, maintains its price to distributors as long as the spot exchange rate does not move more than 5 percent from the rate in effect when the quote was made. If the movement exceeds 5 percent in either direction, Harley and its distributors share the costs or benefits. When enjoying exchange rate gains, some exporters use support tools such as training with their distributors or customers instead of lowering the price. The thinking is that increasing prices after a future currency swing in the opposite direction could be difficult.

Other adjustment strategies include looking to other markets with more favorable situations, streamlining operations by tightening payments or collections processes, focusing on offerings that are less sensitive to exchange rate changes, or shifting production. Companies often increase direct investment when currency shifts are seen as long term.

Where to Find Customer Financing

Most international marketers help their customers secure financing, since financing terms can significantly affect the final price paid by buyers. A variation in the financing rate of just 1 percent can make a big difference on a large sale. Buyers have been known to overlook differences in quality or price to award a contract to the company with cheaper credit.

Financing assistance is available domestically and abroad from both the public and the private sectors.

Commercial banks are a worldwide source of trade financing. Whether or not financing can be secured depends on the bank's relationship with the exporter, the nature of the transaction, the country of the borrower, and the availability of export insurance. In the end, this means that many U.S. international marketers are frustrated with U.S. banks, many of which do not see international trade finance as their core competency. When identifying banks, consider their overseas reach. While money-center banks can provide the greatest amount of coverage through their own offices and staff, they still use correspondents in regions outside the main banking or political centers of international markets. Banks with little overseas exposure use other knowledgeable partners to carry out the transactions and reduce their risk. That way, they can offer to cash an international check or make a transfer to support the international business transactions of their customers.

Some banks have formed alliances to extend their reach to markets their customers are entering. Commerzbank, a large German private-sector bank, has branches in the Far East, Latin America, South America, and Eastern Europe to support its international trade financing activities. Any bank's branches or correspondents are important at all stages of international transactions, from providing market intelligence to processing payments.

Forfaiting and factoring, discussed earlier in this chapter, are other financing options. The benefits of forfaiting include risk reduction, simplified documentation, and 100 percent coverage, which export–import banks do not provide. Forfaiting does not involve either content or country restrictions, but it is not available in high-risk countries and it is usually a little more expensive than public sources of trade insurance. Factoring companies provide a complete financial package that combines credit protection, accounts-receivable bookkeeping, and collection services. Because arrangements are usually made with recourse, though, the exporter is liable for repaying the factor if the importer defaults. Some factoring companies accept export receivables without recourse but they require a larger discount to do so.

The industry is dominated by about a dozen major players which are usually subsidiaries of major banks. The CIT Group Inc. (www.

cit.com) is a leading player. Find factoring companies through the Commercial Finance Association (www.cfa.com). Find forfaiters through the International Forfaiting Association (www.forfaiters.org).

Forfaiting and Factoring Differences

Forfaiting and factoring methods appear similar, but there are significant differences:

- Factoring companies usually want a large percentage of the exporter's business while most forfaiters work on a one-shot basis
- Forfaiters work with medium-term receivables (more than 180 days to five years) while factors take on short-term receivables
- Factors typically lack strong capabilities in developing countries, but since forfaiters usually require a bank guarantee, most will deal with these regions
- Forfaiters work with capital goods and factoring companies work with consumer goods

---

Another option available through governments is known as official trade finance. It can be either a loan or a guarantee, including credit insurance. In a loan, the government provides funds to finance the sale and charges interest at a fixed rate while accepting default risk. When it is a guarantee, a private-sector lender provides the funds and sets the interest rate. The government reimburses the lender if there is a default. The advantages are significant – these programs essentially reduce the risk for corporations while making it possible for commercial banks to participate.

The governments of most developed countries have recognized the importance of credit in export selling by establishing organizations that insure credit risks for exports. Known as export credit agencies (ECAs), they include the French Coface, German Hermes, and the Export-Import Bank of the United States (Ex-Im Bank, www.exim.gov). Some are divisions of government trade missions while others operate as private institutions with government support.

The Ex-Im Bank does not compete with private sector lenders but provides export financing products that fill gaps in trade financing. It assumes credit and country risks that private sector institutions are unable or unwilling to accept. It also helps level the playing field for U.S. exporters by matching the financing that other governments provide to their exporters. Ex-Im Bank provides working capital guarantees, export credit insurance, and loan guarantees and direct loans. The organization has supported more than $400 billion of U.S. exports, primarily to developing markets worldwide, with 85 percent of its transactions directly benefiting U.S. small businesses.

Other public-sector supporters include the Overseas Private Investment Corporation (OPIC, www.opic.gov) in the U.S., which focuses its efforts in developing economies. OPIC supports U.S. businesses that will foster economic development in new and emerging markets when investing overseas. Its work complements the private sector in managing risks associated with foreign direct investment while advancing U.S. foreign policy by supporting projects that expand economic development. OPIC promotes U.S. best practices by requiring projects to adhere to international standards on the environment as well as worker and human rights.

The Agency for International Development administers most of the international economic assistance programs of the U.S. Since most of those programs require purchasing from the U.S., exporters can benefit. The U.S. Department of Agriculture's Commodity Credit Corporation operates export credit guarantee programs that ensure companies or lenders that they will be repaid for export financing to international buyers. The Small Business Administration also administers its Export Working Capital Program and an International Trade Loan Program for small businesses.

Protect Against Dumping

Inexpensive imports often trigger accusations of dumping – selling goods overseas for less than in the exporter's home market or at a price below the cost of production. Accusations of dumping are common, especially in highly competitive industries such as computer chips. It can be predatory or unintentional. Predatory dumping happens when a nondomestic firm intentionally sells at a loss in another country so it can increase its market share. Unintentional dumping usually results from time lags between the date of sale and the product's arrival in the market. If exchange rates have changed and the final sales price falls below the cost of production or the prevailing price in the exporter's home market, it looks like the product is being dumped, even if it is not.

Companies need to watch market developments to avoid dumping their own products, even inadvertently. Minimize the risk of being accused of dumping by focusing on currency shifts. It also helps to reduce misleading transparency by increasing product differentiation. This could involve including services in the product offering.

In the U.S., domestic manufacturers may petition the U.S. International Trade Commission and the U.S. Department of Commerce with a complaint. If the domestic industry is considered threatened or harmed by the situation, the government can impose an antidumping duty equal to the dumping margin. International agreements and U.S. law also work to offset the advantages imports receive from foreign government subsidies. This reaction via duties can cause backlash, though, from countries imposing retaliatory duties.

Responding to a Financial Crisis

No matter what the pricing strategy or situation, global marketers will often need to make major adjustments when hit with a regional or international financial crisis. History shows that financial crises are not uncommon and that companies should prepare for them. A series of currency crises shook emerging markets beginning with the devaluation of the Mexican peso in 1994 and continuing to the Argentine default in 2001. Add to that the global recession that began in 2008 and it is clear that companies must be savvy and resilient to respond, survive, and thrive.

When consumer confidence suffers, marketers have to weigh their strategies closely because recessions have an impact on consumer spending. In a financial crisis, consumers will consume less, be more careful with decision making especially as it relates to spending, do more product research, focus on necessities instead of luxuries, and buy local rather than imported brands. They shop more in discount stores and are less tempted by attention-getting end of aisle placements. Marketers can respond to these changes, in turn, by withdrawing from weakest markets, fortifying strong markets, acquiring weak competitors, or pruning weak products. They might also offer better value by supporting products with warranties, reducing prices while maintaining quality, adjusting promotional campaigns to be more informational, and create customer loyalty programs. For some, it is an opportunity to increase market share.

The global marketplace is becoming increasingly competitive. At the same time, governments are enacting regulations to protect domestic companies, inflation is accelerating, and exchange rates are fluctuating. For all these reasons, marketers must pay particularly close attention to pricing strategy. Whether a company exports the product from the domestic base or from one overseas location to another, or whether the product is sold from one subsidiary to another, it is important to pay attention to manufacturing costs and those associated with filling the order.

FOOD FOR THOUGHT

- Which element of the marketing mix is revenue generating?
- What unique export-related costs might your company encounter? How can you take these costs into account?
- How might the terms of sale and payment affect your success? How can you use these terms as a competitive tool?
- How can currency conditions impact exporter strategies? How might they impact your own strategies?

Further Readings

Dimancescu, Katherine. *Global Transfer Pricing Solutions*. Concord, MA: WorldTrade Executive Inc., 2008.

Gregson, Andrew. *Pricing Strategies*. North Vancouver, BC: Self-Counsel Press, 2009.

Anil, Gupta and Vijay Govidarajan. *The Quest of Global Dominance*. New York, NY: John Wiley & Sons, 2008.

Ruskin-Brown, Ian. *Practical Pricing for Results*. Abingdon, Oxford, UK: Thorogood, 2008.

Online Resources

TradePort: Global Trade Tutorial
An introduction to the different kinds of trade finance and funding
http://www.tradeport.org/tutorial/financing/

Coface
A company that specializes in facilitating business-to-business trade
http://www.coface.com/

Centers for International Trade Development: Trade Reference Tools
Offers numerous useful pages for deciphering trade terminology
http://www.citd.org/trade_info/sections.cfm?sid=5

SME Toolkit: Sales Management
A series of how-to articles on sales
http://www.smetoolkit.org/smetoolkit/en/category/955/Sales-Management

Chapter 10

Discovering Trends in International Business

The Delphi Method at Work

Our goal with this book has been to bridge the information gap for emerging global marketers by outlining many of the most pressing and practical issues and helping those marketers address those issues, challenges, or opportunities with some level of knowledge and structure. Our awareness and wisdom come from decades of global business experience and our ongoing interactions with corporations near and far. In addition, just as we encourage readers of this book to research their markets, we do research of our own so that we thoroughly understand the international business environment. This research includes our most recent Delphi study – a research project we undertake periodically to help us guide and educate the international business community so that global entrepreneurs are as informed as possible about current international marketing conditions.

DELPHI STUDY OVERVIEW

As the significance and magnitude of international business increase, so does the need to quickly identify emerging issues and assess their potential impact. While there are many broad visions concerning tomorrow's international business climate, a more targeted way to predict the future is for the policy, business, and research communities around the globe to collaborate in drafting possible scenarios. By identifying, analyzing, and debating issues, we can develop timely response strategies that help policy-makers and business leaders be proactive.

Despite widespread agreement on the importance of tracking international trends, few companies do so successfully, and information sharing between disciplines is limited. In addition, top management publications do not offer enough articles focused on international business and policy.

To fill the gap in international trend forecasting and to keep our knowledge current, we conducted a Delphi study in 2009 that included 34 geographically diverse participants from government, business, and academia (see box below "What Is the Delphi Method?"). During the past 25 years, we have completed four other Delphi studies used by governments, firms, and researchers to identify key international business dynamics likely to shift during the subsequent decade. Changing priorities between Delphi studies have been significant. For example, from 2005 to 2009, terrorism and corruption issues rose in importance, while trade negotiation declined. The need for reform influences corporate strategy more today than it did four years earlier. Table 10.1 shows the accuracy level – or "hit rate" – for each of them.

The average accuracy level of the four prior Delphi studies is 79 percent. As panel participants became more global and diversified, the accuracy level increased. In many cases, inaccuracies occurred in predicting a specific rate of change rather than in identifying change itself. But the studies did miss predicting some big events – events that were unpredictable, even by the world's finest intelligence agencies. Examples include the fall of the Berlin wall and the disintegration of the Soviet Union. These

TABLE 10.1 International Delphi Study "Hit Rates"

Year of Study	Accuracy Level
1986	82%
1992	80%
1997	65%
2005	89%*

*Might be high because forecast is recent.

"black swans," so named by Nassim Nicholas Taleb in his 2007 book *The Black Swan* (Random House), are conditions or phenomena never encountered before and thus difficult to incorporate in a forecast.

What Is the Delphi Method?

Leading corporations and organizations use the Delphi method to develop strategic guidelines for making investment decisions in new technologies and markets. The 50-year-old technique brings together the thinking of a variety of different communities and integrates the opinions of experts through multiple waves of data collection and respondent interaction. The objective is to achieve consensus among panelists. While there is no ideal size, Delphi panels typically included 10 to 30 experts.

The Process

We identified and recruited 34 panelists from a variety of backgrounds and locales for our three-phase 2009 international Delphi study. Selection criteria included an active career and leadership role in international business, a demonstrated ability to see issues beyond local and current circumstances, and a willingness to engage in intellectual dialogue and debate. The caliber of participants and their willingness to work determines the value of study results. Participants in the panel for this study met the following criteria:

- More than 20 years of experience in their field
- Well connected to global counterparts
- Active in international business for at least ten years
- Play a leadership role within their professional setting
- Have a global vision
- Are accessible and willing to engage in intellectual dialogue.

Some of these individuals had participated in earlier Delphi studies, but most were new respondents. Table 10.2 indicates the number, location, and profile of the panelists.

TABLE 10.2 2009 International Delphi Study Panelists

Panelists	Africa/ Asia	Europe	The Americas	Total
Corporate Chief executives or executive vice presidents	4	4	5	13
Policy Current or former members of the legislative and executive branches of government	3	4	5	12
Research Professors specializing in international business	2	3	4	9
Total	9	11	14	34

Using e-mail communication to facilitate turnaround in a Delphi study and help sustain panelist commitment, we conducted the study in three waves over the course of six months. The first wave used open-ended questions to identify international business dimensions subject to change in the next ten years. The second wave, designed to generate responses to the information gathered in the first wave, presented the first wave findings for discussion. Panelists responded accordingly, ranking issues gleaned from the first wave. During the third wave, we built consensus by working through areas where panelists disagreed.

Some geographic locations or professional communities are more likely to generate or experience change than others; therefore, interaction among respondents across geographic locations as well as corporate, policy, and academic communities is a key element in data collection. This diversity forces respondents to be realistic and think broadly and even beyond their strategic perspective. In the 2009 study, we introduced ideas designed to gauge trends beyond the normal realm of expectations.

To glean results, Delphi study leaders analyze the frequency and intensity of issues identified by panelists and develop a value scale based on events, issues, and regions and their anticipated impact on international business. The highest value is then standardized at 100.

THE FIVE POLICY ISSUES IDENTIFIED IN 2009

The top five policy issues identified by the 2009 Delphi panelists are, with their ranking on a scale of 1 to 100:

1. Terrorism (100)
2. Globalization (83)
3. Corruption (72)
4. Cultural adjustment (55)
5. Information (46)

Panelists had a great deal of information to share on these five areas.

1. Terrorism

A growing emphasis on national interests and local culture will increase terrorism and lead to higher security standards worldwide. Policy-triggered restrictions in global transportation and corporate linkages are likely. Both corporations and policy makers understand that terrorism is an ongoing activity that must be confronted. Panelists saw terrorism as a fact of life that demands continuous multilateral pushback without compromise.

Panelists identified the root causes of terrorism as policies toward immigrants and divisive activities among advocates of specific religions, cultures, regions, or races. Panelists proposed education, improved nutrition, and the ability to control one's own destiny as ways to address these root causes. Increasing emphasis on national interests, however, is likely to limit the efficacy of multilateral solutions. Rather than succumb to populism, governments must diffuse drives toward local and regional protectionism and de-globalization. Developing and maintaining the power to execute peace will be governments' greatest challenge.

Panelists disagreed over key approaches to defeat, or at least contain, terrorism. Some panelists felt strongly that materialism – "having something to lose" – is a key dimension for winning over those who feel excluded from the benefits of globalization. Others suggested that spirituality and understanding cultural differences are of prime importance. Those who can combine these approaches might enjoy more success in the future.

Corporations are likely to revive ethnocentric and polycentric policies and use export activities rather than foreign direct investment to deal with foreign markets. They will either leave countries that lack law and order or service them only at a very high-risk premium. Consumers appear willing to change their consumption patterns as a result of security requirements. Many consumers might shift their preferences in response to cultural diversity and cross-border cultural conflicts, thus giving a new meaning to country-of-origin influence.

2. Globalization

Mobility, a central trend in globalization, might create a new generation of innovators and risk takers. Consumers, intermediaries, and originators who participate in the supply chain can move to different locations to take advantage of low costs and other benefits. Workers, however, are not necessarily able to take advantage of this trend.

Education and training are critical for attaining better and more rewarding employment. When asked how countries can progress on the globalization chain, panelists consistently rated education as the most important component, followed by competition and investment. Panelists were sharply divided, however, on the content of education. Some stressed the importance of acquiring both quantitative and qualitative knowledge. Others believed that attainment of difficult knowledge – for example, physics, mathematics, or chemistry – could be outsourced to those willing to specialize in such areas. Education time could then be dedicated to other pursuits, such as music, art, or poetry. The question of whether learning is meant to satisfy an inner spiritual need or fulfill a societal requirement arose repeatedly. For example, would implementing a "knowledge chip" be better or worse than the acquiring of knowledge the traditional way under difficult conditions?

Because of barriers imposed by governments, workers in low-wage countries are often unable to earn at a developed-market rate. While evidence shows that removing trade and investment barriers raises living standards across the board, distributional effects can still produce winners and losers. Sequencing policy and business shifts will minimize disruption. For example, a lengthy phase-in period will allow people to adjust to change and help those who are hit the hardest. Location-specific differences in the speed of globalization combined with variations in social safety nets will influence how workers experience change. Currently, brawn and assembly are cheap, while knowledge and creativity are expensive. But conditions can change quickly to reward "fighters" more than "thinkers."

Naturally, those who believe they will experience negative effects from globalization will be its fierce opponents. But when confronted with proof that only a small portion of their troubles emanate from international trade and investment issues, the mere fact that these issues are even involved will be enough to fuel vitriolic antiglobalization campaigns. The supportive role played by those who benefit from international economic activity will be crucial. Preoccupation with managing growth, however, will tend to make their support sporadic. A lack of balance between camps can result in a rapid and unanticipated decline in the global economic environment.

Changes in financial reserves and economic relations, accompanied by an unbundling of financial systems between the U.S. and other nations, will lead to financing difficulties in markets that previously depended on an ample supply of money. One consequence will be the exit of marginal participants and the tightening of existing financing rules and expenditures.

The U.S. continues to present new and special opportunities to the world, offering security and safety that have been unattainable for most people in other countries. The U.S. has the vision, flexibility, and capability to adjust to new conditions that other countries aspire to. Global investors who are reluctant to turn away from the dollar know that what determines the value of money over time is the trust and future promise a nation offers those holding its currency. Finding ways to manage investor expectations enables a country to maintain or systematically alter the value of its currency.

The role of international organizations is likely to shift. For example, the World Trade Organization is already under pressure to assume more responsibilities, some of them reaching far beyond trade. Principles addressing child labor, working conditions, and the rule of law in contracts and procurement must be implemented to avoid trade conflicts and the exploitation of local rules for the benefit of nefarious individuals and firms. Enforcement around the world must be consistent and supported by highly motivated activists.

Other international organizations might become weaker. The current overwhelming power of rich countries in the voting systems of international organizations suggests to developing countries that they are considered second-class members. For example, the role of the World Bank might diminish as poor countries decide that they have no stake, no respect, and nothing to gain from the institution. Similarly, the International Monetary Fund might be outperformed by local and regional lending arrangements that do not impose harsh requirements that are of little relevance to long-term performance.

3. Corruption

Corruption detracts significantly from global welfare and local economic development. Its consequences include shoddily built roads, structures that collapse, and equipment purchased at high prices with inappropriate specifications. Under these circumstances, vast public expenditures do not yield promised benefits, incentives for future funding are reduced, and local interests suffer.

Typical "side payments" are 10 percent to 15 percent of major expenditures. Amounts are even higher in the developing world, especially in places such as Latin America, Eastern and Central Europe, and Asia where corruption is implicit in the culture. The social acceptance of corruption is seen as a substantial danger because it protects the elite from domestic scrutiny and control. The Delphi panelists see the U.S. Foreign Corrupt Practices Act and the Organization for Economic

Cooperation and Development as instrumental in reducing or at least containing such misappropriations. More multilateral action is necessary to ensure broad, continuous, and relentless enforcement.

4. Cultural Adjustment

The Delphi panelists believe that cultures around the globe will become more similar, particularly around macro issues such as accountability, performance expectations, social freedom, and product preferences. This cultural assimilation will be profoundly influenced by the U.S. and thus potentially threatening to less-dominant cultures. At the same time, due to an increase in regional and local sovereignty and cultural protectionism, it will be more difficult to export overwhelmingly uniform ways of thinking, even by multilateral organizations such as UNESCO.

History indicates that cultures rise and fall over time amidst social turbulence, regardless of information flow, insights, and learning. If that were not the case, the world would speak a language from one of the great ancient empires – Greek, Latin, or Arabic. Currently, the use of English as a business language can create resentment and hostility. Companies are discovering that language conveys cultural norms that reduce employee creativity and weaken local connections. It is possible that companies will de-emphasize English language skills, with a new multi-polarity in global management as the result.

On a micro level, most Delphi panelists see ongoing culture clashes often advancing fundamentalist beliefs. In some regions, individuals will encounter new cultural groups for the first time. For example, in America, many Caucasians will be exposed to large groups of Hispanics and in some regions might become a minority. Similarly, Western Europeans will experience major competition from the people who used to be their communist neighbors. Some might find these new ethno-cultural experiences unacceptable. Opening up to others on such a grand scale over a relatively short time will create some xenophobia but also flexibility, better understanding, and rising tolerance levels. It is the task of governments to prevent cultural conflicts from becoming irreconcilable and to find ways to keep society cohesive and ready for collaboration.

Governments also must recognize the corporate investment models that evaluate locations and opportunities in terms of risk and return. Higher risk and shorter investment periods require higher returns. Expedited returns lead to higher prices, lower investments, and less investment stability. It is important that governments provide a lower-risk platform and communicate about planning and results so that investors can recognize and reward a less-risky environment. In addition, it is essential to recognize the growing impact of consumer activists on corporate action. Consumers are willing and able to express their views, consolidate their emotions into commercial action, and use their networks to enhance their reach. Consequently, governments must develop and adhere to standards of behavior that comply with global expectations for human dignity.

The corporate challenge is to reap the economic advantages of globalization while preserving local cultural values. Corporate business practices are likely to become more global and, in particular, more Asian due to the growing participation of Asian firms, brands, and managers in world markets. A better understanding of networks and their functions across cultures is crucial. For example, Chinese, Indians, and Russians approach network building differently from Westerners. Increased participation by international players will affect market opportunities for American products and force firms to "glocalize" their strategies. Similarly, corporations will prefer the use of soft power (e.g., corporate philanthropy) over hard power (e.g., penalties) to achieve gains in the global marketplace.

Corporations also must find ways to adjust to different subcultures around the globe. For example, the Archbishop of Canterbury stirred up public sentiment when in 2008 he called for a re-examination of the role of Sharia in British life. Sharia is the body of Islamic religious law that is based on the Koran, the words and actions of the Prophet Mohammad, and the rulings of Islamic scholars. The Archbishop observed that Sharia already figures prominently in the lives of more than 2 million Muslims in the United Kingdom. Informal neighborhood councils provide rulings on family issues such as divorce, and banks such as HSBC already market mortgages that comply with Sharia rules of lending. Perhaps Muslims in Britain would be more comfortable and willing to occupy a more constructive space within British society if they could choose Sharia law to settle civil disputes.

5. Information

Even though greater diversification of information sources might provide for better knowledge evolution, Delphi panelists expect that due to mergers and acquisitions, cost cutting, and limited user willingness to pay, fewer sources will offer increasingly larger quantities of data. This development is likely to affect accuracy and reliability, making data use heavily trust-dependent. Data users might demand more insight into the origin of information, forcing information providers to confirm their sources. Suppliers can then use origin of data to enhance credibility.

With more transparent sourcing, however, some firms and individuals might be less willing to offer information. Nebulous laws and restrictions might increase the threat of lawsuits, and the amount of free information that has greatly helped businesses and individuals over the past 10 years is likely to shrink. Data might become more "organic" – that is, unaltered by manipulation or interpretation. Another alternative might be "comparative" data that provide multi-source perspectives on an ongoing basis. In addition, quantitative data are likely to be combined with qualitative information, resulting in a diagnostic perspective. Once data pass the trust threshold, they can then be used in a much more aggressive and insightful way, going far beyond the traditional retrospective use of statistics.

Advancements in information technology and the convergence of new technologies will make new equipment more sophisticated and cost-effective. Companies will adopt these new technologies faster than ever before but will maintain a competitive edge only if the technology is easy to use and does not distance the customer. Younger consumers will be quick to adopt new capabilities, but more mature buyers will be reluctant to invest in products that require a high degree of additional learning. Excelling in technology alone has no intrinsic value. It is the application of technology that satisfies human needs and values.

LOCATION AND SOURCE OF GROWTH

Emerging market economies will continue to impact the global economy. The threat of polarization and an increase in regional and local trade and financial relations will encourage eventual completion of the World Trade Organization's Doha Development Round of trade negotiations, which began in November 2001 and broke down in 2008. Countries will focus on the issues that are most relevant for their economies, thus leading to a differentiation among players according to a desire to grow, make, create, or coordinate.

Key growth industries, prioritized according to the Delphi panelists' value scale, are:

- Communications/IT (100)
- Coordination of services/demographics (84)
- Pharma/biotech (72)
- Environmental (66)
- Energy (55)

Significant new market opportunities will develop within emerging economies. At the same time, rising capabilities will enable these countries to compete directly with more established goods and services produced in the developed world. Emerging regions will cooperate more, resulting in greater integration and, perhaps, more regional protectionism. Developing nations will seek more diverse partnerships and welcome increased competition among larger players. For some countries, collaboration is likely to introduce new moral and ethical positions based on greater human dignity and freedom. Efficiency will gain in importance. As economic power shifts to Asia, in both investment and output, Asian-style business practices will be incorporated globally.

China will be the player to watch. For firms planning to enter the global market, succeeding in China is a critical indicator of competitiveness. Domestic pressures fueled by weaknesses in the banking system, urban–rural imbalances, and regional political dissonance will encourage Chinese corporations to expand overseas. The Fortune 1,000 will soon include a significant number of China-headquartered companies. Mergers and acquisitions led by Chinese firms also will increase.

India's growth will rival that of China, due to the country's widespread use of English, its commitment to the rule of law, a well-developed commercial infrastructure, and a democratic government. Companies are likely to see India as both a primary source and an important market. Indian linkages in the communications and information sectors are likely to soar.

ENVIRONMENT, CONSERVATION AND SUSTAINABILITY ISSUES

China will demonstrate limited concern for the environment, even though environmental problems will have a major effect on the country's ability to compete as a global manufacturing center. Medical, environmental, and other social costs will dramatically reduce the advantages of manufacturing in China, prompting foreign direct investment in other locations, including the U.S. and Europe.

China's and India's rapid growth and push toward economic progress and better lifestyles for their citizens will cause the ongoing depletion of natural resources. Consequently, control of raw materials will be a vital strategic issue, often leading to preferential bilateral agreements that might contradict multilateral arrangements. Governments will attempt to put more land into grain production and use subsidies and price controls. Scarcity will also drive up the price of consumer alcohol. Protecting materials from theft (e.g., cutting electrical wires to steal copper) will become a priority. Recycling and recovery will become strong business opportunities. As fuel production from food accelerates, farming will become attractive and profitable. The global shortage of potable water will be rediscovered as a priority issue and constraint on global advancement and well-being. Government investment in desalination and reverse osmosis technologies will grow along with emphasis on water conservation.

In light of public concern over climate change, interest in energy-saving technologies will grow. Unusual natural phenomena will be attributed to global warming, a relationship that will be supported by a stream of scientific and nonscientific proof. Public perceptions will lead to changes in living patterns. For example, the population of dry, arid, and hot climate areas might shift due to water shortages and limitations on the use of air conditioning. Such changes will occur even if it becomes generally accepted that global warming is only slightly dependent on human activity.

Africa might offer the most opportunity for green investments and accumulation of carbon credits. Eventually, as governments frown on the transfer of resources resulting from carbon trading, wealthy countries and international operating companies will make agreements (both multi-lateral and bilateral) that create a framework to protect the environment. Key sectors for industry creation and expansion include public health; sustainability; saving energy, water and natural resources; biotechnology, genomics and nano-technology; and the creation and promotion of eco-products, services and processes. For example, sustainable water recycling technologies will spawn new industries, and governments will adopt and encourage more advanced pollution-control policies, par-ticularly for heavy metals and engineered (nonnaturally occurring) substances.

DEMOGRAPHICS

The aging-population trend now seen in North America and Europe will spread to Asia and Latin America. Older people will become a growing market segment for the financial-services sector as well as for providers of health care and certain household products. Lack of public support for the disabled and needy – often the result of cultural traditions – will create problems for generations caught in transition. As baby boomer societies experience waves of retirement, companies will attempt to increase employee longevity and loyalty through new and substantial incentives designed to maintain expertise within the organization. At the same time, major opportunities will emerge as older people seek to fill their increased leisure time with education, entertainment, and activities.

In a world of permeable borders, there will be more opportunities to pick up and move. The ability to prove and improve oneself and to access new resources are powerful motivators for migration. The young and the not so well off are likely to experience the greatest incentives. The moves and behavior of the young will act as a signal to others. Regions can enrich their quality of life by attracting young, upwardly mobile migrants.

REFORMING THE GLOBAL CORPORATION

Corporations are likely to face increasing pressure from a wide variety of stakeholders, governments, unions, media, and the public at large. This pressure becomes more intense as corporations transition from being Western-centric organizations to multi-polar structures. In addition, location will shift from a West-North to an East-South orientation.

Accountability and transparency will form the foundation for change. To facilitate new approaches to corporate capitalization and performance, accounting systems will include procedures for calculating the value of intangible corporate assets, which will become the prime measure of corporate success and have a major influence on cash flow projections and stock prices. Value investors will recognize that building intangible assets is a multi-year, multifaceted endeavor. Buy-and-hold strategies will dominate as quarter-to-quarter performance becomes less important in investment decision making.

Corporate responsibility will be reinterpreted to include broad-based activity and profit sharing. Low-capital manufacturing facilities will become the norm around the world. Stakeholders will demand greater involvement and, for better or worse, will play a major role in corporate image building. Since lapses in ethics or social responsibility will have a major negative impact on brand equity, strong corporations will engage in robust social responsibility programs and demand strict ethical conduct from employees.

A backlash against excessive executive remuneration will come from regulators as well as from shareholders, managers, and employees. Executive compensation will be compared to average level of pay, which might lead to pay raises for employees at lower levels. In addition, the professional education of future business leaders will emphasize morality, ascetics, and the judgment of history. Outsourced back-office and support functions will allow global firms to eliminate internal functions. Global banks will expand into outsourcing by providing high-value-added services such as the oversight of corporate treasuries.

Emerging markets will account for larger portions of corporate profits and sales, particularly because emerging-market populations account for more than two-thirds of global consumers. Corporations will be expected to provide improved product access and help overcome difficulties in logistics and infrastructure. For many products, development strategies will shift from "the latest" to increased affordability.

BUSINESS FUNCTIONS CRITICAL FOR GLOBAL SUCCESS

The most critical business functions for global success according to panelists are:

- Logistics (100)
- Marketing (86)
- Human resources (71)
- Finance (57)
- Communications (34)

Given the commonalities among them, these functions are likely to propel an even more rapid evolution of supply chain management around the globe. The emphasis will be on markets provided by "second-tier cities" – large cities outside the political or economic spotlight, particularly in Russia, China, and India. Firms will need to expand their distribution and market-entry strategies for these cities, thus creating new regional hubs. Companies also must collaborate with the public sector to encourage infrastructure investments, which will increase regional political and economic importance.

Smaller firms can benefit from the globalization by focusing on niche markets, especially those abandoned by large players. What might be uneconomical to produce for a multinational conglomerate might be a viable segment for a much smaller firm. Even small players, however, can face large problems. Strategic alliances and other collaborative efforts will allow smaller players to compete for a larger share of global markets. These companies also will be heavily dependent upon and therefore very concerned about open markets and global standards. Consequently, uniform local codes and enforcement supported by the one-country-one-vote rule are crucial for the success of smaller competitors.

OBJECTIVES FOR THE FUTURE

Panelists participating in the 2009 international Delphi study identified three key objectives for the future of globalization:

1. Reducing global inequality
2. Creating new and widely enforced global rules that provide stability and consistency in basic rights and obligations across borders
3. Supporting individual freedom

Over time, nations, institutions, and individuals worldwide are expected to accept these dimensions as drivers of the "good life." As freedom facilitates international marketing, international marketing will support the cause of freedom.

The world might have come to the point where stability and constancy are seen as "falling behind," but it is important to remember that setbacks are not fatal. Growth does not take place on all levels simultaneously. The current "go-go-grow" economic mentality might not be as important in the future as it is today. In fact, stability might be regaining some currency, thus giving everyone a chance to catch his or her breath.

In addition, the degree to which industries are embedded in society will become more relevant. Countries, regions and/or cities will specialize in developing industry clusters. Firms will open subsidiaries and representative offices in these locations to take advantage of the proximity to competitors, suppliers, and customers. Public policy-makers will encourage this development and place greater emphasis on the special educational needs of the workforce in industrial clusters.

A new worldwide division of labor and specialization will change growth patterns by creating a competitive setting, in which borders are defined by research and development as well as by high standards for workforce education and training. Firms will focus on highly specialized research and service-intensive niche products. To stay ahead, companies will aim for narrow, monopolistic positions. Politics will play a lesser role since whether liberal or conservative, one style of market economy is not necessarily more competitive and efficient than another.

From our perspective as Delphi study researchers but also as educators who work continually to help businesses enjoy the benefits of international marketing success, the study results tell us that the world benefits from global trading.

GLOBAL MARKETING AND FREEDOM

There is, in fact, a direct connection between global trading and freedom. Global marketing is essential to freedom because freedom is about options. Options provide the opportunity to make decisions. With international marketing, companies cross borders to provide more than one choice for customers. Global marketing does so in all corners of the globe, in the glamorous ones as well as in the small and remote ones where the efforts are not seen by others. By operating both in the limelight and well outside of it, international marketers offer freedom by providing options to the seller and the buyer – whether it is in supplying or purchasing, pricing or selecting.

Another key dimension of freedom is the loosening of restrictions that prevent people from going outside the box. National borders usually create the box where business and government find their limits. Global marketers thrive on understanding how to successfully cross national borders, on coping with the differences once the crossing is done, and on profitably reconciling any conflicts.

Freedom also means not being forced to do something one does not want to do. There are economic migration pressures that force people to move from their rural homes into urban areas or from their emerging economies into more developed ones. The developed nations, in turn, speak about immigration pressure. For both sides, little if any freedom is involved here. Most individuals who do the moving would much rather stay home but cannot afford to do so because of economic realities. The recipient countries feel political and humanitarian pressure to welcome the migrants even if they do not want to. Global marketing may have been part of what triggered some of these migrations, but it also can be instrumental in stemming the tide. It can provide the economic opportunity for individuals at home so that they do not need to migrate. It can help individuals become productive contributors to the global economy, free from pressures to change locations.

When the long-standing rivalry between socialism and market

orientation was resolved, market forces and the recognition of demand and supply directly affected human rights and the extent of freedom. With all humility and gratefulness we can conclude: the markets were right. In country after country, market forces have demonstrated typically greater efficiency and effectiveness in their ability to satisfy the needs of people.

International marketers have been instrumental in stimulating these newly emerging market forces. In spite of complaints about the slowness of change, the insufficiency of wealth redistribution, and the inequities inherent in societal upheavals, a large majority of participants in market-oriented changes are now better off than they were before. Without the transition provided by international marketing, these changes would not have come about that swiftly.

The Cost of Freedom

People talk about the large segment of the world population that is poor and therefore supposedly excluded from any international marketing efforts; the World Bank's former president called them the 3 billion $2-a-day poor. By contrast, international marketers see them as an attractive $6 billion-a-day opportunity for valuable exchanges.

What is more is that global marketing provides the opportunity to acquire resources without the deployment of force. Why fight if you can trade? Countries that have been historic enemies such as France, England, and Germany are now all united in their close collaboration through international marketing. The field is, therefore, at the very least contributing to freedom from war while providing additional choices for consumption.

But the cost of freedom is rising. Terms such as "free trade" or "free choice" are misleading since they all come with a price. Global marketers pay that price in terms of preparing their shipments, scrutinizing their customers, and conforming to government regulations.

We all are paying a higher price because of global terrorism – an issue identified by our Delphi study. As freedom suffers, so does international marketing. In most instances, terrorism is not an outgrowth of choice but rather the lack of it. Terrorists may succeed in reducing the freedom of others but not in increasing their own. Who is typically most affected by terrorist acts? Attacks aimed at businesses, such as the infamous bombings of U.S. franchises abroad, do not bring big corporations to their knees. The local participants, the local employees, the local investors, and the local customers are affected most.

Who can protect themselves against such attacks and who can afford to protect targets? Only the more wealthy countries and companies can. They have the choice of where to place their funds, with whom to trade, and whether to hold the enemy at bay through a security bubble created by changing business formats via exporting or franchising. The poor players do not have choices. The local businesses, the nations with economies in development, and the poor customers continue to be exposed to further acts of terrorism with very limited ability to influence events.

But international marketers can enable the disenfranchised to develop alternatives. Multinational firms can invest in the world's poorest markets and reduce poverty while increasing their own revenue. With support from shareholders and the benefit of good governance, global marketers can, and should, continue in their role as social change agents. If it is worthwhile to fulfill the needs of large segments of people, even at low margins, then it will be done. International marketers want to create new customers and suppliers and they are delighted when, in the process, they can bring about freedom from extremes of hunger, sickness, and intolerance.

Values and Freedom

In a global setting, freedom can take on many dimensions. Privileges and obligations that are near and dear to some may well be cheap and easily disposed of by others. The views of one society may differ from views held in other regions of the world. Such differences then account for misunderstandings, surprises, and long-term conflicts.

There are two value dimensions at work here, both of them highly relevant to global marketing. One may be defined as the freedom and values of a market economy. To make them work, governmental, managerial, and corporate virtue, vision, and veracity are required. Unless the world can believe in the messages and behaviors of institutions and their leaders, it will be difficult to forge a global commitment between those doing the marketing and the ones being marketed to. It is therefore of vital interest to the proponents of freedom and international marketing to ensure that corruption, bribery, lack of transparency, and poor governance are exposed for their negative effects in any setting or society. The main remedy will be the collaboration of the global policy community to agree on what constitutes transgressions combined with swift punishment of the culprits involved.

A second and even more crucial issue is the value system we use in making choices. There are major differences among what people value around the world. Contrasts include togetherness compared to individuality, cooperation versus competition, modesty next to assertiveness, and self-effacement compared to self-actualization. Often, global differences in value systems keep us apart and result in spectacularly destructive dissimilarities. How we value a life, for example, can be crucial in terms of how we treat individuals. What value we place on family, work, leisure time, or progress has a substantial effect on how we see and evaluate each other.

Cultural studies tell us that there are major differences between and even within nations. Global marketing, through its linkages via goods, services, ideas, and communications, can achieve important assimilations of value systems. On the consumer side, new products offer international appeal and encourage similar activities around the world. It has been claimed that local product offerings help define people and provide identity and that it is the local idiosyncrasies that make people beautiful. Some even offer the persistence of the specific breakfast habits of the English and the French as evidence of local immutability in the face of globalization.

Yet, we should remember that values are learned, not genetically implanted. As life's experiences grow more international and more similar, so do values. Therefore, every time international marketing forges a new linkage in thinking, new progress is made in shaping a greater global commonality in values. It may well be that international marketing's ability to align global values which makes it easier for countries, companies, and individuals to build bridges between them, may eventually become the field's greatest gift to the world.

How do freedom and international marketing match with today's discontent so forcefully expressed by antiglobalists? Many claim that never before in history has there been so much evidence of such strong opposition to globalization and to Americans as harbingers of international marketing. Perhaps those making such claims are wrong. In looking at other "globalizers" in world history, such as the Vikings, the Mongols, the Tatars, and the Romans, there probably was both intellectual and physical opposition. But protesters were never allowed to become very vocal, or to engage in repeated, large demonstrations or widespread pamphleteering. Because of rather harsh policies toward those who opposed, very few records of resistance are available today.

Today's news is good. The nations, institutions, and individuals around the world are increasingly accepting freedom as the key foundation of the good life. We are discovering that international marketing, both as a discipline and as an activity, is very closely interwoven with freedom – some even call it essential. It is the freedom Thomas Aquinas saw as the means to human excellence and happiness which international marketing helps us reach. In reciprocal causality, freedom causes and facilitates international marketing, while global marketing is a key support of the cause of freedom. It is a productive symbiosis at work.

FOOD FOR THOUGHT

- What capabilities will industry leaders of the future need to be able to adopt, adapt, and build on change?
- What are the social and technological transformations in the markets you are operating in or targeting?
- How quickly and effectively does your organization adapt to external changes?
- How do you manage new information flows within the organization?

Further Readings

Camillus, J. C. Strategy as a Wicked Problem. *Harvard Business Review*, 86, 5, 2008, 98–106.

Duboff, Robert S. The Wisdom of (Expert) Crowds. *Harvard Business Review*, 85, 9, 2007, 28.

Pavlovic Zoran and Charles F. Gritzner. *The Changing Global Economy (Global Connections)*. New York, NY: Chelsea House Publications, 2009.

Sull, Donald. *The Upside of Turbulence: Seizing Opportunity in an Uncertain World*. New York, NY: HarperBusiness, 2009.

Online Resources

Strategies for Achieving High Performance in a Multi-polar World
https://microsite.accenture.com/mcim/Documents/Multi-Polar_World_3_Report.pdf

Economic Conditions Snapshot: McKinsey Global Survey Results
www.mckinseyquarterly.com/Economic_Studies/Productivity_Performance/Economic_Conditions_Snapshot_February_2009_2301

GMID – Global Market Information Database
www.portal.euromonitor.com/passport/magazine.aspx

Country Watch: Country-specific intelligence and data
www.countrywatch.com

Index

Note: page numbers in **bold** refer to figures.